father, his betrothal and his conflict with the Danish Established Church. Part Two contains an analysis of Kierkegaard's spiritual life, which seeks to investigate the bases of his religious experience and to examine the psychological climate of his thought. In Part Three, Kierkegaard's thought is discussed in some detail against a background of the facts established in the two preceding sections.

While Professor Jolivet's treatment lacks none of the qualities of scholarly thoroughness, it is unmarred by that academic aridity which Kierkegaard himself so abhorred; he approaches Kierkegaard, as he says in his Foreword, not as a "subject," but as one would a friend, and he writes of him with sympathy as well as with insight.

INTRODUCTION TO KIERKEGAARD

INTRODUCTION TO
KIERKEGAARD

by

REGIS JOLIVET

*Dean of the Faculty of Philosophy
in the Catholic University of Lyon*

Translated by

W. H. BARBER M.A. Oxon

*Assistant Lecturer in French at University College
Bangor (University of Wales)*

NEW YORK
E. P. DUTTON & CO. INC.
300 *Fourth Avenue, New York* 10

PRINTED IN GREAT BRITAIN BY EBENEZER BAYLIS AND SON, LTD.
THE TRINITY PRESS WORCESTER AND LONDON

Originally published in French by
Editions de Fontenelle, Paris, in 1946

TRANSLATOR'S NOTE

Acknowledgments are due to the Oxford University Press and
the Princeton University Press for their kind permission to make
use of the translations of Kierkegaard's works published by them

W. H. BARBER.

BIBLIOGRAPHICAL NOTE

In this translation the fullest use has been made of the English translations of Kierkegaard's works which have appeared in recent years. Wherever possible, references to, and quotations from, them have been substituted for corresponding references and quotations from French translations of Kierkegaard given by Professor Jolivet. In cases where no English translation exists, the author's references have been retained, and quotations have been translated into English from the French. The following list therefore contains both the relevant English translations of Kierkegaard and those French translations for which no English counterpart as yet exists, as well as some indications concerning the Danish originals and German translations of which Professor Jolivet also makes use.

I. Works

Either/Or, (Vol. I. Translated by David F. Swenson and Lilian M. Swenson. Vol. II. Translated by Walter Lowrie). 2 vols. Princeton University Press, 1944.

Fear and Trembling. Translated by Robert Payne. Princeton University Press, 1941.

Repetition. Translated with introduction and notes by Walter Lowrie. Princeton University Press, 1941.

Philosophical Fragments. Translated by D. F. Swenson. American-Scandinavian Foundation. New York 1936.

The Concept of Dread. Translated with introduction and notes by Walter Lowrie. Princeton University Press, 1944.

Stages on Life's Way. Translated by Walter Lowrie. Princeton University Press, 1941.

Concluding Unscientific Postscript. Translated by D. F. Swenson and Walter Lowrie. Princeton University Press, 1941.

The Sickness unto Death. Translated by Walter Lowrie. Princeton University Press, 1941.

The Point of View, etc. Translated by Walter Lowrie. Princeton University Press, 1940.

Training in Christianity. Translated by Walter Lowrie. O.U.P. London 1941.

Purify your Hearts! Translated by A. S. Aldworth and W. S. Ferrie. C. W. Daniel & Co. London 1937.

For Self-Examination, etc. Translated by Walter Lowrie. O.U.P. London 1941.

The Present Age, etc. Translated by Alexander Dru and Walter Lowrie. O.U.P. London 1940.

Christian Discourses, etc. Translated by Walter Lowrie. Princeton University Press, 1940.

Works of Love. Translated by D. F. Swenson and L. M. Swenson. Princeton University Press. Princeton, N.J. 1946.

Philosophical Fragments. Translated by D. F. Swenson. American-Scandinavian Foundation, New York. 1936.

The Lilies of the Field: Les lis des champs et les oiseaux du ciel. French translation by P. H. Tisseau, Alcan, 1935.

The Gospel of Sufferings: L'Evangile des Souffrances, French translation by P. H. Tisseau, Bazoges-en-Pareds, 1937.

Religion der Tat. Leipzig 1930. (A selection of extracts from Kierkegaard in German, translation by Geismar. Quoted as "Geismar" after reference to the corresponding volume and page of the Danish complete edition of Kierkegaard, *Samlede Värker*, 1901–1906.)

II. Journal[1]

The *Journal* consists of extracts from Kierkegaard's *Scattered Papers*, of which only selections have been translated into English, French, and German. The following have been utilised in the text:

The Journals of Sören Kierkegaard. A selection edited and translated by Alexander Dru. O.U.P. London 1938.

---

[1] From 1831 until his death, with only a few years' interruption, Kierkegaard habitually noted down, on loose sheets or in notebooks, sometimes with the date, the ideas, observations, criticisms, projects for articles, drafts of letters (sometimes fictitious), reflections on his personal life and feelings, prayers and religious meditations, which he hoped to make use of in his books. It is this collection of documents which is called *Scattered Papers* in the complete edition of his works. They have been divided by the editors into three groups: the first (A) contains all those to be described as *Journal* notes; the second (B) embraces everything relating to Kierkegaard's literary work; finally, the third (C) relates to his theological and philosophical reading and researches. Published selections from the *Journal*, such as A. Dru's, are consequently drawn largely from Series A.

(Quoted as "Dru" followed by the number of the extract quoted.)
Kierkegaard, *Journal* (Extraits), 1834–46, French translation by Ferlov
and Gateau. Gallimard. Paris 1941.

(Quoted as "F. & G." and the page reference.)

J. Wahl, *Etudes Kierkegaardiennes*, Aubier 1938. This study contains
numerous extracts from Kierkegaard's text. (Quoted as "Wahl").

P.-H. Tisseau, *Prières*, and *Christ*, Bazoges-en-Pareds, 1937, 1940.
Passages from the *Journal* concerning prayer, and Christ's life.
(Quoted as "Tisseau".)

Kierkegaard, *Die Tagebücher*, in zwei Bänden ausgewählt und über-
setzt von Th. Haecker. 1923. (Tom. II quoted as "Haecker".)

Wherever possible, references have also been given to the Danish
edition of the *Scattered Papers* (1835, I A 46=Vol. I, Series A, page 46),
and of the *Posthumous Papers; Efterladte Papirer*, 8 vol., 1869–81.
(Quoted as "E.P.", with vol. and page number.)

FOREWORD

The name of Kierkegaard, which not long ago was still almost unknown outside a small circle of specialists, is on the way to acquiring a celebrity which will make it equal to the greatest of our present age. As translations of his works appear, admiration increases for a body of writing whose literary perfection, psychological subtlety, wealth of doctrine, and dialectical force assert themselves with singular authority. From another point of view, the concrete, "existential" character of a way of thought which thrusts its roots into the very depths of the human heart and which had at its command a power of psychological analysis truly without equal, holds the attention of an age which appears to have little taste for abstract speculation, and is seeking to recover the meaning of living, the direct contact between reality and experience. The current of Bergsonian thought had already run powerfully in this direction. There had developed a new climate which was to make the public ready to welcome a way of thought which presents itself more as an expression of the soul and of life than as an intellectual structure. Lastly and above all the anxiety which possesses present generations concerning the value of life and the meaning of human greatness, and also the disappointments which have followed the immense effort of the first half of the century to resolve, by means of criticism and history, of scholarship and statistics, of psychology and sociology, the problems raised by the existence of religion and morality, and particularly of Christianity; all this could not but give a powerful sense of topicality to Kierkegaard's work, intended as it was to make men heedful of the original and immeasurable nature of the Christian message, to give them the inclination and the will to "become Christians", that is to say, to live intensely, and to fulfil all the demands of a faith made to govern and transform the whole of life.

Without doubt, Kierkegaard stands out as one of the greatest among those thinkers who, without official authority, have had the noble ambition to be the apostles of Christian truth. He can be compared without hesitation to Pascal. He has the same fervour and enthusiasm, passion and harshness, power and depth, with all the dazzling gifts of genius. They are heroes of equal stature. As he himself remarked of Goethe, Kierkegaard's greatness, like Pascal's, was "to have once seen, once felt, something so incomparably great, that all else seems to be nothing beside it, something one never forgets, even if one forgets everything else." (*Journal*, 1837, I A 58). This "something", again so Pascalian, was "becoming a Christian".

In many aspects of his work, Kierkegaard reminds one of the Jewish prophets. The dramatic struggle in which he himself is engaged, the struggle in which he sees all Christendom involved, taking the risk of allowing his Christian faith to be weakened by the assurance he received from the official, juridical reality of a profession of Christianity: this it is which leads him more and more to thrust aside the moderate and peaceable methods of discussion in favour of a proclamation of the gospel message presented in its original vigour and its essentially paradoxical nature— to the Jews a stumbling block and to the Greeks, foolishness—and one knows that Jews and Greeks abound in Christendom. Instinctively he puts forward the most brutal formulas, summary judgements, heroic solutions. He sees truth only in the enthusiasm of passion and the ardent fervour of the partisan. His Christianity is intransigent from conviction. Let us admit that, for a world which, in every field of activity, has so greatly suffered from the temptation of facility, no lesson can be more salutary than that which Kierkegaard offers us.

The conflicts which overwhelmed him are themselves richly instructive for us. His thought, always in the form of dialogue or drama, excels in brushing aside compromises and illusions, the devices of prejudice, the egoisms of the tribe. But it is first of all in his own heart that this moving drama is enacted, and by that fact itself he invites, and indeed obliges, us to relive in ourselves the disputes which tortured him. These disputes, in truth, are eternal; but the form they assume for Kierkegaard is the form which is also relevant to our own age. The problem of truth and the meaning of life, the problem of God and Christianity, the problem of faith and reason, man's impotence to fulfil himself in immanence, the ineradicable attraction of transcendency, all our anguishes and griefs, our doubts and refusals, the divisions of Christendom and the Christian demand for unity, the struggles and victories of faith, and, above all, the effect of a Love which dominates all the vicissitudes of individual life as it does all the contingencies of history: Kierkegaard's soul has experienced, with prodigious intensity, this drama, at once manifold and simple, which is the drama of the present age.

On many points, undoubtedly, we shall have to leave the paths that Kierkegaard followed. But the fact remains that he expounds the problems with admirable precision and force, that he explores, so to speak, all their out-of-the-way corners, and that even when in our view he goes astray, he casts magnificent light upon them. By the power, above all, of a passionate dialectic, which but for Pascal could be called unique in the history of modern thought, he obliges us less to come to a conclusion than to choose and to choose to make a choice, or rather, if one prefers, to ensure that our conclusion is a choice, that is to say a binding engagement which makes a reality, if necessary by risking everything, of the perfect coincidence of truth and life.

Such is the man of whom, and of whose writings, we wish to give a general, but nevertheless precise, account, so as to facilitate the reading of works which are often difficult of approach. In this study of Kierkegaard's life, thought and spirit, our wish would be to satisfy the condition which Kierkegaard lays down for an Introduction worthy of the name. It should, he says, (*Unscientific Postscript*, p. 18) expound a problem. Now there are three ways of making a problem disappear instead of *expounding* it, that is to say making it clear, visible and living. In the first place, there is the learned introduction; at first this appears capable of bringing great enlightenment, by the detailed erudition it displays. But this is an illusion, for the effort to attain critical perfection is not necessarily the same as that expended upon the problem. This latter is always simple: scholarship moves around it, multiplying points of view and comparisons, but does not enter into the problem itself. There is also the introduction which takes the form of a "rhetorical exposé". It is eloquent and polemical, but it too distracts attention from the problem. Instead of bringing the reader's mind to grips with it, it breaks up the problem into material for its effects. The orator does not reason dialectically. He wishes to impress. As for the systematic introduction, which sets out to synthesize everything by main force, to impose a logical order upon the factors involved, it promises everything and achieves nothing whatever. The problem finds itself in some sense devoured by the system, the question by the answer, life by mathematics. Everything is ordered in advance by the system's hidden postulates.

Let us then avoid these misleading introductions. Let us endeavour to expound in the simplest way possible, without any display of scholarship or rhetoric, the Kierkegaard problem as it appears in the great Danish thinker's works, without attempting to impose any preconceived order upon him: such an order would not be admissible, for the only order he boasts is not that of abstract logic, but of life: the existential order.

Above all, let us approach Kierkegaard as one would a friend. Nothing disturbed him so much as becoming the prey of the professors. He wonders, in a note in the *Journal* (1852, Haecker, p. 293), to whom he should bequeath the intellectual riches, dazzling enough in all conscience, which he has accumulated. Alas, he says, I fear my heritage will revert to that breed I dislike so much, but which up till now has inherited, and will go on inheriting, the treasures of the mind—the professors. No, for us Kierkegaard will never be a "subject", matter for academic discussion and the occasion of abstract speculation. It is of a living thought, an ardent soul, a generous heart, an apostle (although he refused the title). in short of a man, that we wish to speak; and this can be in the form of dialogue, which Plato calls the song of friendship. Thus we may fulfil Kierkegaard's wish, which was never to make disciples, but to move men's hearts to serve truth—by practising it.

Lessing, according to Kierkegaard, (*Fear and Trembling*, p. 135, note), had "an exceedingly uncommon gift of explaining what he himself had understood" and "there he stopped". Nowadays, Kierkegaard adds, people go much further; they explain more than they have understood. No doubt, there is little danger of such excess where Kierkegaard is concerned. With him indeed it is an arduous task to explain what one has understood. That is ambition enough for us. It comprises the whole of our purpose in this study.

CONTENTS

PART ONE

BIOGRAPHICAL SKETCH

YEARS OF APPRENTICESHIP

Kierkegaard's Family.—Sören Aabye Kierkegaard was born on 5 May 1813, the year, he tells us, when the State went bankrupt and "so many other mad notes were put into circulation".[1] His father, Mikaël Pedersen Kierkegaard, was born in 1756 and had married for the first time in 1794. He became a widower in 1796, without having had a child. The following year he married his servant, Anna Sörensdatter Lund, then twenty-eight years old, by whom he had seven children, three girls and four boys. Sören, the youngest, was as he put it, "the son of his old age", his father being fifty-six and his mother forty-four when he was born. His parents both came from the countryside of western Jutland, but when Sören came into the world they had long been settled in Copenhagen. Mikaël Kierkegaard, having succeeded in making a handsome fortune in the linen trade, had retired from business and was living there on his income.

Kierkegaard never speaks of his mother, although he loved her dearly, and felt her loss keenly when she died in 1834. She does not seem to have had any profound influence upon him. His father, on the other hand, was a powerful and durable force in his moral and spiritual life. In his *Journal* and his other works, Kierkegaard continually evokes the tortured figure of this old man, in whom the ardent and arid fervour of Moravian pietism was allied to a mysterious melancholy. It was by him that the young Sören was introduced to an absolute respect for duty, for a duty which was itself an absolute rather than a concrete multiplicity of individual duties,[2] and was at the same time initiated into Christianity, but into a sombre, stern Christianity, in which sin assumed a catastrophic aspect and duty took on the form of drama. Certain of his father's sayings sank deep into his heart and caused him a kind of oppressive anxiety, as when he heard repeated, with all possible solemnity, that people spat upon Christ ("people" meaning here the mass of ordinary Christians).[3] Thus Kierkegaard could note in the *Journal* that his father had filled his soul with anguish concerning Christianity.[4] It is in the light of these childhood impressions that we must understand his affirmation, constantly repeated in so many different ways, that "Christianity with the terror removed is merely a Christianity of the imagination".[5]

A "Crazy Upbringing."—At the same time, the extremely subtle religious discussions which Sören's father liked to indulge in with his friends formed a precocious introduction to the fields of theology and ethics, and trained him in dialectical method. Kierkegaard revealed himself very early as a prodigiously gifted pupil. From his earliest schooldays, he plunged with enthusiasm into the mysteries of Greek grammar and the complexities of construing Latin. The manipulation of ideas gave him immense pleasure; their logical arrangement filled him with a kind of ecstasy; above all he preferred the involved dialectic of the so-called "labyrinthine" problems.[6]

Kierkegaard's imagination, too, was especially stimulated at an early age by his father's educational methods. Often, instead of taking him for a walk as he had asked, his father would propose that they should take one, of any kind he chose, without leaving the room. "So they went out of doors to a nearby castle in Spain, or out to the seashore, or about the streets, wherever Johannes wished to go;[7] for his father was equal to anything. While they went up and down the room, his father described all that they saw; they greeted passers-by, carriages rattled past them and drowned his father's voice; the cake-woman's cakes were more enticing than ever. He described so accurately, so vividly, so explicitly even to the least details, everything that was known to Johannes and so fully and perspicuously what was unknown to him, that after half an hour of such a walk with his father he was as much overwhelmed and fatigued as if he had been a whole day out of doors . . . Johannes soon learned from his father how to exercise this magic power. . . ."[8] He rapidly became a master of the art of conjuring up a setting or a scene, and at the same time he learned to overcome solitude by peopling it with all the fantasies of his dreams and his desires and filling it, too, with the meditations of a reflective mind addicted to "eavesdropping upon the secret murmur of one's thoughts."

All this, Kierkegaard says later, formed a crazy sort of upbringing. He never remembered having been a child.[9] But when, after his father's death, he looked back upon these youthful years, he never dreamt of reproaching him with the upbringing he had received or the influence it had had upon him.[10] The reproach would have been valid if he had been an ordinary child. But he was conscious very early of being "an exception" and life confirmed him in this view. His father was thus justified in having used an exceptional method. And Sören, when he was in a position to appreciate the benefit of it, was immeasurably grateful for it to his memory.

His Studies and Vocation.—His secondary school career completed, Kierkegaard went on to the University. Hegel's influence was preponderant at the time, and rationalism seemed to demand recognition as the perfect form of speculation. Kierkegaard, for whom logic had always been a "passionate delight", felt no difficulty in entering into the subtleties of the Hegelian dialectic. On his return home he reflected with extreme attention upon the sayings of these men who had "a head for philosophy", for it was their company, he writes, which he sought above all else.[11] Yet he was far from being carried away by the idealist current then everywhere prevalent. His resistance began to assert itself in the name of a very powerful sense of what he was soon to call *existence, existential reality*, which idealism prides itself upon turning into a mere abstraction. With his usual humour, Kierkegaard has noted the comic side of the "objective and abstract thinker", that is to say, the Hegelian type of idealist: "There is no special difficulty connected with being an idealist in the imagination; but to *exist* as an idealist itself constitutes a hindrance and an objection. To express existentially what one has understood about oneself, is in no way comical. But to understand everything except one's own self is very comical".[12]

Thus he reached his twentieth year. Neither his life nor his ideas, however, had yet undergone any noticeable change. As in his earliest years, he remained a stranger to the world and always a lover of solitude, for the sake of listening to his own thoughts.[13] Reflection absorbed him for long periods and took a special form in him, which was to characterize all his literary production. He observes in the *Journal*[14] that while either the trivial or the important might catch his attention as starting points for his thought, nevertheless the conclusions were of no consequence to him, for it was only the flux and reflux of the meditations themselves which interested him.[15]

Kierkegaard has noted in *Unscientific Postscript*[16] that it was about this time that he became aware that his vocation was to devote himself to making things more difficult. "You must," he told himself, "do something, but inasmuch as with your limited capacities it will be impossible to make anything easier than it has become, you must, with the same humanitarian enthusiasm as the others, undertake to make something harder." "This notion," he adds, "pleased me immensely, and at the same time it flattered me to think that I, like the rest of them, would be loved and esteemed by the whole community. Out of love for mankind, and out of despair at my embarrassing situation, seeing that I had accomplished nothing, and was unable to make anything easier than it had already been made, and moved by a genuine interest in those who make everything easy, I conceived it as my task to create difficulties everywhere.[17] Nothing, moreover, is more apt to arouse the enthusiasm of noble souls, who can become enthusiastic only over what is difficult".[18]

Let us give Kierkegaard his due: if that was his mission, he has fulfilled it magnificently. As for his literary and speculative talents, they seemed to him, from then on, to find their fullest expression in the practice of introspection and the inner dialogue (which he already practised, but without discipline or method). This alone, he feels, can furnish his thought with the richest nourishment and complete stability.[19]

NOTES TO CHAPTER ONE

[1] *Journal*, 1843, IV B. 1. (Dru 477). Kierkegaard adds: "I can be best compared to one of them. There is something about me which points to greatness, but because of the mad state of affairs I am only worth little. And sometimes notes of that kind are the misfortune of a whole family."

[2] Cf. *Either/Or*, II, 225, where Kierkegaard assigns obviously personal recollections to the assessor William's pen: "When I was sent to this school and the prescribed schoolbooks had been bought, my father handed them to me with the words, 'William, when the month is up, you are the third in your class.' I was exempted from all parental twaddle. He never asked me about my lessons, never heard me recite them, never looked at my exercise book, never reminded me that now it was time to read, now time to leave off. . . . When I wanted to go out he asked me first whether I had time. That I was to decide for myself, not he, and his query never went into details. . . . I had not many duties —and how many children are spoiled by being overwhelmed by a regular ceremonial of duties! So I got a thoroughly deep impression of the fact that there was something called duty and that it had eternal validity."

[3] Cf. *Journal*, 1844, IV A 144 (Dru 457): "I could perhaps reproduce the tragedy of my childhood, the terrifying, mysterious explanation of religion which a frightful foreboding played into my hands, which my imagination worked upon, and the scandal which religion became to me—all in a novel called "the mysterious family". It would begin on a completely idyllic, patriarchal note so that no one suspected anything until suddenly the word sounded which translated everything into terror."

[4] 1848 (Haecker, p. 427).

[5] *Unscientific Postscript*, p. 524. Cf. *The Point of View*, p. 76: "Already in my earliest childhood I broke down under the grave impression which the melancholy old man who laid it upon me himself sank under. A child—what a crazy thing!—travestied as an old man! Frightful! What wonder then that there were times when Christianity appeared to me the most inhuman cruelty."

[6] Cf. *Either/Or*, II. 225, where Kierkegaard explains how his passion for Latin grammar and the high disdain he felt for exceptions to the rule, always branded in red in his notebooks, introduced him to philosophical inquiry, which is fundamentally the art of distinguishing the essential from the accidental.

[7] Johannes Climacus, the pseudonym under which Kierkegaard published the *Philosophical Fragments*, and provided some autobiographical reminiscences in the *Journal*.

[8] *Journal*, 1843, IV B I (Dru 413).

[9] *Journal*, 1843, IV B I (Dru 413, in part, F. and G. p. 194): "When Johannes grew old he had no toys to lay aside, for he had learned to play with that which was to be the serious business of his life, and yet it lost thereby nothing of its allurement. A little girl goes on playing with her doll so long that at last it is transformed into a lover; woman's whole life is nothing but love. Johannes' life had a similar continuity, for it was nothing but thought."

[10] It is possible moreover, as certain notes in the *Miscellaneous Papers* tend to suggest, that Kierkegaard exaggerated the austere and sombre side of his childhood years, especially after 1843, when he was under the influence of a more and more oppressive melancholy.

[11] *Journal*, 1843, IV B I (F. & G.p. 194).

[12] *Unscientific Postscript*, p. 315-6.

[13] Cf. *Stages on Life's Way*, p. 214, concerning these early years: "I have often in my youth smiled inwardly at love. I have not derided it, nor sought with hand or mouth to make it ridiculous, it concerned me too little for that. But I have lived intellectually. . . . The eternal, a God-relationship, relationship to ideals, was what moved my soul".

[14] F. & G. I. p. 194.

[15] Cf., again, the reminiscences of the *Unscientific Postscript*, p. 165 on this period: "I had been a student half a score of years. Although never lazy, all my activity nevertheless was like a glittering inactivity, a kind of occupation for which I still have a great partiality, and for which perhaps I even have a little genius. I read much, spent the remainder of the day idling and thinking, or thinking and idling, but that was all it came to; the earliest sproutings of my productivity barely sufficed for my daily use and were consumed in their first greening. An inexplicable persuasive power constantly held me back, by strength as well as by artifice. This power was my indolence. It is not like the impetuous inspiration of love, nor like the strong prompting of enthusiasm, it is rather like a housekeeper who holds one back, with whom one is very well off, so well off that it never occurs to one to get married. So much at least is certain, that although I am not unacquainted with the comforts and conveniences of life, of all conveniences indolence is the most comfortable."

[16] p. 165-6.

[17] With regard to Christianity, this mission of making everything more difficult becomes the mission of restricting its spread as far as possible. "My task," Kierkegaard writes (June, 1844, Wahl, p. 35), "is something so new that in the eighteen centuries of Christendom there is nobody whose advice I can seek on how to conduct myself. Anything which outstanding individuals have done up till now has been towards the expansion of Christianity; my task is to stop this expansion".

[18] *Fear and Trembling*, p. 189.

[19] Cf. Letter of 6 July 1835, to a friend (*Journal* I A 74, F. & G. p. 30): "To return to our friends' silence, it is favourable to me, then, in so far as it teaches me to fix my gaze upon my own self, it stimulates me to grasp it, this self which is mine, to hold myself steady amid the infinite changeability of life, to turn towards myself the concave mirror in which I formerly tried to capture life outside myself; that silence pleases me because I am capable of this effort and I feel I am of sufficient stature to hold up the mirror, whatever it may show me, an ideal picture or a caricature of myself."

II

THE GREAT EARTHQUAKE

The Temptation of Unbelief.—From this moment onwards, the trusting admiration Sören had for his father suffers quite a long eclipse. The causes are to be sought in Kierkegaard's psychological evolution. By developing his taste for solitary meditation, the education he had received had itself also awakened and stimulated a natural tendency to independence. Even at eighteen he is conscious of the originality and richness of his own personality, and keenly feels the need to preserve it. At this time, his ideas about the world and about life change in a direction which leads him away from his father. He had been set upon the path of theological studies, which were to prepare him for a minister's career, but he applies himself to them only half-heartedly and irregularly, having no clear idea of what career would suit him. His intellectual life, too, seems to take a new course; he appears anxious to draw up an exact balance-sheet of his acquisitions in the fields of doctrine and morals, and above all, he writes, to "find a truth which is true *for me*, to find *the idea for which I can live and die*".[1] He admits, no doubt, the existence of an "imperative of knowledge", that is to say a principle and a rule of objective certainty, analogous to the moral imperative.[2] But this imperative, he says, he must absorb within himself as something living. It was with this in view that he then thought of studying law, to sharpen his discernment in the manifold complications of life. Hence, too, his wish to become a barrister, so as to obtain, by entering into the rôle of another person, "a substitute for his own life".[3]

These uncertainties coincide in Sören with a growing detachment from Christianity, marked by passages in the *Journal* which one might well attribute to Nietzsche[4] if one did not know their author. Even in these passages however one can seize Kierkegaard's method of elaborating, at the same time, a conception of Christianity which will eventually dominate his thought and become the central theme of his work. Christianity, he wrote about this time, is "a radical cure, one puts it off as long as possible".[5] "How is it," he asks again, "that there are many who, so they say, find Christian impulses in their consciousness, but who on the other hand neither are nor give themselves out to be Christians? It is probably because *Christianity is a radical cure* (the italics are Kierkegaard's) which people shrink from, although they do not require those outward representations which in the earliest times resulted in many Christians putting off the decisive step till the last moment—it is probably this, that they lack the strength to make the despairing *leap*".[6]

The exact meaning of this criticism is here apparent: it is directed against what he will later call the "Christianity of Christendom", in opposition to authentic Christianity, which demands "the most fearful of all decisions".[7] But all this is still only suggested.[8] For the time being Kierkegaard abandons religious observances and gives himself up to a life of cafés and pleasure. All the information which scholars have been able to collect on this period of his life[9] tends to present him to us in the character of a young dandy, spending heavily on the "æsthetic futilities" which he affects (perfumes, especially), denying himself nothing in the way of food and drink, dressing exquisitely in accordance with the most trifling demands of fashion. Brandt has calculated, from his expense book, that in 1836 alone Sören put himself into debt for 1262 rixdaler,[10] of which 235 was for a café account.

Physically Kierkegaard was of poor appearance. Thin, frail-looking, a little bent and giving the impression of being a hunchback, he knew he was ugly. In a letter to his fiancée, with which he had enclosed a caricature of himself, he remarked to her that after all he was better looking than the picture he was sending her! Nature had endowed him with an odd voice, very high-pitched, reminiscent of a eunuch's, with abrupt changes in its intonation. He described his own voice as "uncircumcized, not an evangelist's"; it is, he says, "a night-hoarseness like a seagull's cry, a dying voice like the benediction on a dumb man's lips".

Morally Kierkegaard had a difficult character. He was of a caustic, mocking turn of mind, and rarely amiable; his sense of superiority often found expression in satirical remarks or hurtful attitudes. In company he enjoyed displaying a dazzling vivacity, and knew how to employ with enormous éclat a store of knowledge which was already extremely varied and extensive. Israel Levine, who was his secretary from 1845 onwards, declares that he seemed constantly impelled by a spirit of contradiction; he maintained with vehemence the most extravagant opinions, and rarely revealed his true thoughts. His talk, too, was of the freest; the liveliness of his imagination allowed him to recount his "visions" "with remarkable eccentricity and indecency, and a degree of frankness which was horrifying". He used to assert, Levine adds, that where paintings were concerned it was only lubricity of thought, not liberty of expression, which was to be avoided, "poetry being made not for babes in arms, or little girls, but for mature minds". So he was both admired and feared. Generally speaking, his sarcastic cast of mind and his susceptibility cut him off from all friendship.[11]

This style of life was far from affording him any great satisfaction. He was trying, no doubt, in this way to dispel or at least to conceal from himself the melancholy and sadness which formed the basis of his nature. A Don Juan in all appearance, tempted too by Faust's spirit of knowledge and doubt, he felt deep within him the anguish of the Wandering Jew, that is (in his conception) of the man whose life develops wholly apart from the things of religion. As we shall see later on, when we attempt to analyse his psychology more closely, the truly prodigious powers of reflection which were vouchsafed to him prevented him from really losing himself in the pleasure of the moment. "It is certainly true," he writes at this time, "that Faust includes in himself Don Juan; but nevertheless his amorous life, his sensuality, can never be the same; with Faust the latter is already mediate, something he is driven by despair to throw himself into".[12] He has said of these youthful years ("the road to perdition") that after noisy banquets where, with his dazzling wit, he had drawn forth the admiration of his companions in pleasure, he would go home with despair in the depths of his soul. "I have just returned from a party of which I was the life and soul; wit poured from my lips, everyone laughed and admired me—but I left—and the dash should be as long as the earth's orbit—and wanted to shoot myself".[13]

All this explains well enough why his studies lagged. Examinations were constantly deferred till later. Sören's father looked on sadly at these excesses, which were in such sharp contrast with the austere life of the family circle. Kierkegaard gives this as the moment when "communication" with his father broke down. Disagreement between them even became such that in September 1837 an amicable separation became necessary. It was agreed that Sören should receive from his father an annual allowance of 500 rixdalers,[14] which would permit him to live on his own, and in comparative comfort, thanks to the fees from some lucrative work,[15] until he had chosen his career.

The Thorn in the Flesh.—Henceforth, then, Kierkegaard had complete freedom, and the rupture with his father seemed complete and final. During all this period (1837–8) he is "increasingly out of sorts, abashed, discouraged", as his elder brother puts it in his *Journal*, and for his own part he notes: "It seems as though I were a galley-slave, chained to death; every time life moves the chains rattle and death withers everything—*and that happens every minute*".[16] What exactly does he mean? There are several hypotheses. Did Sören suffer from some physical defect, like that which had by then already carried off five of his brothers and sisters? Was it suffering of a moral order? or the anguish of feeling that a curse lay upon all the Kierkegaards? or, again, that melancholy whose weight never ceased to oppress him secretly, a melancholy which turned all the flowers of his heart to ice-flowers?[17] or, even, the somehow breathless, jerky character imparted to his life by the morbid exaltation of his feelings? "This is my misfortune," he notes, "all my life is an interjection; nothing is firmly fixed in place (everything moves, there is nothing motionless, no *dwelling*), my sadness is wailing despair, my joy an exalted lyricism, an upward leaping".[18] "The thorn in the flesh" to which the *Journal* so often refers contained something, no doubt, of all these. Kierkegaard moreover experiences, as his analysis of it will show later with such lucidity in *The Sickness unto Death*, the radical failure of the æsthetic life; that is to say, of the life which makes enjoyment its principle. "No less than in the bottomless ocean of pleasure," he writes, "I have sounded in vain for a spot to cast an anchor in the abysses of knowledge. I have felt the almost irresistible power with which one pleasure drags another after it, the kind of adulterated enthusiasm which it is capable of producing, the boredom, the torment which follow".[19] But at the same time Kierkegaard returned to Christianity, or at least to the public act of communion, which formerly he had been wont to perform in the company of his father and elder brother, which he had abandoned for some time and which he would in future perform alone.

His Father's Secret, and Death.—It was in these circumstances, in 1838, that he was reconciled with his father, shortly before Mikaël Pedersen died, at the age of eighty-two.[20] It was an event which overwhelmed him, and he has provided us with only fragmentary and somewhat mysterious information concerning it. What is certain is that he learned from his father a secret of the latter's conscience which threw new light upon the old draper's whole life, and whose revelation was a blow of incredible violence to him. "Then it was," he writes, "that the great earthquake occurred, the terrible revolution which suddenly forced upon me a new and infallible law of interpretation of all the facts. Then I suspected that my father's great age was not a divine blessing but rather a curse; that the outstanding intellectual gifts of our family were only given to us in order that we should rend each other to pieces; then I felt the stillness of death grow around me when I saw in my father, an unhappy man who was to outlive us all, a cross on the tomb of all his hopes. There must be a guilt upon the whole family, the punishment of God must be on it".[21] Mikaël Pedersen thought that for him the punishment for his sins consisted in seeing all his children die before him. Sören had adopted this point of view and was convinced that in any case he would not live beyond thirty-three, the maximum age of those of his brothers and sisters who were already dead. He was consequently very surprised to have to celebrate his thirty-fourth birthday on 5 May 1847. It is this conviction which explains the title of his first work, published in 1838, *Papers of a survivor*; Kierkegaard, who was twenty-five at the time, explains that he expects to die soon.

It has been supposed that it is to this tragic secret of his father's that Kierkegaard alludes in a passage in the *Journal* where he tells the terrible story of the man who "once as a little boy, while herding the flocks on the heaths of Jutland, suffering greatly, in hunger and in want, stood upon a hill and cursed God—and the man was unable to forget it even when he was eighty-two years old."[22] Hence, once admitted to the paternal secret, Sören could at last grasp the meaning of the melancholy which he had always observed in his father: it was the despair of a conscience which dared not absolve itself, and in which solitary meditation had monstrously magnified the sense of guilt. It can be assumed that he devoted himself to restoring to his father the comfort of hope, and that in this task of filial love he himself re-discovered the faith and the joy which he believed he had lost. The *Journal* for this period contains many echoes of this new spiritual state.[23] His Christian fervour was henceforth to be associated with the feelings of veneration and admiration which he had formerly had for his father, and to whom he now offered them again, transformed by understanding of his fault and his repentance.[24]

NOTES TO CHAPTER TWO

[1] *Journal*, 1 August 1835, I A 75. (Dru 22.)

[2] Kierkegaard always thought however that no certainty was afforded by the senses. "The apparent trustworthiness of sense," he writes, (*Unscientific Postscript*, p. 280), "is an illusion. This was shown adequately as early as in Greek scepticism, and modern idealism has likewise demonstrated it." It is from this that Kierkegaard later deduces that historical knowledge is at best an approximation.

[3] *Journal*, 1 August 1835, I A 75. (Dru 22.)

[4] Cf. *Journal*, 1835, I A 101 (F. & G. p. 39 and 41): "In many cases, when I look at Christian lives, Christianity, instead of giving them strength, seems to have emasculated them as compared with pagans, and these Christians seem to me henceforth as geldings to stallions. For my part, I have an idea which has always seemed to me beneficial in quite another way; I should like to see the world's great geniuses, who put their shoulders to the wheel of human history assembled together again; I am filled with enthusiasm at the idea of such a sublime academy, of such a republic of letters. . . . Yet Christians have always feared to admit these great men among them, lest the company should become too mixed, so that only one note shall be sounded; and so they sit in a closed circle, rejoicing that they have built an impenetrable wall of China against the Barbarians."

[5] *Journal*, 9 October 1835, I A 89. (Dru 27.)

[6] *Journal*, 1835, I A 101. (Dru 32.)

[7] Cf. *Unscientific Postscript*, p. 333: "Becoming a Christian is then the most fearful decision of a man's life, a struggle through to attain faith against despair and offence, the twin Cerberuses that guard the entrance to a Christian life."

[8] On many points, however, Kierkegaard adopts positions at this time which he will later abandon for others exactly contrary to them. Thus he thinks that present-day Christians, after eighteen centuries, enjoy a privileged position as compared to those of the early years: "When one expounds the idea of inspiration, one speaks of the apostles' personal contact with Christ as though they enjoyed a privilege in understanding him well, in advance of other men, but one forgets that on the other hand those who live after Christianity has lasted eighteen centuries have a great advantage in the very fact that it has penetrated into every field, that it has progressed, while the apostles had to struggle against a multitude of abuses, errors, etc., precisely because Christianity was then only just beginning." (*Journal*, 1835, I A 50, F. & G., p. 19). Similarly *Journal*, 1835, I A 108, Wahl, p. 583: "It is certain that he who remains close to the source must receive the strongest and most immediate impression; but does it follow that it is the purest? Here I must perforce point out the essential circumstance that now, after this period of eighteen hundred years, the Christian element has impregnated the whole of life, so that in the Christian church the whole of life is permeated with the Christian element (Christian philosophy, Christian aesthetics, Christian history) and furthermore I must point out that it

is now undoubtedly easier to discover the essentially Christian element. One must study not the undeveloped bud but the plant in flower." We shall see how Kierkegaard will later oppose to this view his notion of contemporaneity. He writes again (*Journal* 1835, I A 58, Wahl, p. 584): "It would be absurd for the Church to say: 'I am conscious of my existence, therefore I am the original Apostolic Church.' The Church must be prepared to substantiate, to prove this latter assertion, since it is a question of history." Soon, however, he will exclude all possibility of proof and refuse all value to historical criticism. On 2 May 1835 Kierkegaard writes (Journal, I A 49, F. & G. p. 19): "Christians who to-day consider Judaism realize that it was only a transition, but who can prove that this is not also the case with Christianity?" Kierkegaard is not long in replying to this objection, showing that within the religious field Christianity is a climax and an absolute, ordered by nothing external, but by which everything is ordered.

9 Especially Fr. Brandt, in his word *Der Junge S. Kierkegaard* (The Young Kierkegaard).

10 About £300.

11 It seems, however, that Kierkegaard gradually succeeded in correcting the asperities of his character, and that the agreeableness of which he was also capable triumphed in his later years over the caustic and polemical tendencies of his youth.

12 *Journal*, 1836, I A 227 (Dru 71).

13 *Journal*, 1836, I A 161 (Dru 53).

14 About £130.

15 During the winter of 1837-8 Kierkegaard taught Latin to a senior form in the Copenhagen lycée.

16 *Journal*, 1837-9, II A 647 (Dru 136).

17 *Journal*, 1837-9, II A 641 (Dru 132).

18 *Journal*, 13 March, 1839, II A 382 (F. & G. p. 89).

19 *Journal*, 1835, I A 85 (F. & G. p. 33).

20 Between October and December 1835 has sometimes been proposed as the date, and certain psychological reasons would seem to make this plausible. On the other hand, however, it is difficult to reconcile this date with the events of 1836-7, when relations between Kierkegaard and his father became so strained that they led to their separation.

21 *Journal*, 1837-9, II A 805 (Dru 243).

22 *Journal*, 1840, VII A 4 (Dru 556). Sören probably knew another secret of his father's, namely that before he married his second wife (his servant) he had had marital relations with her.

23 Cf. *Journal*, 19 May 1838, 10. 30 a.m., II A 228 (Dru 207): "There is an indescribable joy which enkindles us as inexplicably as the apostle's outburst comes gratuitously: 'Rejoice I say unto you, and again I say unto you rejoice'. Not a joy over this or that but the soul's mighty song . . . a heavenly refrain, as it were, suddenly breaks off our other song; a joy which cools and refreshes us like a breath of wind, a wave of air, from the trade wind which blows from the planes of Mamre to the everlasting habitations."

24 *Journal*, 11 August 1838, II A 243 (Dru 215): "My father died on Wednesday (the 9th) at 2 a.m. I had so very much wished that he might live a few

years longer, and I look upon his death as the last sacrifice which he made to his love for me: for he did not die from me but *died for me* in order that if possible I might still turn into something. Of all that I have inherited from him, the recollection of him, his transfigured portrait—not transfigured by the poetry of my imagination (for it did not require that) but explained by many an individual trait of which I can now take account—is dearest to me, and I will be careful to preserve it safely hidden from the world."

THE BETROTHAL TO REGINA OLSEN

Regina Olsen.—Kierkegaard resolved to put his life in order and comply with his father's desire to see him take his theological degrees and become a pastor. On 3 July 1840, indeed, he successfully sat the examination in theology necessary for the exercise of the ministry, and preached his first sermon in a Copenhagen church in early January 1841. Finally, on 29 September of the same year, he maintained before the University his thesis *On the Concept of Irony.*

For a short period, his religious life was of intense fervour.[1] At this time, too, he decided on marriage, which was to lift him permanently from the rut in which he was struggling and establish him among "the generality" (upon well-trodden paths). In 1840, when still a theological student, Sören became engaged to Regina Olsen, supplanting another suitor. This engagement was the starting point of an extraordinary adventure, whose repercussions upon his life and his works were immense. In fact, he had been engaged for only a few months when he felt how impossible it would be, without deception, to involve an open-hearted, simple young girl of seventeen in the destinies of a young intellectual marked down, apparently, to be an "exception", and in addition burdened with a melancholy which bore all the signs of fatality.

Kierkegaard's confidences on the subject, his numerous writings relating to the event, allow us to be even more precise. He loved Regina Olsen deeply and sincerely. He seems, however, to have been obsessed by the difference in age (ten years) between his fiancée and himself. He looked upon himself as an old man recalling a youthful passion with feelings of melancholy tenderness. Regina gradually assumed for him the form of an exquisite picture shrouded in the mists of the past. His passion (as he explains in *Repetition*) was no longer anything but recollection, and consequently it was no longer Regina whom he loved, but the image she had left in his memory, or rather the absolute spiritual ideal to which he had raised himself from that time on.[2]

The Obstacle of Melancholy.—Kierkegaard also keenly felt his melancholy to be an obstacle,[3] and it had taken on a new meaning for him through the revelation of his father's secret. Its source, no doubt, lay in his physical make-up. But it was at the same time the outward sign and the effect of the dramatic circumstances which had left their mark upon his father's life.[4] As such it became for him a matter of conscience, the sacred continuation, as it were, of a despair and a repentance which he had inherited.[5] How could Regina be associated with a spiritual condition at once so complex and so exceptional? To explain himself upon this point, he notes in the *Journal*,[6] would have been to initiate Regina into "terrible things": his father's melancholy and the eternal night which brooded over him, his own relations with this father whom he both loved and feared, his own irregularities, his desires and excesses, which were not perhaps such very great faults in God's eyes, for it was really anguish of spirit which had led him astray—and where should he have looked for support, when he knew or at least suspected that the only man whose force and energy he might have admired wavered in such dramatic fashion himself!

Thus Kierkegaard argued with himself. It seems, however, according to *Guilty? Not Guilty?*, that he at first thought that marriage would be possible if he admitted Regina Olsen to the dreadful secret of his melancholy. But that implied that they should both agree in centring their lives upon religion. He applied himself, then, to endowing his fiancée with a deep religious life, and to this end read to her freely from works of piety. The results were inconsiderable; Regina Olsen did not appear to be desirous (or capable) of following him along this path. She was lacking, it seemed, in religious inclination.[7] It was then that he understood that in the absence of any spiritual harmony between his fiancée and himself the marriage was decidedly impossible: a marriage in such circumstances—any marriage at all, no doubt, in his case—

would be a kind of moral death for him, to which nothing would make him resolve himself.[8] "By such a union," he told himself, "I become unhappy, I feel apprehensive with regard to my deepest existence. If now I could, if I were morally compelled to go through with this, well then, what further, what of her happiness for which I am to risk all this? Am I then to stake everything upon a fond illusion? If only anyone could assure me that she would be happy—but to be in an illusion, is that to be happy?"[9]

The Rupture.—All the obstacles thus appeared insurmountable to Kierkegaard. Consequently he decided to break off his engagement. In August 1841, returning her ring, he sends Regina the following note: "Let this be an accomplished fact, so that there may be no further renewal of attempts at what must nevertheless happen, and which, once it has happened, will provide the strength which is necessary. Above all, forget the author of these lines; forgive a man who, though able to do much, is incapable of making a young girl happy."

The engagement, however, was not broken off immediately. Regina was so deeply hurt by Sören's decision that he agreed to return to her. But if he did so it was with the intention of applying other tactics, designed to discourage Regina's love and to alienate her from himself. He thought that the rupture would be less painful if Regina ceased to love and even respect him. Hence he affected for several months an attitude of coldness and apparent indifference towards his fiancée (of being "tired of her, a deceiver, crack-brained", he defines it in *Guilty?*) and even (if one goes by the *Seducer's Journal*) of having a new attachment elsewhere.[10] As he had foreseen, this behaviour eventually proved too much for Regina's constancy. In October 1841 the final break occurred.

It seems however that, in spite of everything, Regina Olsen wished to preserve some hope that her former fiancé might return to her.[11] In this attitude Kierkegaard discerned both the failure of his efforts and lack of pride, thoughtlessness and vanity in Regina. For, he writes, "if there had really been any buoyancy of character in her, the way in which I broke off the engagement would

have finished everything completely. My method was intended
to give her precisely that kind of resiliency. But see how my
beauty behaved: at first distant and stand-offish, from pride and
arrogance, and afterwards cowardly".[12] These terms are undoubtedly excessive. However that may be, the affair ended as he
had sometimes wished: in 1843 Regina Olsen became engaged to
Fritz Schlegel, whom she had known and loved before Kierkegaard. Their marriage took place four years later. One final
episode, in the summer of 1855, marked the end of Regina Schlegel's relations with her former fiancé. Regina's husband had just
been appointed governor of the Danish West Indies, and his
wife was preparing to leave with him. Regina contrived to meet
Sören in the street and said to him tenderly: "God bless you, and
may everything go with you as you would wish." Kierkegaard
stepped aside and answered only with a bow.

   This love story, so involved and so strange, throws remarkable
light upon Kierkegaard's psychology. The explanations of it
which he subsequently furnished[13] are scarcely successful in putting us off the scent and making us forget how much there was
that was morbid in his way of studying his behaviour and his own
feelings. It is very true that he was conscious of this morbidity, of
what he calls in the *Journal* (1847) "the bizarre depths of his
machinery", and that this consciousness explains and justifies the
rupture. "Ought a soldier of the advanced guard to be married?"
he asks. "Dare a soldier on the frontier (spiritually understood)
take a wife, a soldier on duty at the extremest outpost, who is
fighting day and night, not exactly against Turks and Scythians,
but against the robber bands of an innate melancholy, a soldier
of the outpost who, even though he does not fight day and night,
though for a considerable period he has peace, yet never can know
at what instant the war will begin again, since he cannot even
dare to call this quiet a truce?"[14] All that is understandable, but by
itself it scarcely justifies his manner of breaking with her, and the
cold cruelty it implied. Kierkegaard has repeated that it was his
love for Regina which led him to behave so unfeelingly towards
her.[15] Once the affair was ended however he was not long in
becoming anxious over the results of his strategy. He felt himself

henceforth responsible for the consequences of the rupture.
Every day he wondered what his former fiancée's reactions might
be. He wanted to give an explanation of his actions and make her
understand the reasons underlying them, to show that his face
preserved its true features behind the impostor's mask he had been
obliged to assume. These are the feelings and anxieties which fill
the works which he wrote at this time with such surprising fecun-
dity, especially *The Seducer's Journal*, *Guilty? Not Guilty?*, *Fear
and Trembling*, and *Repetition*, which all date from 1843, and whose
operative source he located in the experience of his engagement,
as well as in his father's influence. "If it were inquired," he writes,
"how, relations with God apart, I was led to become the writer I
am, I would reply—that has depended upon an old man, the man
to whom I owe most of all, and upon a young girl, to whom I
owe a very great debt—hence upon what must have been part of
my nature as a potentiality, the union of old age and youth, the
rigour of winter and the mildness of spring: the one educated me
by his noble wisdom, the other by her sweet futility".[16] Thus
Kierkegaard became at once master of his art as a psychologist
and an analayst ("an expert at reflection", he says), and conscious
of the nature of his genius.[17]

"All Things are New in Christ."—A further result was that henceforth Kierkegaard's thought centred upon the problem of
Christianity and the Christian life. He became convinced both of
his own exceptional nature and of the message he was to address
to his contemporaries.[18] The *Miscellaneous Papers* of this period,
in fact, contain a note in which he gives the plan of a "speculative
exposition of Christian knowledge".[19] The point of view which
he proposes to develop is that "all things are new in Christ",
"new", he explains, "not merely as being other, but as being renewed; the rejuvenated as opposed to the aged, the obsolete".
This point of view Kierkegaard proposes to present both polemic-
ally and ironically. (The object will be to show that Christianity
is not a peep-hole restricting the vision to a single object, nor a way
of thinking and feeling which admits only one state of mind, but
on the contrary a permanent source of rejuvenation and life.)

Contemporary philosophy, on the other hand, had concerned itself with reducing Christianity to the known and classified forms of the past. The comparative method had appeared to justify the calling into question of its originality. There is nothing new under the sun, it had been said. But that, Kierkegaard remarks, is a negative position which can be defended only by reducing the Christian religion to the abstract outlines which it necessarily has in common with all religious forms. It would be more rewarding to consider the concrete realities comprised within these outlines: then the wonderful novelty of Christianity would be understood.

However, this very impotence of rationalism to discover in Christianity anything that exceeds the common denominator is a tribute to its humanity: from the moment he first receives it, it is essential that in one way or another Christianity should be "natural" to man, that is to say that he should find in it a connecting link and a bond of sympathy. Was it not in this sense that Tertullian spoke of "the naturally Christian soul"? But the mistake consists in not grasping with equal force the other equally necessary aspect of the Christian phenomenon, namely that "Christianity is what has never entered any man's head".

The Religious Poet and the Hermit.—Such were the thoughts upon which Kierkegaard never ceased to meditate, and the plan of the work which he wished to write. In reality, this project, like all his literary activity, was the result, as he later explained,[20] of the union which took place in him at this time between the poet which he became by "following his nature" and the religious feeling which had dominated him continually since childhood. The fact which determined his career as an author and the forms it took was therefore "dialectic", like everything else in him, as he says. From the human point of view, he had by-passed childhood and youth. In default of having been young, he became a poet, which is a second youth. But his Christian antecedents, together with his "essentially religious" character, intervened at the same time with all their weight to give a religious orientation to his poetic vocation. Thus the poetic was in some sense absorbed into the religious, or, to be more precise, it was led to begin in two places at once, and yet in such a way that the poetry was only the instrument and the expression, in disguise, of his religious re-awakening. It is this which explains the apparent duality of his work, and the real unity it possesses. [21] Kierkegaard, however, did not think immediately of becoming a religious author. He wished to exhaust as rapidly as possible the poetic impulse which possessed him, and then obtain an appointment as pastor in a little country parish. But he soon came to realize that he ought to devote himself entirely to his vocation as a religious author.

This project imposed a new way of life upon him. He had to accept solitude. (He remarks moreover that "the need of solitude is a sign that there is spirit in a man after all, and it is a measure for what spirit there is.")[22] Only a solitary life could assure him both leisure for reflection and study and the perfect liberty which the expression of his ideas demanded.[23] Henceforth, apart from four journeys to Berlin, of which one immediately followed the break with Regina Olsen, Kierkegaard lived permanently in Copenhagen, where his patrimony allowed him to live in comfortable independence and to devote himself to literary work with no other care than that of expressing his thought.[24]

However, solitude did not shelter him from public curiosity. Not only had his early writings drawn attention to him, but he acquired a kind of celebrity in his native city at this time by the eccentricities of his dress and his way of living.[25]

A well-known stroller through the Copenhagen streets, whose charms he has sung in some fine lyrical pages, he would reveal all the brilliancy of his prodigious animation and passionate discussion as he wandered through the town, usually in the company of friends encountered on the way. At other times, and more and more frequently in his latter years, he would have himself driven far into the country, as far as the north of Zeeland, to enjoy at leisure the melancholy tranquility of its dull skies and sombre woods.[26] "If one seeks consolation," he writes, "where the lily flowers in its gracefulness—in the fields, and where the birds dwell in their freedom—under the open sky, one will find the silence that is never interrupted, away from every importunate presence, in the bosom of persuasion unalloyed."[27]

Apart from these excursions, Kierkegaard lived at home in solitude behind closed doors. He preferred to work at night. "At night I was no longer alone", he writes. As soon as evening came, all the rooms in his vast apartment were brightly lit; in each one there was always ink and paper. Then he would write, when all outside was wrapped in silence, poring over his touching, mysterious memories of his past, heedful of the call which determined his life's mission.[28]

NOTES TO CHAPTER THREE

[1] Cf. *Journal*, 30 October 1838, II A 285 (Tisseau, p. 1): "Heavenly father! Our thought turns to Thee, it seeks Thee again at this time, not with the hesitant step of a lost traveller, but with the sure flight of a bird which knows it is in its homeland; grant then that our confidence in Thee may not be a fleeting thought, a momentary outburst, deceptive soothers of the fleshly heart; grant that our aspirations to Thy kingdom, our hopes of Thy glory may not be still-born, may not be like empty rainless clouds, but that in the fullness of our heart they may rise up to Thee, and that, being granted, they may refresh our life like dew and satisfy us continually like Thy manna from Heaven."

[2] Cf. *Journal*, 1840, III A 64 (Dru 333): "Altogether my misfortune is that at the time when I went about pregnant with ideas I was frightened by the ideal; and so I gave birth to deformities, and therefore reality does not answer to my burning desires—O God, grant that that should not also be the case in love; for there too I am seized by a mysterious dread of having confused an ideal with a reality."

[3] Cf. *Stages on Life's Way*, p. 326: "Our relationship cannot become a marriage. Why not? Because in my melancholy I am morbidly reserved."

[4] Cf. *Journal*, 1844, V A 33 (Dru 483): "And the father believed that he was the cause of the son's melancholy, and the son believed that he was the cause of the father's melancholy, and so they never discussed it."

[5] Cf. *Stages on Life's Way*, p. 192: "There was once a father and a son. A son is like a mirror in which the father beholds himself, and for the son the father too is like a mirror in which he beholds himself in the time to come. However, they rarely regarded each other in this way, for their daily intercourse was characterized by the cheerfulness of gay and lively conversation. It happened only a few times that the father came to a stop, stood before the son with a sorrowful countenance, looked at him steadily and said: 'Poor child, thou art going into a quiet despair.' True as this saying was, nothing was ever said to indicate how it was to be understood. . . . Then the father died, and the son saw much, experienced much, and was tried in manifold temptations; but infinitely inventive as love is, longing and the sense of loss taught him, not indeed to wrest from the silence of eternity a communication, but to imitate the father's voice so perfectly that he was content with the likeness."

[6] IV A 107 (Dru 444).

[7] Cf. *Stages on Life's Way*, pp. 211-5, 222-8, 286, 291.

[8] *Stages on Life's Way*, p. 282-3: "But what power she has over me! To gratify her every wish, to employ the days in giving her joy, that indeed is a pleasure, had I been permitted to do it; but my thought which is my very life and the loss of which is my spiritual death—if that is to be taken from me! . . . Oh, yes, here you have a real man who resigns himself up to a certain point, and then in turn consoles himself up to a certain point! But no, be still, thou passion,

which would stir my mind to rebellion, though there is good reason for it. For that which to the point of desperation I require of myself—not as something extraordinary but simply as the right thing—I cannot endure to see confused with something different, I cannot chaffer.'

[9] *Stages on Life's Way*, p. 296. This is the meaning of the words on the title-page of this section of the work. *Periissem nisi periissem*: "I would have perished if I had not perished."

[10] Cf. *Journal*, 1841–2, III A 159–61. (Dru 377, 379): "To remain with her was my one desire; but from the moment I felt it would be wrong, and that moment came all too soon, I decided to make her believe I did not love her; and now I am hated by all men for my faithlessness, the seeming cause of her unhappiness, and yet I am faithful to her as always".—"My relation to her may, I truly believe, be called unhappy love—I love her—I own her—her only wish is to remain with me—her family implore me—it is my greatest wish—and I have to say no. In order to make it easier for her I will, if possible, make her believe that I simply deceived her, that I am a frivolous man, so as if possible to make her hate me; for I believe that it would always be more difficult for her if she suspected that the cause was melancholy—how like are melancholy and frivolity."

[11] Cf. *Journal*, 1843, IV A 97 (Dru 439).

[12] *Journal*, 1843, IV A 107 (F. & G. p. 174).

[13] Cf., especially, *Journal*, 1843, IV A 107, 133, 142 (Dru 444, 453, 456)— *Guilty?, Fear Trembling*, p. 144–66.

[14] *Stages on Life's Way*, p. 188: "For a moment Kierkegaard had also thought of putting an end to his life, after having "fanned her love into fire" though it was not a guilty love. But he came to realize that by so doing, far from solacing her grief, he would gravely harm Regina, for she would not fail to blame herself for her fiancé's death. (*Journal*, 1842, III A 166, Dru 383.)

[15] Cf. *Journal*, 1842, III A 179 (Dru 392): "It is hard indeed to have made someone unhappy, and hard that to have made her unhappy is almost the only hope of making her happy."

[16] *Journal*, 1849 (Haecker, p. 51).

[17] The reflections in the *Journal*, 1839, II A 806 (Dru 244) date from an earlier period than that of his relationship with Regina Olsen, but convey feelings which the aftermath of his rupture with her must have greatly strengthened: "Inwardly torn asunder as I was, without any expectation of leading a happy earthly life, ("that I should prosper and live long in the land"), without hope of a happy and comfortable future—as it naturally springs from and lies in the historical continuity of family life—what wonder then that in desperate despair I grasped at nought but the intellectual side in man and clung fast to it, so that the thought of my own considerable powers of mind was my only consolation, ideas my one joy, and mankind indifferent to me". Cf. *The Point of View*, p. 98: "I know that (in respect to genius) extraordinary gifts were bestowed upon me".

[18] Kierkegaard grew more and more convinced that celibacy was the natural condition of an apostle's vocation and even, more generally, of any decision to work for a great idea. Cf. *Journal*, 1847 (Wahl, p. 25): "Other men are too secure in life and consequently do not learn to know God. They have assured

positions; they never go to extremes; they are comforted by wives and children. I shall never speak ill of this happiness, but I believe my task is to dispense
with such things. . . . Every time the history of the world takes an important
step forward and crosses a difficult pass, a formation of remount horses ad-
vances in support: the unmarried, solitary men who live only for an idea". Little
by little, especially in his latter years, Kierkegaard came to feel that his relations
with Regina had been destined by Providence to reveal his vocation to him.
Cf. *Journal*, 1852, X⁵ A 21 (Dru 1281): "My engagement to her and the break
are really my relation to God, they are if I may say so, divinely speaking, my
engagement with God"—1854, XI¹ A 288 (Dru 1338): "A girl was used against
me in a quite unusual way, as an intermediary, in order to get me out (into
existence), and in the interest of ideas."

[19] *Journal*, 1840, III A 211 (F. & G. p. 149).

[20] Cf. *The Point of View*, p. 84 ff.

[21] Cf. *The Point of View*, p. 84–5: "Here the reader can easily perceive the
explanation of all the difficulty of the authorship, but he must note that the
author was at the same time conscious of this. What was to be done? Well,
obviously the poetical had to be evacuated, anything else was impossible for
me. But the whole æsthetic production was put under arrest by the religious.
The religious agreed to this elimination, but incessantly spurred it on, as
though it were saying, 'Are you not now through with that?' While the
poetical works were being produced the author was living under strict religious rules."

[22] *The Sickness unto Death*, p. 102.

[23] Cf. *Journal*, 1851 (Haecker, p. 230): "In the same way that one says one is
bewitched, I might say that I was—wounded by ideas."

[24] On his father's death, Kierkegaard received 31,000 Rx. (more than
£6,000). It has been reckoned that his royalties subsequently amounted to
5,000 Rx. In point of fact he spent his capital so regularly from year to year
that by the time he died he was reduced to the point of poverty. This conduct
has sometimes been explained by his indifference to practical matters. Brandt's
researches have established, however, that this indifference was a very relative
affair; Kierkegaard seems to have watched closely over his own interests
(especially by assuring himself a regular income from his capital), and his con-
tracts with his publishers show that he took good care to insist upon his rights.
There is also the fact to be considered that he believed he was destined to die
young. He explains himself on the subject, moreover, in a note in the *Journal*
(1853, X⁵ A 146, Dru 1294): two things, he says, have discouraged me from
watching over my income. "The first is that there are men whose qualification
is to be sacrificed, in one way or another, sacrificed for others in order to forward the idea—and that, with my particular cross, I was such a man. The other
thought is that I should never be tried by having to work for my livelihood,
partly because I thought that God, considering my particular cross, would
withhold that suffering and task from me. I cannot say where one gets such
ideas; but this I do know, I did not get them out of books or from other men."
In the last resort, the surest explanation of Kierkegaard's penniless condition at
the end of his life is to be found in the enormous expenditure he continually
incurred in keeping up a luxurious style of living.

[25] In one of the aphorisms of the *Diapsalmata* (*Either/Or* vol. I, p. 30) Kierke-gaard notes one aspect of his physical appearance in picturesque terms: "The disproportion in my build is that my forelegs are too short. Like the kangaroo, I have very short forelegs, and tremendously long hind legs. Ordinarily I sit quite still; but if I move, the tremendous leap that follows strikes terror to all my acquaintances, friends and relatives."

[26] Cf. the page quoted by Koch, *Sören Kierkegaard* (French translation by Nicolet and Jansen, Paris, 1931, p. 30): "In the forest of Gribskov there is a place called Eight Road Corner; only the diligent seeker can find it, for it is not shown on any map. Its very name, indeed, seems to involve a contradiction, for how can the intersection of eight roads form a corner? How can something public and much frequented be reconciled with the idea of a remote and hidden spot? . . . This contradiction has the effect of making it even more isolated, for contradiction always leads to solitude. Nobody uses this road, except the little insect in a hurry, crossing it *lente festinans* . . . eight roads and no travel-lers! Truly, one would think that the world was uninhabited. . . . Every-thing one can hear in the world and everything that deserves to be heard is audible, with all possible clarity and charm, in a lonely place where the ear must be on the alert. So I have often been back to my secret place. I have known it for many long years past, but now I know that one has no need of the night to find silence, for there it is always quiet, always beautiful, and at present more beautiful than ever. It seems to me, then, that the autumn sun marks the even-ing hour, and the blue of the sky grows languid, while all creatures draw breath anew after the heat of the day, and coolness spreads into the air and the leaves in the meadow tremble with delight, while the forest fans itself. Then towards evening the sun's thoughts turn towards the coolness of the sea, and the earth prepares itself for rest, and gives thanks. Then before they part the sun and earth unite in a tender embrace, which makes the forests darker and the fields more green."

[27] *The Lilies of the Field* (French translation, p. 40).

[28] Cf. *Stages on Life's Way*, p. 307: "Therefore I love thee, thou quiet among the graves, for the dead sleep there, and yet this quiet is the form for the eternal consciousness of their works! Therefore I love thee, thou quiet of the night, when the inmost character of nature betrays itself more clearly than when it loudly proclaims itself in the life and movement of all things! Therefore I love thee, thou quiet of the hour of spiritual exercise here in my chamber, where no sound and no human voice sets limits to the infinity of thought and of the thoughts to which Petrarch's words apply: 'The sea has not so many creatures in its waves, never did the night behold so many stars in the vault of heaven, there dwell not so many birds in the forest, nor are there so many blades of grass in the field and meadow, as every night my heart has thoughts!' . . . Therefore I love thee, thou quiet of loneliness, rather than all that is multi-farious, because thou art infinite!"

THE CONFLICT
WITH THE ESTABLISHED CHURCH

Christendom and Christianity.—Kierkegaard published new works unceasingly for nine years. It provided a kind of relief from the melancholy which continually oppressed him. "As Scheherazade saves her life by telling stories," he writes, "so I too save mine, or keep myself alive, by producing".[1] This whole period is marked by desperately hard work and intense reflection upon religious problems. Kierkegaard is alone and not understood. Solitude helps him to become more acutely conscious of the demands of true Christianity and, by contrast, of the crying insufficiencies of the established Church. More and more, official religion seems to him designed to provide the faithful with the necessary compromises to allow them to live as pagans beneath the convenient shelter of the respectability attached to the name of Christian. Even the clergy, when they have delivered their Sunday sermon, for which they receive a comfortable salary, go out into the world again and apparently forget that they should bear witness to the truth they teach. The evil is so widespread and so deep, the divorce so complete between Christ's doctrine and the lives of believers and clergy, that if one calls *Christianity* our true relationship with God, and *Christendom* what Christians call the "Christian" organization of life, we are bound to say, Kierkegaard assures us, that Christendom is alien to Christianity. "Luther," he writes, "had ninety-five theses. I have only one: Christianity has not been made a reality".[2] "Nothing is more true than Pascal's remark, the aptest ever made about Christendom—that it is a society of people who with the help of certain sacraments evade the duty of loving God".[3]

These sentiments find expression in Kierkegaard's later writings, and especially in *Training in Christianity* (1850). From 1845 onwards, in particular, they take a polemical form, and involve him in a struggle which was to shorten his life.

The Fight Against the "Corsair".—Before he came into conflict with the established Church, Kierkegaard had been engaged in a violent quarrel with a very widely-known Danish satirical paper, of which P. L. Moller was the editor-in-chief. Kierkegaard thought that the *Corsair*—"the loathsome organ of loathsome irony"[4]—was intellectually and spiritually demoralizing the Copenhagen public. He felt himself obliged to interfere to make an end of such a scandal. He consequently published several articles, between May and December 1845, in the daily paper *Faedrelandet* (*Fatherland*), to protest against the conduct of a press whose literary poverty was equal to its moral degradation. These vigorous, mordant articles had one certain result: P. L. Moller was rendered harmless and the *Corsair* did not recover from the blow. But Kierkegaard did not have the laugh on his side. The *Corsair*, before it foundered, retaliated by a series of articles designed to hold him up to ridicule, and printed numerous caricatures, for which he offered so many easy opportunities. Kierkegaard became famous over-night, but to his own disadvantage, for in the streets of Copenhagen, with his slovenly dress, especially his trousers, which the *Corsair* had heavily lampooned, and the umbrella without which he was never seen[5], he was an object of derision to the urchins and of mocking curiosity to passers-by.[6]

In actual fact, if we accept the explanations which Kierkegaard provides in *The Point of View*, written in 1848, the eccentricities in his dress and his way of living which were remarked upon and laughed at were neither mania, mannerisms, nor negligence, but habits specially designed to serve his aims in life. In the same way, it was apparently quite deliberately, in accordance with a premeditated plan, that he entered into conflict with the *Corsair* and the public to whom it owed its success. This whole plan itself formed part of a general strategy which was necessary, according to him, for the effectiveness of his writings. From the outset of his career, he says, religion had been not merely his chief, but in some sense his unique, concern. The difficulty, however, was to force the religious message of Christianity upon the attention of men who, though born and classified as "Christians", lived at one and the same time in a state of real paganism and in the placid security which their official, public description as "Christians" assured to them. Now to obtain a hearing from these people it was desirable to approach them by means of æsthetics, their familiar medium, without at first presenting a Christian point of view, and also to adopt a personal way of life which corresponded, in appearance at least, with the æsthetic sort of literary work.[7]

After 1845, however, after the completion of the *Unscientific Postscript*, when the religious element emerged from the disguise which had concealed it in the earlier works, especially *Either/Or*, which was a popular favourite, Kierkegaard realized that his personal style of living had to undergo a transformation, because worldly approval is incompatible with the religious cause, which obliges a writer to become a *controversialist*. "A victorious religious author who is *in the world* is *eo ipso* not a religious author".[8] Whoever puts himself at the service of true Christianity must do so at his own risk. The religious author must even "take care to be the object of persecution by the masses", "to be hated by the mob, which is the evil and the chaos which threatens us".[9] In his decision to attack the *Corsair* he found a favourable opportunity to effect the revolution necessary for this new aspect of his work. It would infallibly, he thought—and events proved him right— bring upon him, the master of irony, the gibes of the populace and the dislike of all those who exploited its baser instincts; for it would apparently justify them in changing their attitude towards him from favour to hatred because of the abrupt change he made both in his work and in his life. He would thus oblige them, he told himself, to "pay attention" to the message he had to deliver.[10]

These explanations are plausible if one allows for the complications of Kierkegaard's psychology. Some doubt remains, nevertheless, when one takes note of the bitterness with which the *Journal* frequently dwells upon the sarcasm and the mockery of which Kierkegaard was the butt throughout this period. Thus he remarks concerning the *Unscientific Postscript* (1846): "The book was published in Denmark. It was not so much as mentioned in a single paper. About fifty copies were sold, so that including the proof-corrector's fee of 100 Rx. the publication cost me 400 to 500 Rx. in addition to my time and energy. And in the meanwhile I was caricatured by a vulgar rag, which in the same little country had a circulation of 3,000, and another paper (also very widely read, *Flyveposten*) continued discussing my trousers".[11] It is thus certain that Kierkegaard was painfully aware of the hostility his intervention had provoked. This experiment, in which his devotion to the interests of justice and morality turned to his own disadvantage, finally confirmed him in his melancholy and his isolation, but also convinced him that great tasks demand great sacrifices.[12] Above all, the lack of support for his campaign which he found among the leaders of the Church was especially painful to him, and the disappointment which he felt on that score was to have a notable influence upon the early stages of a new episode, which was to bring him to grips with the established Church itself.[13]

The Adler case.—The initial occasion of this conflict seems to be attributable to the "Adler case". A pastor of Bornholm of the name of Adler experienced a profound religious crisis in 1843, and abruptly abandoned the philosophical and theological works upon which he was engaged in order to devote himself exclusively to the spiritual life. "Jesus," he declared, "ordered me to burn my writings and keep henceforth to the Bible." Little by little Adler came to consider himself as the immediate vehicle of Christ. Various subsequent works by him, however, gave rise to doubts about his mental condition, and he had to be relieved of his pastoral duties.

Kierkegaard was greatly struck by these events: he reflected at length upon Adler's writings, and even undertook the composition of a book on the case. In his view, the Adler case raised the whole problem of the established Church. Here, he thought, is a man who over a period of years has made a thorough study of theology, who has been given an official position by the Church, and has carried out its duties. Now it is only later on that this man eventually discovers Christianity, by virtue of a living, personal experience. What is more, it is because of this very discovery that he is dismissed. Does not the established Church seem thereby to place it self outside Christianity? Kierkegaard wondered continually whether the Church and the whole of so-called Christian society, if it were to be regenerated, ought not to go through a crisis similar to Adler's, and whether he, Sören Kierkegaard, had not been singled out by Providence to precipitate this salutary crisis.

Little by little this conviction grew upon him. It must be proclaimed loudly and clearly, he thought, that there is no Christianity in the country and that it must be introduced. The clergy would be furious—but at the same time glad that I am already at odds with the populace, a fact of which they would take advantage. But "that Christendom certainly needs a jolt of this kind I do not doubt for a moment, or rather, I am absolutely sure. That I shall succeed in administering it, I am also convinced. That this is the greatest thing, humanly speaking, which can come of my life, I well understand."[14]

The break with the Church.—Such were the thoughts which occupied Kierkegaard, when on the death in January 1854 of Bishop Mynster, a worthy representative of bourgeois respectability, Hans Martensen, the professor of theology (who was to succeed Mynster as Bishop of Copenhagen) declared in his funeral oration upon the deceased that Mynster had been "a witness to the truth". Kierkegaard, after some months of hesitation, thought it his duty to make a public protest (18 December 1854), in which he severely censured the bishop, who seems to have concerned himself only with obtaining from his formidably responsible postion the honours and profits attached to it, who went so far astray as to identify Christianity with the established order and to reduce his vocation to the exercise of a public office. How could one see in this bishop a "witness to the truth"? "A witness to the truth", Kierkegaard wrote, "is a man whose life has brought him profound knowledge of inner conflicts, fear and trembling, temptations, spiritual distress, moral suffering. A witness to the truth is a man who bears witness to the truth in poverty, in humiliation and contempt, misunderstood, hated, mocked at, despised, ridiculed. A witness to the truth is a martyr."

This incident, and the bitterness which Kierkegaard showed over it, would be difficult to explain without knowing that Mynster, with whom he was in personal touch, had long since, on several occasions, shown himself unworthy of his respect and confidence. Before he became a bishop, Mynster had been in contact with the Kierkegaard family, and especially with Sören's father, who had the greatest admiration for him, and had inspired similar feelings in his son. Thus during his engagement, when Sören found that Regina Olsen lacked religious education, he read her Mynster's sermons every week.[15] After his father's death, Kierkegaard's relations with Mynster had continued, but he had never ceased to feel how little he could rely upon the bishop's support or even friendship. The *Journal* makes frequent allusions to these difficult relations.[16] Kierkegaard notes that Mynster seems to be afraid to talk to him, as though he wished to avoid his interlocutor's penetrating gaze.[17] But Kierkegaard had been particularly shocked by the bishop's failure in the *Corsair* affair. The fact that he was so obviously defending the common interest of Church and society ought to have obliged Mynster to support him in the hard struggle he had had. Mynster however, had held aloof. A little later (1850), when Kierkegaard published *Training in Christianity*, Mynster let him know that the book had greatly vexed him by its impious badinage upon sacred matters. In fact, Mynster had well realized that part of the work was concerned with, and censured, his own compromises with secularism, the rest being taken up with combating the theological rationalism of Martensen.[18] These repeated incidents explain the terms in which Kierkegaard speaks of the bishop of Copenhagen. This Mynster, "the epitome of a whole generation", was in reality, he writes, "only human wisdom, worldly intelligence, weakness, ambition for pleasure, with no greatness beyond oratory; and the misfortune of my life, my misfortune, is that having been brought up by my father on Mynster's sermons, I too, from filial piety towards the dead, endorsed this false bill, instead of protesting".[19]   From 1851 onwards, moreover, he had clearly foreseen that a conflict with Mynster was inevitable. He explains that had times been different he could have waited, but that his financial embarrassments have become such, and his future so uncertain, that he must hasten to launch his offensive, if he wishes to accomplish what appears to him to be a duty.[20]

However this may be, Kierkegaard's intervention marks his public break with the established Church. Henceforward, in a broadsheet entitled *The Instant*, of which nine numbers appeared from May to September, 1855, he attacks religious conformism, setting out to show that the time has come when the Christian must accept the double condition of conduct which is absurd in the eyes of the world and a testimony which goes as far as martyr-dom. The established Church, which coincides with the State, which assumes, although it stands for development, the static character of the State, [21] this Church continually adds to the number of its compromises with secularism, and betrays its sacred mission. Present-day Christendom is "the caricature of true Christianity, or a monstrous amount of misunderstanding, illusion, etc., mixed with a sparing little dose of true Chris-tianity".[22]

Kierkegaard's Last Days.—Throughout the course of this polemi-cal activity, Kierkegaard was keenly conscious of the paradox and the strangeness of his position. A defender of Christianity against the established Church, a preacher without any mandate or official authority, the poet of an absolute, crucifying Christianity, in conflict with the world, he did not believe he was able to call himself a Christian. The inconsistency of his life with his work, or rather, to be more exact, what the combined effects of his melancholy, his meditation and his faith made him feel to be an inconsistency, was a greater internal torture than ever to him. Alone against everyone in this ardent struggle, he felt his strength failing. Lacking all further resources, sick in body and soul, he was obliged to seek admission to the Frederik hospital, where he died after a few weeks' illness, at the age of forty-two. He had realized, and repeatedly declared, that death was necessary to his cause, for it seemed to him to place upon his work the only seal which was a valid testimony in his eyes: that of martyrdom.[23]

Concerning his last days we have the remarkably moving account of a friend of his youth, Emile Boesen, then pastor at Horsens, who visited him assiduously in hospital. After each visit Boesen made notes summarizing their conversation. Boesen asks: "How goes it?"—Kierkegaard: "Badly, it is death. Pray for me, that I may die soon, and well. I have been a toy in the hands of Providence, which put me into the world to serve. It has lasted a few years, and then curtains. Here is Providence stretching out her hand and taking me back into the ark. Such is always the fate of envoys extraordinary." Another day, Boesen asks him if he has nothing more to say. "No . . . Yes, greet all men for me, I loved them all. Tell them my life has been a great suffering, incomprehensible and unknown to everyone but me. I may have given an impression of pride and vanity; it was not that. I am no better than the rest, I have said so and I never said anything else. I had my thorn in the flesh, that was why I did not marry and could not take up any duties. I became 'the exception'. In the daytime I lived in a fever of work, and at night I was alone: that was my life as an exception".—"Can you pray to God in peace?"—"Yes indeed I can! First I ask for remission of sins, that all may be forgiven. Then I ask that I may be spared from despairing in the moment of death. I often remember a verse which says that death should be pleasing to God. And then I ask what I have always so much wanted, that I should be allowed to know a little before hand the moment when death will come."—"When you sit up like that and talk, you look as fresh as though you were going to get up and go out."—"Yes, there's only one thing I lack, the power to walk. The only means of transport left to me is to be lifted up. I have the impression of becoming an angel, of having wings. That's what will happen: finding oneself astride a cloud singing *Alleluia alleluia, alleluia*! All the rest is bad. I don't think it is bad, what I have said, but I have only said it to drive away evil, to arrive at the *Alleluia, alleluia, alleluia*!"— "And it is all because you believe in God, and rely upon his mercy in Christ?"—"Yes, of course. What else?"—"Have you made any arrangements about your papers?"—"No, that can be left to chance. . . . I am ruined and have nothing left, except for my funeral. I could have used influence to get a pastorate; as an old candidate I should have obtained one; but I couldn't take it up (it was my thorn in the flesh) . . . The doctors don't understand my illness. It is psychological, but they want to make everything fit in with their pet medical theories". A nurse brought him some flowers, and he said when he saw them: "It is the fate of flowers to bloom, to give their perfume, and then to die".—Returning to the subject of Mynster, Kierkegaard said to Boesen: "You have no idea what a poisonous weed Mynster was; it's monstrous, the corruption he spread. He was a colossus. It needed great strength to break him, and the blow was sure to rebound upon the man who struck it".

On Friday 19 October, Boesen asked Kierkegaard: "Don't you wish to receive Holy Communion?"—"Yes, but not from a pastor, from a layman."—"That will be difficult."—"Well then, I will die without it."—"That is not right!" —I can't argue about it. I have made my choice; I have chosen. Pastors are royal officials; royal officials have nothing to do with Christianity."—"That is not true; that is not in accordance with the truth, with reality."—"Look. God is sovereign; but then all these men intervene, behaving as though Christianity were made for them."

On Thursday 25, Kierkegaard said that he felt increasingly weak, and that his hands and his whole body were trembling continuously. Boesen said to him: "What wonderful things have happened in your life."—"Yes, that makes me very happy, and very sad, for I can share that joy with nobody." On the following days Kierkegaard spoke only a few words. On 11 November he gave up his soul to God.[24]

The Lutheran Church was ready to overlook the dramatic controversies of his latter years, and granted the deceased the funeral honours it accords to those who die in its bosom. But the young intelligentsia, whose ear and admiration Kierkegaard had eventually won, formed a guard of honour round his coffin in the church, and at the cemetery a protest was raised against this final intervention by the established Church.

Strange, fiery, and brief, such was Sören Kierkegaard's life. After a long period of neglect his work, unique in its kind, was to exercise a powerful and ever-growing influence not only in Denmark but in the whole word. As he himself had foreseen, in humility before God but also in the conscience of his own genius,[25] it was to make of Kierkegaard a hero of modern thought.

NOTES TO CHAPTER FOUR

[1] *Journal*, 1848. Cf. Ibid., 1843, IV A 110 (Dru 447): "I will try to rid myself of all the black thoughts and dark passions within me by writing 'The leper's meditation'."

[2] Review article, 1854-5, XIV, 45 (Geismar, p. 242).

[3] *Journal*, 1854.

[4] *The Point of View*, p. 57.

[5] *Journal*, 1840-2, III A 221 (Dru 346): "My umbrella, my friendship. It never leaves me, only once has it done so. It was a terrible storm; I stood alone abandoned by all on Kongens-Nytorv; then my umbrella also turned on me. I was at my wits' end, not knowing whether I should let go of it for its act of perfidy and become a misanthrope or not. It has become so dear to me that I always carry it whether it is rainy weather or sunny; and so as to show it that I do not love it merely from utilitarian motives I sometimes walk up and down in my room and behave as though I were out, lean upon it, open it up, lean my chin against the crook, put it up to my lips, and so on and so forth."

[6] Four years later this still went on. Cf. *Journal*, 1849 (Haecker, p. 38): "Four years have now passed, and Copenhagen is still interested in my trousers and my legs, with the same passionate curiosity it has for Tivoli, the masquerades at the Casino, or for war."

[7] Cf. *The Point of View*, p. 51-2: "This is the first period: by my personal mode of existence I endeavoured to support the pseudonyms, the æsthetic work as a whole. Melancholy, incurably melancholy as I was, suffering prodigious griefs in my inmost soul, having broken in desperation from the world and all that is of the world, strictly brought up from my very childhood in the apprehension that the truth must suffer and be mocked and derided, spending a definite time every day in prayer and devout meditation, and being myself personally a penitent—in short, being what I was, I found (I do not deny it) a certain sort of satisfaction in this life, in this inverse deception, a satisfaction in observing that the deception succeeded so extraordinarily, that the public and I were on the most confidential terms, that I was quite in the fashion as the preacher of a gospel of worldliness. . . . This satisfaction, which was my secret and which sometimes put me into ecstasy, might have been a dangerous temptation. Not as though the world and such things could tempt me with their flattery and adulation."

[8] *The Point of View*, p. 59.

[9] Ibid.

[10] Cf. *Journal*, 1847, VII A 221, and VIII A 23 (Dru 626, 638): "It is clear enough that I shall be sacrificed. . . . But to God all things are possible. From now on, humanly speaking, I must not only be said to be running into uncertainty but to be going to certain destruction—and, in confidence in God, that is victory. . . . I do not mean that I am going to strike them (alas, one

40

cannot strike the masses): I mean to make them strike me. And in that way I all the same compel them through evil. For if they once strike me they will be made aware; and if they put me to death—then they will certainly become aware of their position, and I shall have won an absolute victory."

[11] *Journal*, 1849, X¹ A 584 (Dru 945).

[12] Cf. *The Point of View*, p. 129, note. *Journal*, 1849, X¹ A 120 (Dru 880): "I have been made a laughing-stock, that is the martyrdom I have suffered; I even dare to say something else, more profound about myself: I am the martyr of laughter; for not everyone who suffers being laughed at, even though for an idea, is strictly a martyr of laughter. . . . I am the martyr of laughter and my life is arranged for that purpose . . . it is in the martyrdom of becoming a laughing-stock that I recognize myself. And in order to become it I am the wittiest of all, possessed in a high degree of *vis comica* . . . quite rightly I had to command laughter to turn on me (just as Ney commanded the soldiers to fire on him)."

[13] Kierkegaard's pessimism concerning the influence of the press was also greatly increased. Cf. *Journal*, 1849 (Haecker, p. 37): "That one man, every week or every day, can in an instant lead 40 or 50,000 men to say and think the same thing, that is what is frightening. And we can never seize the guilty man in person, and the thousands of individuals he stirs up against someone are in a sense innocent. Woe, woe to the press! If Christ returned to earth, as true as I live, he would not accuse the high priests, but the journalists."

[14] *Journal*, 25 April 1849 (Haecker, p. 39)—cf. Ibid., 1849 (Haecker, p. 91): "I expound what Christianity is; for that I have, to an extraordinary degree, everything that is necessary, and in that, quite literally, I find my vocation, to which I have been led, from my earliest years, in an altogether special manner."

[15] Cf. *Journal*, 1843, IV A 142 (Dru 456).

[16] Cf. *Journal*, 1850, X³ A 453 (Dru 1133): "Mynster bears a certain resemblance to Louis Philippe: he is without inspiration or pathos, but makes a clever use of little means and understands that what really rules the world is the question of a living, and that the person who has livings in his gift rules quite securely." *Journal*, 1849, X¹ A 591 (Dru 948): "Socrates loved the young, and why? Because there is a breath of eternity in them, and that is what he wished to preserve. Take Mynster, he certainly does not love the young, he likes demoralized men, those who are demoralized by having to make finite ends into the serious things of life—one can also rule over them."

[17] Cf. *Journal*, 1851, X³ A 742 (Dru 1179): "I, who would like so very much to do everything to please him—if only truth does not suffer as a result; I, who feel obliged by filial piety towards one who is dead to do everything to please him, if only it can be done—and that I, of all people, should without the slightest doubt be the most dangerous light in which he could be seen!"

[18] The work appeared under the pseudonym of *Anticlimacus*. In the *Journal*, 1849, X¹ A 510 (Dru 936), Kierkegaard explains the significance of this new pseudonym, already employed for *The Sickness unto Death*: "The pseudonym is called Johannes Anti-Climacus in contrast to Johannes Climacus (the pseudonym of *Philosophical Fragments*, 1844, and of the *Unscientific Postscript*, 1846) who said he was not a Christian. Anti-Climacus is the opposite extreme, being a Christian in an extraordinary degree—whereas I manage only to be quite a

simple Christian." In an earlier passage, Kierkegaard states that "his own personality corresponds to neither pseudonym."

[19] *Journal*, F. & G. p. 164, note 2. (The translation from the original has been corrected on a few points by the author.)

[20] *Journal*, 1852 (Haecker, p. 273).

[21] Cf. *Journal*, X[1] A 552 (Dru 941): "The 'Church' ought really to represent 'becoming', the 'State' on the other hand 'establishment'. That is why it is so dangerous when Church and State grow together and are identified. . . . 'Becoming' is more spiritual than 'existing'; the servants of the Church ought not, therefore, to be officials, probably not married, but those *expediti* who are fitted to serve 'becoming'." By *becoming* here is not to be understood an evolutionary conception of the Church, which is foreign to Kierkegaard's thought. The term "becoming" serves only to characterize the Church *militant*, whose proper function is to work unceasingly, in the struggle against the age, for "Christian becoming", which is never an accomplished reality, but an effort continually renewed. Cf. *Training in Christianity*, p. 206: "Wherever there seems to be, or people assume that there is, an established Christendom, there is an attempt to construct a triumphant Church, even if this word is not used, for the Church militant is in process of becoming, *established* Christendom simply *is*, does not become."

[22] *The Point of View*, p. 77.

[23] G. Brandes (*Sören Kierkegaard, ein literarisches Charakterbild*, Leipzig 1879) quotes the notes which the house physician of the Frederik Hospital made in the hospital diary: "He considers his illness as fatal. He thinks his death is necessary for the completion of the task to which he has devoted all his intellectual powers and the whole of his works. If he does not die, he says, he will have to pursue the religious struggle, but it will be more feebly. His death, on the other hand, will bring it new strength, and even victory, he thinks."

[24] *Journal*, 1855, Appendix (Haecker, p. 406–15).

[25] *The Point of View*, p. 98: "So it is I represent myself. Should it prove that the present age will not understand me—very well then, I belong to history, knowing assuredly that I shall find a place there and what place it will be. Humble as I am before God, I also know this—and at the same time I know it is my duty definitely not to suppress this in silence."

PART TWO

KIERKEGAARD'S SPIRITUAL LIFE

KIERKEGAARD'S SPIRITUAL LIFE

Before beginning the study of Kierkegaard's thought we must try to see more deeply into his psychology than the biographical sketch has allowed us to do. For if biography is an indispensable means of approach for anyone who wishes to grasp Kierkegaard's thought in its originality and its complexity, if it makes many aspects of his work understandable, nevertheless one cannot claim that it is able to account for the whole of that work. To explain the deep repercussions which the great events of Kierkegaard's life, few as they are—the discovery of his father's "guilt", the engagement to Regina Olsen and the break with her, the conflict with the established Church—had upon his spiritual life, to explain first of all these events themselves, which were primarily internal, it is necessary to have recourse to Kierkegaard's psychology. This latter is consequently, far more than external and adventitious circumstances, the key to his whole work.

This psychology is difficult to seize. Like Descartes, Kierkegaard wished to appear in a mask. *Larvatus prodeo.* Repeated remarks in the *Journal* bear witness to it. Not only, as he warns us, is his paper "watermarked",[1] but his writings conceal an impenetrable secret, which still remains inviolate. "No, no, my silence, my secret, cannot be broken". He resembled those heroes whom his own imagination conceived in such numbers, who are "burdened with a deep secret which they may impart to no one".[2] Incognito is his element.[3]

The pseudonymous works complicate the problem further. How is one to account for the truly astounding perseverance Kierkegaard shows in concealing himself, not only behind a fictitious name, but behind a fictitious character? Various explanations can be put forward. One, which he often employed himself, is to present the pseudonyms as so many ways of bringing readers face to face with themselves. "I proclaim the truth," he writes, "and I place my readers in a situation where they have no alternative but to make it their own. Personality is only ripe when a man has made the truth his own whether it is Balaam's ass speaking or a laughing jack-ass with his loud laugh, an apostle or an angel."[4]

A second explanation, which does not exclude the first however, relates to a gift and a state of mind peculiar to Kierkegaard, which his father's education had greatly developed, and which sometimes assumed a somewhat morbid form. From his childhood years, Kierkegaard was accustomed to the introspective and the fictitious. He had never ceased to make up tales, to imagine scenes, to invent themes for novels and short stories, as almost every page of the *Journal* proves, and also to sketch characters (the Wandering Jew, Don Juan, Faust, etc.) which symbolized his different affinities and his manifold possibilities. Kierkegaard saw in them so many "temptations". All these possibilities, moreover, struggle towards reality. Hence in order to rid himself of them he gives them a literary form. This constitutes for him the deliverance which he needs. "I will try to rid myself of all the black thoughts and dark passions within me by writing *The leper's meditation*."[5] On this basis one can explain Kierkegaard's surprising assertion that the pseudonymous works contain not a word by him, not a single word.[6] For a very long time, he says, his melancholy prevented him from being on familiar terms with himself. "It kept me far away from myself while I went off to discover an imaginary world, rather like the heir of a vast estate who is perpetually at the stage of being *initiated* into the field of possibilities."[7]

The pseudonyms thus serve at once to show the reader that the author is not exactly the same as Sören Kierkegaard, to furnish Kierkegaard with intermediaries who help to distinguish him from himself and to realize, in poetic form, the manifold possibilities which he finds within himself.[8]

Plainly, the existence of these various planes in Kierkegaard's work, which often intersect, sometimes confuses the vision and casts shadows which hinder a clear perception of Kierkegaard's true personality. Nevertheless the fact remains that beneath all these disguises we can discern the authentic features of his psychology. The disguise itself reveals the man who is disguised. Moreover Kierkegaard is continually alluding to his personal life, to his feelings, to his inner crises, to incidents in his career, especially to his relations with Regina Olsen. Often these allusions appear as "watermarks"; that is, they are attached to fictitious characters, like the Nameless Man in *Repetition*. In one way or another, it is possible to see quite deeply into his inner life, in spite of all the obstacles deliberately piled up to bar the way to a secret which he was determined to the end to keep inviolate.

The questions which arise here can be reduced to three main problems, concerning firstly what might be called Kierkegaard's inner conflict, secondly his melancholy, and thirdly his faith. Studied from these three points of view, closely bound together as they are, Kierkegaard's psychology may be sufficiently illuminated to explain many aspects of his life which seem at first mysterious, and the genesis of works apparently so strange and so disparate.[9]

NOTES

1 *Journal*, 1839, II A 413 (F. & G. p. 90).

2 In the *Notebooks* and the *Papers*, many pages were destroyed or torn out by Kierkegaard, in many cases certainly because he thought later that they ran the risk of giving a glimpse of that secret which he had determined to keep absolutely to himself.

3 *Journal*, 1851 (Haecker, p. 232).

4 *Journal*, 1843, IV A 87 (Dru 432). Cf. in the same strain, *Unscientific Postscript*, p. 552: "So I am in a position of indifference: that is to say, it is a matter of indifference what and how I am. . . . My facsimile with portrait, etc., like the question whether I go abroad with hat or with cap, could be the object of attention only for those to whom the indifferent has become important—perhaps as compensation for the fact that the important has become indifferent." Cf. also the reflections which conclude the minor work entitled: *Has a man the right to let himself be put to death for the truth?* (1847) and which are valid *a fortiori* for all the pseudonymous works: "The foregoing, as has been said, reports 'this man's many thoughts in brief compass' (the work is supposed to have been written by H. H. . . .). Since the whole of it is poetic, 'a poetic experiment'—but, be it observed, by a thinker—the thoughtful reader will surely find it natural that I say nothing about the man himself . . . lest by talking in novelistic fashion I might perhaps say something which would divert attention from the essential thing, the thought-content". (*The Present Age*, p. 134–5.)

5 *Journal*, 1843, IV A 110 (Dru 447). This *Meditation* was inserted in *Guilty?*

6 Cf. *Unscientific Postscript*, p. 551: "What is written therefore is in fact mine, but only in so far as I put into the mouth of the poetically actual individuality whom I *produced*, his life-view expressed in audible lines. For my relation is even more external than that of a poet, who poetizes characters, and yet in the preface is himself the author. For I am impersonal, or am personal in the second person, a *souffleur* who has poetically produced the *authors*, whose preface in turn is their own production, as are even their own names. So in the pseudonymous works there is not a single word which is mine, I have no opinion about these words except as a third person, no knowledge of their meaning except as a reader, not the remotest private relation to them. . . ."

7 *Journal*, 1847.

8 Cf. *Journal*, 1852 (Haecker, p. 315), where Kierkegaard returns to this question of the pseudonyms. They are poetic personalities, he says, to be understood poetically, so that everything they say is to be taken as characteristic of their poetic individuality. It would therefore be an error to attribute their remarks to him. If anyone attempted to do so, he adds, he would be led into the "joke" of making me a kind of madman, given up to contradicting himself without respite. This sort of exegesis would reveal a charlatan or a mere literary bungler.

9 Kierkegaard has himself stressed the necessity of distinguishing two levels of explanation in his work, as well as the close solidarity between them. Cf.

The Point of View, p. 9: "It goes without saying that I cannot explain my work as an author wholly, i.e., with the purely personal inwardness in which I possess the explanation of it. And this in part because I cannot make public my God-relationship. . . . In part because I cannot wish to obtrude upon anyone what concerns only my private person—though naturally there is much in this which for me serves to explain my work as an author".

I

THE INNER CONFLICT

A "Problem Man."—Kierkegaard's work appears to us at first as a long discussion with himself, as the expression of a conflict.[1] Kierkegaard was a problem even in his own eyes. Everything in his life is mysterious, ambiguous, and, to use a favourite word of his, dialectical. What is the explanation of the curse which weighed down his father, the shepherd who cursed God on the lonely, desolate Jutland heath? Whence comes the melancholy which lay upon him unceasingly from his earliest youth? How did he come to be driven by a series of strange events, in spite of himself as it were, from the æsthetic phase to the religious? And how, in this latter phase, did he receive a mission without having, officially, the necessary authority? How was he, the lover and the poet of religion and the Church's son, led to begin a struggle against the Church? Secretly bruised by his thorn in the flesh, discredited and despised, humiliated and flouted, how could he believe, in spite of his distress and his despair, that he was called to preach to others a truth and a greatness in which he was never confident of participating himself?

Such are the questions which fill Kierkegaard's pseudonymous writings and miscellaneous papers. These questions however, and the replies they evince, seem to be merely the forms or expressions of the inner conflict with himself which Kierkegaard pursues. He has noted that "no task, no effort, is as difficult as those which are necessary to escape from the temptations of reflection".[2] In fact he is torn between the attraction of the æsthetic, subject to the primacy of the moment, and of the religious, which imposes the primacy of eternity; and within the religious itself, between its poetical and its truly Christian form. Faith and doubt dispute the possession of his heart, and we shall see him resolving the conflict, as he thinks, by setting up doubt in the very heart of faith. He knows he has a mission, but he is distressed at lacking the authority to fulfil it. He loves the Church, but like an unhappy lover, and strife will become the very pattern of his love. Luther seems to him the master of subjectivity; but subjectivity risks bringing the Church and Christianity to ruin. Kierkegaard is keenly conscious of his genius; but he wonders if it may not be an illusion caused by pride. His melancholy lies upon him with all the weight of a hereditary disability, but it might possibly be in the nature of a sin. His duty seemed to oblige him to give up Regina; but he is not sure that an unwavering faith on his part would not have made the marriage possible. Guilty? Not Guilty?

Thus everything is dialectical in his case. *Pro* and *contra* present themselves together, and the debate is endless. Hence it is always himself whom Kierkegaard addresses. It is against himself that he argues and inveighs, trying by his writings to calm the inner struggle which an extraordinarily lucid intelligence, linked with a morbid sensibility, continually provokes and quickens within him.[3] The written word is at once a witness to the conflict and an attempt at deliverance from it, a means of provisionally resolving it in fiction.

Many incidental remarks of Kierkegaard's bear this out. In the *Journal*, when he reviews his efforts and struggles to gain acceptance for a truly Christian conception of Christianity, he takes up the objection that the rigidity of his views exposes him to charges of one-sidedness, of being unable to understand his opponent's position. He replies: by no means, for the contrary point of view to that which I maintain has always had its warmest advocate in me.[4] It is in this sense that he repeatedly remarks that his pseudonyms signify so many "possibilities", types of life which transposed his own conflicts and gave intellectual solidity to Christianity. "In between my melancholy and myself," he writes, "lay a whole world of the imagination. That is, in part, what I rid myself of in the pseudonyms".[5] Parallel to the pseudonymous writings, the *Edifying Discourses*, signed with his own name, indicate the "duplicity" of Kierkegaard's works. Kierkegaard notes that he is really only "his own sermonizer".[6] "What is it really

that made me into a religious speaker?" he says. "The fact that I
am a listener. That means to say, that my life is so involved and
such an effort that I really felt the *need* of hearing words of light
and leading. I listened and listened, but if what I heard was
Christianity, I was beyond help. So I became a speaker myself.
And so I know for certain what our parsons rarely know, that
there is someone who benefits from these addresses: myself. I am
the very opposite of other speakers: they are eager to address
others—I speak to myself. And it is also certain that in so far as
others do not think they profit by my addresses it must be because
their lives are all too easy, without effort and free from danger".[7]

Faith and Doubt.—All this may seem too general. Let us, then,
take some examples. The Kierkegaardian conception of faith will
serve as the first such example.

The Demands of Reason.

We shall first observe that a considerable part of Kierkegaard's
work is devoted to emphasizing the rôle of faith in the approach
to Christianity, and the gratuitous and totally irrational character
of faith. The polemic against Hegel derives essentially from this.
Every attempt to rationalize faith, Kierkegaard notes, ends in
destroying the very roots of Christianity. Faith is adherence to a
paradox, a leap into absurdity. (Kierkegaard has brought new
recognition to Tertullian's *Credo quia absurdum*). The man who
wishes to prove belief, he writes, has something further to learn,
namely that he does not believe. "Faith does not need it; aye, it
must even regard the proof as its enemy."[8]

In these texts, with their peremptory tone and their obviously
polemical form, can be found the echo of the debate taking place
within Kierkegaard's soul between the tendencies of a prodigiously exacting and analytical mind on the one hand, seeking in
spite of itself to "conquer" faith dialectically and falling foul of
mysteries which it defines *en bloc* as the "paradoxical" and the
"absurd"; and on the other hand a profound wish to make subject to faith a reason which never ceased to insist upon its rights.
This conflict is visible in the compromises which Kierkegaard

sometimes outlined; in his remarks, for example, concerning infinite resignation.[9] He thinks in fact that before faith, which God alone can communicate to man, a first step towards faith can be achieved by the "movement of infinite resignation". He adds, it is true, that the knight of infinite resignation is not the knight of faith. The fact remains, however, that by his own initiative and his own effort man can force an entry at least into the anteroom of faith. There is discernible here, it would seem, a secret movement impelling Kierkegaard towards a rational justification of faith, but a faith, as we shall see, understood in a rationalist sense and as such ruinous for that very faith which is to be established or supported. The *Journal* contains the clearest evidence of this conflict, and the Kierkegaardian doctrine of faith as a paradox and an offence merely expresses Kierkegaard's efforts to escape from himself. It conveys Kierkegaard's impassioned dialogue with himself. If he proclaims, with Pascal, the necessity of "holding contrary principles" it is perhaps primarily because contrary principles have hold of him. For the realization of this nothing is more valuable than a further study of Kierkegaard's doctrine of faith.

The Dark Night of Faith.

Faith, says Kierkegaard, is defined as an anxiety, an uneasiness, a doubt.[10]. Whether it is a question of faith as belief or of faith as confidence, one can speak of "the dark night of faith" as St. John of the Cross speaks of "the dark night of contemplation".[11]

Faith, indeed, is subject to temptations, and Kierkegaard tells us that the hours when they appear are full of terror and anguish.[12] He is speaking here, it must be understood, of those who profess the faith, not as orators (or as poets), but as witnesses. The orator's anguish is only factitious, the poet's merely imaginary. The witness, however, that is to say the imitator of Christ, knows torturing doubt, and in this very doubt experiences and feels his faith. This doubt by the hero of faith is thus very different from the doubt of the arguing rationalist (of Hegelian pattern), for this latter has nothing to do with anxiety, since it operates upon the plane of reason; that is to say, Kierkegaard observes, upon a plane which is foreign to Christian reality. Moreover, our learned

doubters have only a conventional, methodical, prudently regu-
lated doubt; they doubt for one hour every term in their professorial chairs and the rest of the time they think of other things.[13]
The doubt of faith has the duration and the intensity of faith itself,
because it is within faith and assumes its existence, and at the same
time tests it and perfects it.[14] Luther, then, was right to present
faith as a "perturbing thing".[15]

Faith, in fact, for Kierkegaard (and for Luther), is *contrary* to
reason and not merely above reason. It is the death of reason[16]
and it dwells in the very heart of this death.[17] Its path is thus prepared by doubt, which marks the defeat of reason, and this is why
doubt and anguish are inseparable from faith, as (human) despair
is from (Christian) hope.

It is important, however, to distinguish religious doubt from
demoniac doubt (incredulity in its different forms). Superficially
the two may resemble each other, for they both manifest themselves in anguish. But from a concrete point of view it can be seen
that the anguish of the religious man and that of the demoniac are
contraries. The pious and believing Christian, in fact, is drawn
heart and soul towards that which his doubt would deprive him
of, namely faith and confidence. The demoniac on the other
hand, yielding to his stronger desire, which is the desire to dis-
believe, turns away from the goal to which he would be led by his
weaker desire, namely the desire to believe, which he cannot
entirely renounce.[18]

The term *paradox* (contrary to reason) which Kierkegaard uses
to denote the dialectical activity of faith, that night of despair[19]
which recalls, we said, the "night of the soul" of St. John of the
Cross, must therefore be taken in its most literal sense. "The life-
giving hope of the soul," Kierkegaard writes, "is contrary to the
hope of the reason".[20] In fact, to use a more exact expression it
would be better—as Kierkegaard remarks in *Training in Christianity*, where he corrects his own terminology—to speak of
"offence" rather than doubt, for, he says, "the relationship of
the personality to Christ is not: either to doubt or to believe; but
either to be offended or to believe".[21] The fact remains that,
whatever the risk or possibility of offence, for Kierkegaard faith,

whether in the sense of belief or of confidence, is the choice of "the absurd".

The Proofs of Credibility

How is one to explain a position so disconcerting in the terms in which it is expressed? It may seem at first that it merely translates into polemical language Kierkegaard's sharp reaction against Hegelian rationalism. But it is also apparent that the Kierkegaardian thesis concerning existential faith rests upon a great truth, corrupted by a grave error. What is true is that Christianity cannot be acquired by scientific, philosophical, or even theological means; in fact, it cannot be *acquired* at all, it can only be *received* by the *gift* of faith. And if this is so, it is because the object of supernatural faith is absolutely beyond human reason. In a very real sense it can be said, with Kierkegaard, that the object of faith is "paradox" (to the Jews a stumbling-block, and to the Greeks, foolishness)—the essential paradox being Christ, that is, the Man God.

This thesis, directly opposed to the Hegelian rationalist system which postulates the absolute primacy of reason over faith, is perfectly admissible. By the unconscious influence of his Lutheranism, however, Kierkegaard considers it as the equivalent of another thesis, whereby a fact—even the fact which is the basis of faith in the divinity of Christ—does not need to be objectively certain in order to be admitted. In fact, according to Kierkegaard, objective uncertainty becomes subjective truth as soon as it is embraced with full and passionate sincerity. Faith, in this sense of adherence to what is uncertain or absurd if looked at objectively, becomes wholly legitimate as soon as the act of adherence takes place with the ardour of total sincerity.

All this is summed up in a kind of dilemma concerning the proofs of credibility. For the believer, says Kierkegaard, every attempt at a rational demonstration of the bases of faith is a questionable affair, a species of temptation. How, indeed could argument justify—or destroy—what is beyond reason and even contrary to reason? Whoever consents to argue, thereby renounces faith. All apologetic is a sign of unbelief, or at least of an unsteady

<u>faith.</u>) But on the other hand the unbeliever cannot claim to establish the fundamental concepts of the faith, such as the inspiration of sacred literature, by means of critical considerations. Such notions are accessible only to faith; no scientific inquiry, however learned, can make them credible, let alone give them a rational basis. If science therefore wishes to "prove" them, it is because it has admitted them as postulates. Faith is at the source of the demonstration; it guides it, but does not result from it. And by a fatal contradiction, faith itself is ruined in the attempt at self-demonstration. Thus, Kierkegaard concludes, "uncertainty is really a profitable schoolmaster for faith"—"whose most dangerous enemy, on the other hand, is to be found in certainty".[22]

The psychological conflict within Kierkegaard himself can easily be discerned here. The fundamental error which produces it is also plain: it consists in identifying the following two very different procedures: the rational demonstration of the truth of something which transcends reason, and the rational demonstration of the reasons for belief in something which transcends reason. Kierkegaard's confusion is well revealed in the texts where he objects to every attempt to "prove Christianity" and unremittingly condemns apologetics.[23]

"The whole of this antique arsenal," he writes, "the whole of apologetics, serves only to betray Christianity." To undertake to prove the divinity of Christ is an absurdity.[24] Similarly, the truth of Christianity will never be demonstrated by its good effects, for that would be to place it upon the level of human history,[25]— nor by its duration, for duration has nothing to do with the matter (and when would duration become sufficient to demand a *divine* origin?)—nor by the facts of history, which, as such, can never be more than approximations.[26] So Kierkegaard argues. One can see, however, how the whole question is misplaced. It is clear that one cannot "prove" the divinity of Christ, which is a mystery and absolutely transcends human reason, but one can prove that Christ gave himself out to be the Son of God and acted like God. One cannot "prove" the divinity of the Church, which is a matter of faith; but it is quite possible to show that whoever claims to explain the Church historically in terms of purely human causes fails completely to do so. Apologetics does not assume the senseless task of proving mysteries; it applies itself solely to assembling and establishing the proofs of credibility. Faith always remains the gift of God, and no apologetic argument can beget it in the soul merely by virtue or its own strength.

Thus, the view that all belief is "something deeper than what are considered to be its foundations",[27] that belief upholds the foundations and is the foundation, is undeniably true if one means that the *content of faith* is incommensurable with rational arguments, for from this point of view faith comes first absolutely and constitutes the foundation. It is no less certainly erroneous however if it is meant that faith, as a *human act*, is not itself founded upon motives which make it reasonable and prudent. These motives do not produce faith, but they influence the soul and justify it in admitting the gift of faith. Kierkegaard confuses these two things, and as a result of this mistaken identification constantly affirms that every attempt to establish the credibility of revelation amounts to rationalizing faith. Consequently he asserts that one must believe without reason, and even that faith is the more perfect the more it goes against reason, that it is truly, in the strict sense of the word, a "leap into the absurd".[28]

Thus when Kierkegaard seeks, in spite of himself, to "conquer" faith dialectically, admitting, in such very un-Lutheran terms, that dialectic can lead to the threshold of faith,[29] we must understand that his reason is spontaneously attempting to escape from the truly desperate conditions which the logic of his Lutheranism wishes to impose upon belief. The conflict which troubles him finds expression on many occasions, as is shown by this remark in the *Journal*, which clearly holds an echo of the continual debate he carries on within himself: "There will always remain," he writes, "one thing to be considered, which cannot be passed over: to what extent is one to consider reason as a temptation with regard to faith? To what extent is it sinful, to what extent is a harmonious conjunction of faith and reason in itself a point of faith?"[30] Thus the dispute is here between good sense, that is, the demands of sound and right reason, and pure absurdity. In the last resort Kierkegaard chooses the absurd, but at the same time brings himself into conflict, not only with himself, but with Christianity itself.

This whole dispute over faith and doubt is deeply rooted in Kierkegaard's psychology and personal history. It is merely the translation into abstract terms of an inner conflict which lasted all his life. It is not by chance that he notes in his papers, in various ways, that belief can be purchased only at the cost of profound sufferings, and that its value is exactly in proportion to these sufferings, that it is conditioned by scandal, that not only, is the way of belief strait, but that straitness and affliction are themselves the way.[31] The revolts of his youth, romantic and rationalist in their inspiration, continued in him long after his conversion. While they had at first, however, been in a sense outside faith, they eventually entered into faith itself as one of its elements, as a principle of tension and pathos. Kierkegaard never ceased to writhe upon the horns of the dilemma he had created for himself, which opposed reason to faith upon a plane where they could not meet without clashing. As a result of this persistent rationalism, even though its appearance is different, we see him continually stressing the dramatic character of belief and placing its origin—an origin which is the work of every moment —at the heart of anguish and terror. Here at least he delivers up his secret to us; we can understand why he writes in the *Journal* that in going through religion to his real task he has merely turned his own acuteness against himself.[32]

The Ambiguity of the Immediate.—There is a further example which may serve to illustrate the point of view we have put forward. Kierkegaard insists throughout his work upon the category of the immediate. He excludes it when it supervenes upon the æsthetic plane, signifying momentary enjoyment at the impulsion of instinct; he exalts it in the sense of that second immediacy, acquired and conquered, which is the privilege of the religious life at its highest, and which can be defined as intuition and passion, in opposition to reasoning and mediation, to talk and to abstract dialectics. "Every movement of infinity," he writes, "comes about by passion, and no reflection can bring a movement about. This is the continual leap in existence which explains the movement, whereas it is a chimera which according to Hegel is supposed to explain everything, and at the same time this is the only thing he has never tried to explain."[33]

Reflection and Immediacy

Now immediacy was least of all familiar to Kierkegaard. He declares: "I have never had any immediacy, and therefore, in the ordinary human sense of the word, I have never lived. I began at once with reflection; it is not as though in later years I had amassed a little reflection, but I am reflection from first to last".[34] Here again, one may perhaps discern an expression of Kierkegaard's inner debate. It seems that this attachment of value to the immediate, the importance assigned to this category, is merely a sorrowful admission of what he himself lacks. This lack is either upon the æsthetic plane, where reflection always prevented him from being a true æsthetician, possessing, in Barrès' phrase, the most unclouded awareness together with the keenest capacity for enjoyment (an insoluble contradiction for Kierkegaard, in whom analysis destroys the immediate and pleasure destroys awareness); or upon the religious plane, where immediacy was for him an inaccessible ideal which he even sometimes goes so far as to repudiate on the same grounds as he does the immediate in æsthetics.[35] His deepest sorrow was that he failed to achieve that degree of inner unity which would have allowed him, with a new spontaneity wrested from the spontaneity of nature, in one single ardent, confident leap, to become the knight of faith.

The Lure of the Forbidden Fruit

One is reminded of Amiel, whose oscillations of character and contrasts in feeling can be defined in very similar terms. But here things are very different. In Amiel, the variation is to some extent accidental. In Kierkegaard it is essential; ambivalence and contradiction, uneasiness and conflict are constituent parts of his being. He has often remarked upon it himself. "To me there is something so inexplicably happy," he writes, "in the antithesis Climacus-Anticlimacus (the pseudonyms of *Philosophical Frag-*

ments and *The Sickness unto Death*), I recognize myself, and my
nature so entirely in it that if someone else had discovered it I
should have thought he had spied upon me. The merit is not
mine, for I did not originally think of it".[36] Conflict and contradiction, then, are the effect of a spontaneity which reveals his
nature.

If all is dialectic however in Kierkegaard, that is, if everything
assumes the form of dialogue, and even, as we have seen, of
polemic, is there not also to be found in him a secret liking for
attempts at mediation? Such an inclination would give the fullest
significance to his polemic against Hegel, which would then
appear as a polemical attack by Kierkegaard upon himself. For
the impossibility of the immediate undoubtedly leads to conflict,
but it might also lead towards mediation, which is the overcoming
of conflict. Indeed, might not Kierkegaard's profound and admirably subtle taste for states of transition, moments of uncertainty, doubtful positions, be taken as a replica, on the existential
plane, of Hegel's rational mediation?[37] Kierkegaard protests, no
doubt, in the *Concept* of *Dread*, that the "vertigo of possibility"
cannot account for the qualitative leap constituted by sin; this
category, none the less, has all the appearances of mediation. The
same observation would hold good for the category of irony,
which seems to form the link between the æsthetic and the ethical,
and for that of humour, which appears to bridge the interval
between the ethical and the religious. Often, moreover, Kierkegaard yields to the attraction of well integrated, wisely ordered
concepts. He remarks upon it himself. "My misfortune," he
says, "or the thing that made my life so difficult, is that I am
strung a whole tone higher than other men, and where I am and
what I am about does not have to do with the particular, but
always also with a principle and an idea. At the best, most people
think which girl they ought to marry; I had to think about
marriage. And so in everything."[38] In short, the immediate
always remains an ideal which Kierkegaard contemplates with
melancholy as a promised land rarely attained.

Moreover, there is a further aspect to be considered here.
Every poet is involved in contradiction, for as a poet he is in

touch with the absolute, but as soon as he speaks he loses contact with it, since by definition the absolute cannot be mediatized, that is, if one prefers, rationalized. Thus St. John of the Cross warns us that it is impossible to convey in words the experiences of the divine darkness. The poet wishes to express the immediate by means of an instrument which implies rupture with the immediate. Kierkegaard is thus doubly harnessed to an impossible task, first by virtue of his own psychology, and secondly by virtue of the very nature of the poetic vocation.[39]

NOTES TO CHAPTER ONE

[1] On this point cf. J. Wahl, *Etudes kierkegaardiennes*, p. 46.

[2] *A Literary Discussion*, VIII, 72 (Geismar, p. 232).

[3] Cf. *Journal*, 1851, X[4] A 130 (Dru 1191). "But then too I am a fundamentally polemical nature."

[4] *Journal*, 1849, (Haecker, p. 95).

[5] *Journal*, March 1847, VIII A 27 (Dru 641).

[6] *Journal*, June 1849, X[1] A 483 (Dru 931).

[7] Cf. *Unscientific Postscript*, p. 545. "In the aloofness of the experiment the whole work has to do with me myself, solely and simply with me. . . ." "I ask how I am to become a Christian. I ask only for my own sake, yes, certainly that I do, or rather I have asked this question." Thus he is not to be invoked as an authority, which is ill suited to "an experimental humorist."

[8] *Unscientific Postscript*, p. 31.

[9] Cf. *Fear and Trembling*, pp. 49–68.

[10] *For Self-Examination*, p. 42 and 44.

[11] Cf. *Journal*, 1854, XI[1] A 95 (Dru 1308), where Kierkegaard speaks of "The Night of the Absolute" and of the horror men experience when they enter it.

[12] *For Self-Examination*, p. 44–5.

[13] *Fear and Trembling*, p. 170.

[14] Cf. Pascal, *Pensées*, fr. 233:"Who then will blame Christians for not being able to give reasons for their belief, when they profess a reason for which no reasons can be given? They declare, when they expound it to the world, that it is foolishness, *stultitiam*; do you then complain that they do not offer proofs? If they proved it, they would not keep their word: it is their lack of proof which shows they do not lack sense." Fr. 234: "If one were obliged not to act except in cases of certainty, one ought to do nothing about religion, for it is not certain (the "certain" here, for Pascal, is the mathematically demonstrable). But how many things does one undertake in uncertainty, sea voyages, battles! I say, then, that one would do nothing at all, for nothing is certain."

[15] *Journal*, 1845, VI A 108 (Dru 540): "Luther, as is well known, was shaken by the lightning which killed his friend beside him: in the same way, his expressions always sound as though the lightning were continuously striking down behind him."

[16] Cf. *For Self-Examination*, p. 101.

[17] On this point, undoubtedly, Kierkegaard is far removed from Pascal, whose anti-intellectualism is neither so far-reaching nor, above all, of the same kind. "If the principles of reason are shaken," Pascal writes, "our religion will be absurd and ridiculous." For Kierkegaard on the other hand, faith is properly speaking a "leap into absurdity"; which Pascal will not admit, for faith to him is above reason, not contrary to it. (*Pensées*, fr. 265.) When reason humbles

itself before faith, it sees that it must so humble itself, so that the submission is itself reasonable (*Pensées*, fr. 267–73.)   The opposition between Pascal and Kierkegaard is no less noticeable in another connection. "One must first show," says Pascal, (*Pensées*, fr. 187), "that religion is not contrary to reason; then that it is venerable, and one must inculcate respect for it; then one must make it *lovable*, one must make men of good will wish that it were true; and then one must show that it is true." The difference between their methods and points of view will be well brought out by the following passage from Kierkegaard, (*Training in Christianity*, p. 71): "But if the Christian life is something so terrible and frightful, how in the world can a person get the idea of accepting it? Quite simply, and, if you want that too, quite in a Lutheran way; only the consciousness of sin can force one into this dreadful situation—the power on the other side being grace." Kierkegaard, it is true, at once adds: "And in that very instant, the Christian life transforms itself and is sheer gentleness, grace, lovingkindness and compassion." None the less, this remains very different from Pascal's view, for Kierkegaard will not admit that it is possible to show that Christianity is not contrary to reason, nor that it can be presented to the unbeliever as something lovable, nor that it can be shown to be true.

[18] Cf. *The Concept of Dread*, p. 127, note.

[19] Cf. *For Self-Examination*, p. 101.

[20] Cf. *For Self-Examination*, p. 102: "The spirit which giveth life (which the understanding does not do) declares and bears witness: ' "The hope" is against hope.' O thou who perhaps to the point of desperation art fighting hopelessly and in vain to find hope, it is this, is it not, which makes thee indignant that in thine opinion thou canst absolutely victoriously make it evident even to a child or to the stupidest man that for thee there is no hope; and perhaps it is precisely this that embitters thee, that they will contradict this. Well then, entrust thyself to the Spirit, for with it thou canst talk, it acknowledges at once that thou art in the right, it says: 'That is quite right, and to me it is very important, that this be insisted upon, for it is precisely from this that I, the Spirit, educe the proof that there is hope: hope against hope.' "

[21] *Training in Christianity*, p. 83, note.

[22] *Unscientific Postscript*, p. 30.

[23]Without however ceasing to have recourse to it, and to make brilliant use of it. Cf. *Journal*, 1845, VI A 109 (F. & G. p. 242): "A proof of the truth of Christianity. This proof is that one has often seen its worst enemies turn into its warmest defenders. Conversely it often happens to philosophical doctrines and the like that their most ardent partisans become hostile and abandon them. It is precisely the double reaction produced by Christianity, which irritates as strongly as it attracts, which shows its absolute truth. Elsewhere the adherent's first attitude is simply that of being not hostile but friendly, he is attracted (while with Christianity he is repelled), and it is only later that he wearies of it, With Christianity, the reverse is true; its importance is such that it begins by repelling and then afterwards attracts, and the violence of the change is the measure of its inwardness."

[24] *Journal*, 19 April 1835, I A 53 (Dru 14). Kierkegaard none the less thinks (*Journal*, 1849) that by proving that only a God can allow himself to be killed by men (Cf. *Has a Man the Right to let himself be put to Death for the Truth?*) he

has furnished "an indirect demonstration of the divinity of Christ".(Haecker, p. 47).

25 The argument whereby Christianity's eighteen centuries of existence themselves constitute a proof of the divinity of the Christian religion, so that belief ought to become easier and easier as the centuries pass, particularly angers Kierkegaard, (not without reason). Cf. *Training in Christianity*, p. 143: "And verily the eighteen centuries, which have not contributed an iota to prove the truth of Christianity, have on the contrary contributed with steadily increasing power to do away with Christianity. It is by no means true, as one might consistently suppose when one acclaims the proof of the eighteen centuries, that now in the nineteenth century people are far more thoroughly convinced of the truth of Christianity than they were in the first and second generations—it is rather true (though it certainly sounds like a satire on the worshippers and adorers of this proof) that just in proportion as the proof supposedly has increased in cogency . . . fewer and fewer persons are convinced."

26 Kierkegaard does not wish to eliminate all recourse to history. On the contrary, an essential element in his doctrine is that the paradox consists in the fact that the eternal becomes the historical and that belief is the act of founding eternal bliss, in a decisive manner, upon relationship to a historical fact. Thus he states, (*Journal*, 1846, VII A 130, Dru 602): "The historicity of the redemption must be certain in the same sense as any other historical thing, but not more so, for otherwise the different spheres are confused." On the one hand, however, all history demands belief (in the widest sense of the term) by the very fact that it rests upon evidence and by definition excludes direct verification. On the other hand, and this is of supreme importance, the historical element in Christianity relates to something which transcends history and thereby necessarily requires belief in the strictest sense of the term, that is, faith. Faith, therefore, must not be made dependent upon historical considerations, otherwise it could be acquired by means of knowledge and criticism.

27 *Journal*, 1849, X¹ A 481.

28 Cf. *Christian Discourses*, p. 375: "No glance is so sharp-sighted as that of faith, and yet humanly speaking, faith is blind; for reason, understanding, is, humanly speaking, the faculty of seeing, but faith is against the understanding."

29 Cf. *Training in Christianity*, p. 98: "The proofs might lead a man—not to faith, ah, far from that, but up to the point where faith may come into existence."

30 *Journal*, 1844, IV A 191 (F. & G. p. 188).

31 Cf. *The Gospel of Suffering*, (p. 113–35, Fr. edn.).

32 *Journal*, 1843, IV A 160 (Dru 463).

33 *Fear and Trembling*, p. 59, note.

34 *The Point of View*, p. 81—cf. ibid., p. 67 ff, where Kierkegaard observes that he has never written under the influence of *inspiration*, which would have been an "immediate relationship" with God, but that he has always carried out his work as a methodical, rigorous and exact task, closer to reflection than to inspiration.

35 From another point of view moreover, Kierkegaard thinks (*The Point of View*, p. 90) that "immediate pathos" is scarcely suitable for the religious author of his time. Even if he has the gift, he should refrain from making use of

it. The modern world is too reflective and too clever, not simple and artless enough, to be moved by it. "Even for a martyr to accomplish anything in these times he must possess reflection, in order to so intrigue the age that it cleaves to him even when it puts him to death—that thus the awakening may follow."

[36] *Journal*, 1849, X^2 A 195 (Dru 1000).

[37] Kierkegaard also has a notion of *development* as continuity which exactly corresponds with the reflections Newman had just published in 1845 in his *Essay on the Development of Christian Doctrine*. Cf. *Journal*, 1849, X^2 A 207 (Dru 1003): "The human race, like individuals, also needs examinations or examiners in order to preserve its continuity. Geniuses are really the examiners. They develop much more slowly than other men, they really go through all the fundamental historical forms of existence. And therein lies their significance as correctives. While geniuses prophetically show the future they do so in fact owing to a profounder recollection of what has gone before. Development is certainly not a step back but a return, and that is originality."

[38] *Journal*, 1849, X^1 A 476 (Dru 928).

[39] We have already noted that one of the objects of the pseudonyms, in Kierkegaard's view, is to eliminate at least one form of mediation, namely that of the author *qua* author, between absolute reality and the reader; that is to say, the question is one of creating the most favourable conditions for immediacy in the reader.

II

KIERKEGAARD'S MELANCHOLY

The preceding remarks will perhaps allow us, if not to solve the problem of Kierkegaard's melancholy, at least to shed some light on a field which is in many respects obscure, especially in view of the constant precautions he himself took in order to conceal the deep secret of his life. He has noted that he found consolation in the thought that no one after him would succeed in discovering in his papers a single clue to that which had filled his life. "No one will find among my papers," he says, "the words which explain everything and which often made what the world would call a bagatelle into an event of tremendous importance to me, and what I look upon as something insignificant when I take away the secret gloss which explains all."[1]

With these reservations, one can nevertheless perhaps attempt to discern what was the nature and the meaning of the melancholy whose influence Kierkegaard never ceased to feel. The problem is of capital importance for his psychology and also for the interpretation of part of his work.

From the first it is as well to distinguish melancholy from what Kierkegaard called "religious anguish", that is, the state of anxiety and suffering bound up with faith and the profession of Christianity.

Melancholy itself is of several kinds. Kierkegaard seems to have experienced them all, or rather, to be more precise, to have been subject to a "melancholy complex" whose many aspects and various causes were never clearly distinguished, even in his own mind, in spite of the abstract precision of his self-analysis.

The Burden of Heredity.—First consideration, without a doubt, must be given to Kierkegaard's temperament. It had many morbid aspects, on which we are informed either by Kierkegaard himself or by the accounts of those who came into close contact with him and were able to see something of his intimate life. Thus in the *Diary of the Seducer* Kierkegaard writes, analyzing the psychology of the "seducer", who is himself: "He had suffered from an *exacerbatio cerebri*, for which reality did not afford a sufficient stimulus, at most only a temporary one. He did not break down under reality; he was not too weak to endure it, not at all, he was too strong, but this strength was really a sickness."[2] From another point of view, his secretary and copyist Levine, who was admitted into the intimacy of his domestic life, tells of the eccentricities he witnessed: Kierkegaard's phobia for the sun, "the barricaded windows; his hysterical fear of fire and his frantic precautions, sweating and trembling; his mania for sprinkling eau-de-Cologne on the stove before beginning work; his excessive love of hot baths, sugar and coffee; the luxury of his table; his style of living, which cost him fantastic sums; his silver; his innumerable walking-sticks; the collection of cups, from which a fresh pair had to be chosen every day with all seriousness; finally his absurd tips, not to mention his acts of charity".[3]

Kierkegaard often quoted the Latin adage according to which "there has never been a great genius without a touch of madness". His acute awareness of his own genius was to lead him to apply this old saw to himself.[4] He says, too, by way of definition, that "this *dementia* is the suffering allotted to genius in existence, it is the expression, if I may say so, of the divine jealousy, whereas the gift of genius is the expression of the divine favour". All this raises general problems of great interest: "What relation has madness to genius? Can we construct the one out of the other? In what sense and how far is the genius master of his madness? For it goes without saying that to a certain degree he is master of it, since otherwise he would be actually a madman." Here, converted into the abstract form of a problem, one can hear Kierkegaard's dialogue with himself on the subject of a melancholy which is "dialectical" like everything else in him, and which in some sense oscillates between madness and genius. What is certain is that he was constantly aware of its weight, and that it took root in the darkest depths of his physical constitution and made him struggle endlessly and without respite against "the pale, bloodless, hard-lived, midnight shapes", to whom he himself, he says, gave life and being.[5] The *Journal* (1850) even states specifically that at certain times of "monstrous melancholy" Kierkegaard had been attacked by suicidal impulses.[6]

It is true that he makes Judge William[7] dispute the physiological nature of this melancholy. But he is concerned to assert that it "dwells in the intellect", that is to say, that it is a mental ailment, rather than to deny that it has a physical basis.[8]

Can an exact name be given to this condition? It has been attempted on several occasions, in particular by Hjalmar Helweg, who has studied Kierkegaard's case from the psychiatric point of view.[9] Helweg speaks of a manic-depressive psychosis, marked by periods of dormancy interrupted by crises of extreme intensity, but never such as to overpower him completely. The peculiar characteristic of this psychosis is that it involves more or less frequent attacks either of excitement (mania) or of depression (melancholia), or of both alternately. Kierkegaard would appear to have been especially subject to the depressive form, accompanied by deep emotional disturbance, with acute manifestations of grief and anguish, delusions of inferiority, ochlophobia (horror of crowds) and desire for solitude, and sometimes suicidal impulses. What is certain is that the effect of this morbid condition (more or less well defined) was to plunge him into the intoxication of literary production, which became a powerful derivative from it. He himself moreover was aware of this effect, since he always thought that his melancholy was one of the decisive factors in his genius.

The Defeat of Aestheticism.—Another very frequent form of melancholy results from "æstheticism", from a life dominated by the urge to enjoyment and pleasure, whose final defeat it marks. From this point of view the character of Nero, a notorious æsthete, is melancholy itself.[10] Here melancholy involves guilt, since it is the final outcome of a permanent refusal to choose, of a persistent desire to live in the immediate.[11]

One must be careful not to take this melancholy for a form of religious or even ethical experience. It sometimes has their appearance, but not their reality, for the latter have sources of a much purer nature, in the first place in a deep sense of sin, while the latter involves only a feeling of regret, and sterile regret, at a setback. "I can imagine nothing more excruciating," Kierke-gaard notes,[12] "than an intriguing mind which has lost the thread of its continuity and now turns its whole acumen against itself, when conscience awakens and compels the schemer to extricate himself from this confusion, for what is even the pain of remorse in comparison with this conscious madness? His punishment has a purely æsthetic character; for even to say that his conscience awakens is too ethical an expression to use about him. Conscience exists for him only as a higher degree of consciousness, which expresses itself in a disquietude that does not, in a more profound sense, accuse him, but which keeps him awake, and gives him no rest in his barren activity."

Romantic sadness.—One can also distinguish, closely related to that which we have just discussed, a romantic melancholy, which is the awareness we have at times of the anxiety of nature, and also of the brevity of our own lives, ceaselessly threatened by natural death.[13] Nature, beautiful, young and graceful, where life assumes a thousand shapes and teems in joy and happiness, nature yet contains a deep sadness, a kind of sigh which is the mark of a captive thing unable to breathe or find expression. In nature everything, it seems, calls forth a smile; everything is carefree. And yet, this same nature, is it life, or death? Brief, full of songs and flowers, but incessantly a prey to victorious death: such is the life of nature.[14]

It is this feeling of the ambiguity of nature which forms the basis of romantic sadness. This malady, Kierkegaard observes in *Either/Or,* [15] coupling it with the defeat of æstheticism, is very common nowadays, when everyone feels bound to wear his heart on his sleeve: it makes "all young France and Germany" lament. It is certain, indeed, that the Romantics made much of this kind of melancholy. But Kierkegaard for his own part constantly felt its grip, by virtue of his singular sensitivity to the sighing of creation, to the mute despair of things, the dialectical aspect and the uncertainty of the temporal; and by virtue also of his conviction that he was destined to have only a brief, tormented life.

This melancholy however is at the most but a stage to be passed through. To remain there permanently would be to confuse true human sadness with "childish whimperings". There is only one sadness worthy of man, the sadness brought him by his awareness of eternity and his own state of sinfulness. And this does not have the effect of overwhelming man, but on the contrary of raising him above himself, by forcing him to adoration. By this means, confessing the infinite greatness of God, he finds within himself his true greatness.

The Feeling of Sinfulness.—There is, therefore, a melancholy which is bound up with the condition of humanity, corrupted by sin. To be precise, it is the feeling of inherited sin within us, every man's inability to become transparently pure in his own eyes.[16] This melancholy exists even for those whose life is the calmest, the most peaceable, the most harmonious imaginable. As such it is a sign or at least a principle of perfection, since it induces us to move on to the religious stage, not in order to be rid of it, but on the contrary to strengthen it and see it transformed into that anguish and despair which is the gateway to salvation. "But the strange ideas of melancholy I do not give up; for these, which perhaps a third person would call crotchets, which she perhaps would sympathetically call distressing fancies, I call pulls—if only I follow them and hold out, they lead me to the eternal certainty of the infinite."[17]

Kierkegaard's torture, it seems, was that he could not convince himself that he had succeeded in raising his natural melancholy to this level—a melancholy which he had come to regard as the sacred fruit of his father's heritage. For this, according to a favourite view of his, it would have had to reunite the general and the particular, that is to say the anguish proper to Adam's race and his father's sadness, both nourished by the sense of sin. From a very early age, Kierkegaard undoubtedly had the feeling that if to triumph is to conquer in the infinite sense, it is also, and necessarily, to suffer in the finite sense. But suffering could acquire value and meaning only if it was in some sense the counterpart and as it were the reverse side of the movement of the infinite. In a certain way Kierkegaard obtained "profound understanding of his melancholy", according to which he was good for nothing, properly speaking, in the finite sense; this put him on the road towards the decisive choice, in total renunciation and solitude with God.[18] This choice, however, was to be itself the object of a choice. Kierkegaard has frequently repeated that the choice must be chosen, and not undergone. His melancholy would have had, so to speak, to change its sign in order to be genuinely religious. "I shall try," he writes in a revealing passage in the *Journal*, "to . . . really think out the idea of my melancholy together with God here and now".[19] He always doubted if he had carried out the leap, from a melancholy lying on the fringes of the æsthetic and the moral to the profound anguish which is the specific mark of the religious. He never completely succeeded in ridding himself of the feeling that the melancholy which lay so heavily upon him contained some impurity, that it drew nourishment from sources other than faith. "The hardest trial of all," he writes, "is when a man does not know whether the cause of his suffering is madness or guilt. While in other cases freedom is what he fights with, in this case it has become dialectical in its own most terrible contrary."[20] It was understanding this, with a prodigious keenness of observation, which caused Kierkegaard's anguish, which thus became anxiety at the absence of anxiety, or, what amounts to the same thing, the anguish of experiencing an anguish which does not proceed directly from faith, but, to a great extent at least, from flesh and blood.[21]

The Category of the Ordeal.—None the less, Kierkegaard may have found some alleviation here by placing his deep-rooted melancholy in the category of an ordeal. Certain remarks in *The Repetition*[22] seem to point in this direction. Thus his inherited melancholy and also the profound sadness engendered in him by his brief relationship with Regina Olsen ("the loss of the beloved") take on the appearance of ordeals properly so called, susceptible as such of "repetition": melancholy might no doubt yield to the appropriate physical and psychological treatment, and perhaps the beloved might be given back to the lover who had left her but never forgotten her?

But is not this pure illusion? Or rather, would not the peace of mind brought by a conviction that the ordeal was only temporary be merely another way of escape from the demands made by the Christian life? An ordeal of this kind does in fact develop and resolve itself temporally: Job recovers house, flocks, and children, increased and multiplied.[23] But the religious man expects nothing on earth, except anguish and suffering.[24] The ordeal, then, is at most on the borders of faith.

Moreover, the ordeal is not voluntary. Whether accepted or not, it is undergone. Now Kierkegaard, in spite of the moral value he sometimes attached to his suffering, [25] always wondered whether he were not himself responsible for his melancholy. "And was not this sickness," he writes, "hard enough for me to bear in time, that I not only should suffer but become guilty through it? The deformed man has after all only to bear the pain of being deformed, but how dreadful if being deformed made him guilty!"[26] This doubt was constantly nourished in him by the disparity which he felt to exist between his conception of the demands of Christianity and his personal conduct. The remarks on the poetic life in *The Sickness unto Death* are enriched by painful experience on this point. Poetic existence in its religious form, Kierkegaard notes, is situated in sin and despair, for it consists in the æsthetic treatment of the religious categories. The poet loves religion only as an unsuccessful lover, without being strictly speaking a believer in it. His melancholy, which is real, is not identical with the despair of faith, but is in a sense a thing of his own, which he wishes to enjoy in order to be himself (that is, to remain a poet), or in order not to be himself before God (that is, not to become as God wishes and as he should be). Such is exactly, in his own eyes, Kierkegaard's position, a poet who has succeeded in giving religious realities "an enchantment, a lyrical *élan*" unattained by any official bard,[27] but who at the same time has felt

to the point of anguish the contradiction of "always poetizing instead of being", of interpreting for other people's benefit a reality
which he himself does not experience with all the necessary intensity and truth. "Feeling my wings clipped in the fullest sense of
the term," he writes, "I have accustomed myself to the pleasures
and comforts of life, in order to be able to work productively in
the best possible conditions. I dislike touching upon this point,
because my whole existence is artificial".[28] Here is "the thorn in
the flesh" which, in one respect at least, explains Kierkegaard's
work.

There is no question, however, of depreciating the value of the
poet's rôle. In *Either/Or* Kierkegaard compares it to that of the
prophet. The poet, he says, is an unhappy man who bears secret
torments deep in his heart and whose lips are so formed that sighs
and groans sounding against them produce harmonious music.
The poet, he observes again in the *Journal*, is "a living telegraph
between God and man", and his rôle is to awaken men to consciousness of serious things, of eternity. It must none the less be
admitted that in general the poet is a man whose personal life
develops in categories quite different from those which he expounds poetically. He himself lacks an existential relationship
with God. He is, indeed, "before God", which is the characteristic of seriousness, but he is there in a sense which derives rather
from the æsthetic than from the religious.[29] The serious is itself
poetic.

This must be understood to apply even to the highest form of
poetic existence there is, namely that which has a religious orientation, which is entirely given up to the expression of religious
categories.[30] This poetic life is always sinful for the Christian, for
it consists of dreaming instead of being, of having only an æsthetical imaginative relation to the true and the good, instead of a real
relation. "A poet-existence as such," Kierkegaard writes, "lies in
the obscurity which is due to the fact that a beginning of despair
was not carried through, that the soul keeps on shivering with
despair and the spirit cannot attain its true transformation. This
poetic ideal is always a sickly ideal, for the true ideal is always the
real. So when the spirit is not allowed to soar up into the eternal

world of spirit it remains midway, and rejoices in the pictures reflected in the clouds and weeps that they are so transitory. A poet-existence is therefore, as such, an unhappy existence, it is higher than finiteness and yet not infiniteness. The poet sees the ideals, but he must flee away from the world in order to rejoice in them, he cannot bear about, in the midst of life's confusion, these divine images within him; cannot tranquilly pursue his course un-affected by the caricatures of these ideals which appear on all sides, not to speak of having the strength to clothe himself in them.''[31] Hence it can be said that the poetic life is on the frontier of despair and sin, sin consisting here as elsewhere, for whoever is before God, in not wishing to be oneself according to eternity, or in wish-ing to be oneself according to the finite. This wish is itself the form taken by despair. The poet, then, is in despair, even though he has the idea of God and even a deep need for religion—because he enjoys his torment, while God's demand, as he knows, is that he should abandon it, that he should humble himself beneath his torment as the believer does; that is to say, if one prefers it, that he should adopt it instead of exploiting it.

Such was the inner discussion which filled Kierkegaard's days and nights. "If I lived in a strongly religious age," he writes, "when it was recognized, as it used to be, that Christianity con-sists in the fact that the whole of human life must be suffering, then I should discover more easily whether in my religious feeling there is not a certain pleasure in self-torture".[32] Except for a few moments of comparative calm, Kierkegaard always remained uncertain of the fundamental significance of his melancholy, unable to place it in the category of an ordeal and attempting, without ever succeeding fully, to transfer it from the poetic plane to the religious, from talk to life.[33]

To sum up, Kierkegaard's melancholy is at once the effect of a morbid constitution and the result of an inner conflict, represent-ing his uneasiness at not succeeding in giving a religious meaning to his natural gloom.[34] In reality, what was involved was indeed an ordeal, and of the severest kind.[35] As soon as he could re-nounce "repetition", the ordeal established him really and truly in the religious sphere, in spite even of his doubts which were bound up with the morbidity of his mental condition and his prodigious talent for introspection; until the moment when a lonely death in the hospital at Copenhagen, putting the seal of complete sincerity upon his sufferings, resolved before his conscience the doubt which had so long tortured him.[36]

NOTES TO CHAPTER TWO

[1] *Journal*, 1843, IV A 83 (Dru 431).

[2] *Either/Or*, tom. 1 p. 253.

[3] Quoted by J. J. Gateau in the preface to his French edition of the *Diary of a Seducer*, p. xx.

[4] *Fear and Trembling*, p. 165 f.

[5] *Journal*, 1840, III A 218 (Dru 345).

[6] At the same time Kierkegaard felt this melancholy to be absolutely insurmountable. Cf. *The Point of View*, p. 78: "I have never at any instant in my life been deserted by the faith that one can do what one will—only one thing excepted, all else unconditionally, but one thing not, the throwing off of the melancholy in whose power I was."

[7] Cf. *Either/Or*, vol. II, p. 159.

[8] Cf. *Stages on Life's Way*, p. 356: "What is my sickness? Melancholy. Where is the seat of this sickness? In the power of the imagination, and possibility is its nutriment."

[9] S. Kierkegaard, *En Psykiatrisk-psychologisk studie*, Copenhagen, 1933.

[10] Cf. *Either/Or*, vol. II, p. 156 ff.

[11] Cf. *Either/Or*, vol. II, p. 159: "What, then, is melancholy?" Judge William asks. "It is hysteria of the spirit. There comes a moment in a man's life when his immediacy is, as it were, ripened and the spirit demands a higher form in which it will apprehend itself as spirit. Man, so long as he is immediate spirit, coheres with the whole of earthly life, and now the spirit would collect itself, as it were, out of this dispersion and become in itself transformed, the personality would be conscious of itself in its eternal validity. If this does not come to pass, if the movement is checked, if it is forced back, melancholy comes. One may do much by way of inducing forgetfulness, one may work, one may employ other expedients more innocent than those of Nero, but melancholy remains. There is something inexplicable in melancholy. . . . Herein lies the infinity of melancholy. . . . But melancholy is sin, really it is a sin *instar omnium*, for not to will deeply and sincerely is sin, and this is the mother of all sins."

[12] *Either/Or*, vol. I, p. 255.

[13] Cf. *Journal*, 1836, I A 294 and 306 (Wahl, p. 581): "Romantic effort is an effort which consumes itself; and I cannot make it eternal, since then I should have an eternity consisting of an infinite series of moments." "The romantic element is a perpetual effort to seize something evanescent."

[14] *Christian Discourses*, p. 351 f.

[15] Vol. II, p. 160.

[16] Cf. *Either/Or*, vol. II, p. 160.

[17] *Stages on Life's Way*, p. 345.

[18] *The Point of View*, p. 78.

[19] 1847, VIII A 250 (Dru 694).

[20] *Journal*, 1844, V A 49. (Dru 491.)

[21] Cf. in this connection some incidental remarks in *The Gospel of Suffering* (p. 54-55): "Just as the Christian is always to be recognized by his gentleness, so also is of the nature of Christianity to be an object of faith only in gentleness. All exaggeration, whether caused by melancholy or frivolity, is an immediate sign of lack of faith. . . . The melancholy man does not want to forget (sin): he does not want to remember that it has been forgiven him; he wants to recall his fault to mind; that is why he cannot believe."

[22] P. 128 ff.

[23] *Repetition*, p. 132-4.

[24] *Journal*, 1837, II A 99: "Yes, if my suffering, my weakness, were not the condition which made my whole spiritual activity possible, I would make a fresh attempt to attack it with medical assistance. But here is the mystery: there is a correspondence between suffering and the meaning of life." Similarly, *Journal*, 1853, X^5 A 72 (Dru 1287): "I prayed for everything . . . yet one thing excepted, exemption from the deep suffering beneath which I have suffered from my earliest days, but which I understood as belonging to my relation to God."

[25] Thus he asks himself, *Journal*, 1849, II A 82 (Haecker, p. 82): "Do you believe if you had been in good health you would have attained perfection easily, or, at least, more easily? Oh! quite the contrary. You would have given yourself up just as easily to your passions, if not perhaps to more besides, such as pride and increased vanity. Suffering, although it is a burden, is a useful burden, like the splints used in orthopædic treatment. . . . Physical health, immediate well-being, are a far greater danger than wealth, power and consideration."

[26] *Stages on Life's Way*, p. 336-57.

[27] *The Sickness unto Death*, p. 125.

[28] *Journal*, 1850. Pascal's case, Kierkegaard remarks (*Journal*, 1852, X^4 A537, Dru 1246) was quite different: "Who in modern times has been used so much by parsons and professors as Pascal? His ideas are appropriated—but Pascal's asceticism and his hair-shirt are omitted."

[29] *The Sickness unto Death*, p. 123-6.

[30] In the *Unscientific Postscript*, p. 545, Kierkegaard writes that he is not a Christian, even though he has passed beyond the poetic stage. He is, he says, "a humorist", that is to say a man able to grasp the contradictions which simulate the position which is called Christian but is in fact unrelated to paradoxal suffering.

[31] *Either/Or*, II, 177.

[32] IX, 392 (Wahl, p. 441). Cf. *Journal*, 1849, X^1 A 513 (Dru 937): "That is the fault I have a disposition for—forcing myself almost demoniacally to be stronger than I am. As a man of sanguine humour is required to hate himself, so perhaps I am required to love myself and renounce the melancholy hatred of myself which in a melancholy man can be almost a pleasure."

[33] Cf. *Journal*, loc. cit. "This fault I also have, that I constantly accompany myself poetically and now require of myself almost in desperation that I shall act so as to be in character."

[34] Cf. *Journal*, 1850, (Haecker, p. 167): "Melancholy, meditation and fear of God form in me a unity, which is my very being."

[35] Kierkegaard has noted on several occasions that he had always been able to conceal his melancholy from others, and that his very success in this way had been a revelation to him of his capacity to deceive. Cf. *Guilty?* (p. 20): "Melancholy is natural to me, it is true, but blessed be the power which, in spite of the bonds with which it has thus fettered me, has also given me a consolation. Certain animals are entirely defenceless against their enemies, but nature has endowed them with a wiliness which preserves them. A similar wiliness has been bestowed upon me, and its power makes me as strong as all those with whom I have come into conflict. It consists in dissimulating my melancholy, a melancholy whose profundity gives an exact measure of my ability to deceive." Similarly, *The Point of View*, p. 76: "This proportion (the equally great magnitude of melancholy and of the art of dissimulation) signifies that I was relegated to myself and to relationship with God."

[36] From 1853 onwards Kierkegaard had no further hesitation about the meaning and the religious value of his melancholy. Cf. *Journal*, 1853, X^5 A 72 (Dru 1287): "How foolhardy my soul was in desiring, and daring—for this is how I thought of it—one must not make the all-powerful petty; I prayed for everything, even the most foolhardy things, yet one thing excepted, exemption from the deep suffering beneath which I have suffered from my earliest days, but which I understood as belonging to my relation to God."

III

KIERKEGAARD'S FAITH

We have now been brought to the threshold of another problem, bound up at many points with that raised by Kierkegaard's melancholy—the problem of knowing whether he really had faith, in the strict sense of the term. Doubts have sometimes been raised on the subject[1], and many passages in which he declares that he does not possess the full and complete faith of the Christian might seem, at first glance, to bear them out. At the end of his life he was still writing in *The Instant*: "I have always said that I do not possess faith".[2] The Journal, moreover, often gives the impression that Kierkegaard is seeking or summoning faith, rather than that he has it. "Teach me, oh God," he says, "not to torment myself and make myself a martyr with stifling meditation, but rather to breath freely in faith".[3] It is true that one can wonder, with Kierkegaard himself, if "anyone ever has the right to write that he has faith". This remark has both a moral value, in that it marks the self-distrust and the humility of the believer, and a psychological application, in that faith, for Kierkegaard, is itself an object of faith. I can only believe that I believe, because faith does not belong to the sensible and rational order of things. In other words, faith is, it is true, an act of the intelligence, but of the intelligence moved by the will, through the entry of grace. To believe, then, is always to perform an act of faith in God's grace.[4] Nevertheless, from a more objective point of view—in the sense in which Kierkegaard's subjectivity becomes an object of study and not of secrecy—the question of his faith may well be raised. In order to answer it, in so far as that is possible, several periods in his life must be distinguished.

The Temptation of Unbelief.—We have already noted that for a time in his youth Kierkegaard had, if not abandoned all personal

79   7

belief, at least allowed his childhood faith to grow very weak. *The Point of View* gives some details on the subject.[5] Kierkegaard. observes that because of the nature of his upbringing Christianity had made him extremely unhappy from the human point of view. This, however, must not be taken to be the reason which temporarily alienated him from the Christian faith. Nevertheless, Kierkegaard does not tell us what the reason was. The difficulties which put his faith to test, he says, were not to be found in books, and he had never heard them expounded. But his respect for religion was so profound that he had resolved never to pass them on to others, especially if he had to decide not to become a Christian. Even at the time when he was furthest from Christianity, he never dreamed of attacking it or of doing anything which might diminish its prestige.

It was after the break with Regina Olsen that Kierkegaard again turned to Christianity, but without immediately recovering the faith of his early years. He wrote in the *Journal*: "If Christianity is to dwell in me, it will surely be accomplished according to the heading of to-day's Gospel: 'Christ enters through closed doors'."[6] At about the same period, a kind of examination of conscience, set down in the *Journal*, provides us with some more precise information concerning his position: "*Theology*. This seems to have been the easiest choice, but here again one meets with great difficulties. In Christianity itself the contradictions are so great that, to say the least, they prevent a clear view. As you know, I grew up, so to speak, in orthodoxy, but as soon as I began to think for myself the tremendous colossus began to totter. I call it a colossus with purpose, for taken as a whole it is very consistent, and in the course of centuries the different parts have fused so tightly together that it is difficult to quarrel with it. I could of course agree with it on certain points, but these would have to be treated like shoots, found in the cracks of a rock. On the other hand, I could also see what was wrong with it at many different points, but I had to leave the fundamentals *in dubio* for a time".[7]

However, from the summer of 1838 onwards Kierkegaard experienced strong feelings of a pious nature, which are expressed in numerous moving passages in the *Journal*. Thus on 9 July 1838 he sets down his resolution to impregnate his whole personal life with Christianity, at the same time emphasizing the anxiety which never ceased to trouble him on this very point: "I mean to labour," he says, "to achieve a far more inward relation to Christianity; hitherto I have fought for its truth while in a sense standing outside it; in a purely outward sense I have carried Christ's cross, like Simon of Cyrene".[8] It seems that from this point onwards Kierkegaard really returned to the Christian faith, and there are no grounds whatever for thinking that he subsequently ever left it again. The passages where he declares he cannot accomplish the last step to faith[9] can be understood in their true sense and bearing, only if it is borne in mind that he puts the Christian ideal higher and higher, especially after 1848. Thus the *Journal* states that it was in 1848 that Kierkegaard suddenly came to feel what was "the most high", in a kind of revelation which overcame him (like Saul on the road to Damascus). (Certainly, he notes, this is not given to many in each generation!) But almost at the same moment he was abruptly overwhelmed by another obvious fact, namely that "the highest is not to understand the highest, but to do it".[10] It is in judging himself with respect to this ideal that he confesses that he is not a Christian, that he is still far from Christianity.

It should also be noted that this assertion itself has often in a way a double sense or a double application. In the first place, indeed, it has a purely polemical or tactical sense, when Kierkegaard is concerned with destroying the illusory belief of "Christians" in the mass that they are in true accord with Christianity. This illusion, he says, can never be dispelled by direct means.[11] Only the indirect method can be effective: the man who sets out to dispel the illusion must himself declare that taking everything into account he is not a Christian. For the victim of illusion must be allowed the advantage of his alleged Christianity, a position of inferiority to him must be accepted. He must be taken "from the rear".[12] That is why the author of the *Unscientific Postscript*, Johannes Climacus, clearly asserts that he is not a Christian.[13]

These passages, however, and others in the same strain which are to be found in the *Journal*, have another sense, in which they must be taken literally, no longer as a polemical device, but as the expression of Kierkegaard's spiritual condition. There is fiction in them, if one likes, but the fiction coincides with reality. One might well apply generally Kierkegaard's reflection in the *Journal* that *Fear and Trembling*, which is an expression of the poetical element predominant in him, none the less represents his own life, so that the mystification of the pseudonym (Johannes de Silentio) consists precisely in the fact that it does not mystify.[14] Thus Johannes Climacus is also Kierkegaard, but from another angle, and incognito; a Kierkegaard who is always forced to admit that his faith remains far removed from what could be called a profound, true faith.[15]

Towards the Heights of Faith.—The texts in the *Journal* show clearly enough the stages in the movement which led Kierkegaard towards the heights of faith. An important date here is Easter Day, 19 April 1848, when he writes: "Now I am in the faith in the deepest sense", that is to say that henceforth his faith will be translated into action, without care for risk or danger, without fear of the world's hostility, persecution and death. It is at this moment that he thinks of writing *Training in Christianity*. There are men, he thinks, whose vocation is to sacrifice themselves in the advancement of an idea. But for that intrepid faith is needed. Henceforth, Kierkegaard possesses such faith, or more precisely is possessed by it, and in his career as a writer it will bring about, if not a new orientation, for in a sense there is also continuity, at least a marked accentuation of the religious character of his writings.

This is borne out irrefutably by *The Point of View*, written for the most part in 1848, and unpublished in Kierkegaard's lifetime (it was published only in 1859, by his brother Peder Christian, bishop of Aalborg). Kierkegaard, reviewing his work as a whole, attempts both to indicate its unity and continuity and to underline its various stages. A first group of writings, he says,[16] extending from *Either/Or* (1843) to *Stages on Life's Way* (1845), derives more especially from the æsthetic point of view, without however excluding the religious, which is present from the first, but as it were *incognito*. The *Unscientific Postscript* (1846) forms a *turning-point*, in that it propounds and discusses the central problem of Kierkegaard's work, namely the necessity of becoming a Christian—that which one *is not*, but which one *becomes*. The third group is purely religious, that is to say it relates only to this central and, in truth, unique problem. Now the date of the *Unscientific Postscript* fits in perfectly with the indications which are to be found in the *Journal* and the *Miscellaneous Papers*. There can therefore be no doubt whatever upon the point that Kierkegaard's faith is not only complete and profound, but also that from this time forth, after some period of hesitation and abatement in fervour, it will so to speak polarize the whole of his activity, which is given up henceforward, without limitation or reserve, to the essential task of bringing Christianity into the bosom of Christendom.

At the same time, however, Kierkegaard felt more and more acutely the torment of remaining unable, in his personal life, to fulfil the demands made by the new insight with which reflection had endowed him. "I have been blessed by Providence," he writes, "with an outstanding comprehension of the truth, such as has rarely been granted to any man, and I was also furnished by Providence with outstanding gifts for expounding this truth. In this matter, I have reason for humility in only one respect: it is that I have not had the strength to be myself what I understood".[17]

The more Christian he became, the less he was disposed to call himself a Christian. Many texts from this period might cast doubts upon his faith if no account were taken of a spiritual condition which made him always discover some remnants of the poetic form in the very heart of his burning zeal for Christianity, as though his faith still lacked the necessary intensity, as though the passion which animated him sprang rather from the mind than from the heart. Thus in 1848, summing up his whole career in *The Point of View*, he notes that he "has had far too much of a poet about him to dare to be called in a stricter sense a witness for the truth". No doubt, too, ethics occupied him too fully for him to be able to remain upon the poetic level. But "he is too much of a poet to be a witness for the truth". He is on the borders of these positions.[18] The fact is that his profound faith was not in question, except in so far as it had not sufficed to take him to the fullest extent of his demands, that is, to total renunciation, which is the crucial test of the Christian.

He was obliged to admit moreover that the ambition he had sometimes cherished, of carrying Christian witness to the point of martyrdom and dying for the truth, involved a good deal of presumption. Not only was it a kind of usurpation of the rights of God, since no *man* had the right to let himself be put to death for truth.[19] Such an ambition was also far beyond his powers. He remains still too far from the Christian ideal. His task will, therefore, be to be the poet of Christianity, attempting at the same time, however, to go much further than the mere poet, in a direction in which, more and more for him, poetry will become truth.[20] Such are the thoughts expressed in a long note in the *Journal*: "Now all is in order. On the path where one wishes oneself to be the object represented, I have to take a step back, and I have my task. I shall lean all the more heavily upon Christianity. I am becoming an unhappy lover in so far as *being* the ideal Christian oneself is concerned, and that is why I am becoming the poet of that ideal. I shall never forget this humiliation, and I shall thereby be different from an ordinary orator who, in the emptiness of his thoughts, confuses the fact of chattering about a thing with being that thing. I have not the strength to become a witness to the truth who is put to death for its sake. My natural disposition did not fit me for it either. I am becoming a poet and a thinker, that is why I was born, but with reference to Christianity and the ideal of being a Christian . . . I have been much, much further than the generality of poets. This also was necessary in order to have this task: Christianity, the ideal of being a Christian".[21]

This, no doubt, is only a somewhat humiliating compromise and as it were a renunciation of that vocation for sacrifice which Kierkegaard had discerned on Easter Day 1848. At least one can say that the very uneasiness which he feels and shows on the subject is a clear enough sign of the reality and sincerity of a faith struggling to reach an ever higher pitch of inwardness and fervour.[22]

Kierkegaard's piety.—Moreover, we have many indisputable proofs of Kierkegaard's ardent piety. The numerous prayers in his works, in the *Journal*, would in themselves be sufficient evidence of the intensity of a faith capable of discovering such accents.[23] He himself has confided in us, however, in a passage in *The Point of View* which, one feels, is admirably sincere, that prayer, meditation, the reading of devotional works, were one of his daily occupations and formed the basis of his life.[24] Thus he can write, speaking of himself in the past tense in the epilogue of a book which was not to appear until after his death: "His purity of heart was to will only one thing".[25]

As for the polemic against the Lutheran Church, in which Kierkegaard went so far, in his radical denial, as to write that as long as there was a pastor left, Christianity could not be realized, and that in fact the realization of Christianity is still in the future— this polemic, far from meaning that he had renounced the Christian faith, marks in him, deeply disappointed as he was in the established Church, the highest summit of his faith in Christ and his determination to assist the coming of Christianity into Christendom, even if it were by the witness of his own death.[26]

Kierkegaard's spiritual life, whatever its complexity, finally appears as unified in some degree by the double ambition (which at bottom was really only one) of "becoming a Christian" and of persuading the members of Christendom, pastors and flocks, to become Christians. Kierkegaard's dialogue with himself, no doubt, remains always as passionate and troubled, down to the last days of his life. The conditions under which his thought and activity developed prevented him from achieving tranquillity in calm certainty and peaceful contemplation. Undoubtedly a mystic, as we shall show below, Kierkegaard is a mystic of tempestuousness. He knows joy and peace, but he seems less at ease with them than with terror and dread, whereby his faith is tested and—whatever he may say—proved in his own eyes. Yet, as he more clearly discerns the meaning of his life, the religious value of his melancholy, his vocation as a religious poet, Kierkegaard more and more gives the impression of controlling the dialogue and arbitrating in the conflicts which excite it. The debate, at first turned inwards, assumes concrete form in definite individuals and institutions. From an inner event, the polemic becomes a public matter.

It must be understood moreover that Mynster is one of the possibilities for Kierkegaard, one of the characters which dwell within him, which partly explains the violence of his attack. At the same time, however, Mynster is a Lutheran bishop, a flesh and blood individual. So in a sense he tears Kierkegaard away from himself, at the very moment when Kierkegaard, with a violent gesture, plucks him from his own heart. The objective both expresses and conceals the subjective. The same could be said of the polemic against the *Corsair*, of the Adler case, and of the conflict with Luther and the established Church. More and more, Kierkegaard's conflict with himself tends to become a conflict with others. It is always the same dispute. But the new form it assumes accentuates its objective, universal character.

It is this very fact which gives it its essential value for us. Kierkegaard's greatness, indeed, is to have given a new breadth to the dialogue which every man, and especially every Christian, carries on within himself, between the flesh and the spirit, the æsthetic and the religious, the individual and the institution, the temporal and the spiritual, subjectivity and law, contemporaneity and history, reason and faith. The dramatic disputes which racked Kierkegaard's soul and darkened the last years of his life can help us to understand ourselves better and to take up a position, in order to choose and to choose choice, in the face of the eternal problems.

NOTES TO CHAPTER THREE

[1] Thus Jaspers writes (*Vernunft und Existenz*, p. 16): "In Kierkegaard's work, which breathed a new life into the formulas of theology, one may perhaps discover an extraordinary art employed by an unbeliever in order to force himself to believe."

[2] Gesammelte Werke, XII, p. 306.

[3] 2 April 1850, X² A 632 (Tisseau, p. 24).

[4] Cf. *Journal*, 1850, X³ A 298 (Dru 1123): "Faith has become 'hidden inwardness' and to such a degree that, in the end, we shall require a new kind of faith in relation to faith, the faith to believe that I have faith. Yes, one surely needs an extraordinary dose of faith to believe that man believes, he himself needs an extraordinary dose of faith to believe that he believes." But where is one to stop in this regressive process? Can belief that I believe dispense with an ulterior belief, and this of yet another? As we shall have to show later on, subjectivity is self-consuming. Kierkegaard, thus observes, very logically, that it lacks all support and is a sort of balance, filled with terror, over a void (the 70,000 fathoms of water).

[5] P. 75-6.

[6] *Journal*, 1836.

[7] *Journal*, 14 January, 1837, I A 72 (Dru 16).

[8] *Journal*, 1838, II A 232 (Dru 211).

[9] Cf. *Journal*, III A 48 (Wahl, p. 730): "Whether it be a duty or not, I find it absolutely impossible to take the final step towards belief; yet I would do so more than willingly." *Stages on Life's Way*, p. 242: "I am not actually a religious individual, I am only a properly and completely formed possibility of such a thing". "I am good enough as a possibility, but in the catastrophe when I would appropriate to myself the religious patterns, I encounter a philosophic doubt which I will not pronounce as such to any man". By "possibility" must here be understood the abstract, or the poetic point of view. "It has to do," Kierkegaard rightly adds, "with the factor of appropriation", the art whereby the possible or the abstract becomes an effective reality, personal and concrete (existential reality).

[10] *Journal*, 1852, (*Haecker*, p. 278).

[11] *The Point of View*, p. 24.

[12] Cf. *The Point of View*, p. 25-28: "Supposing that a religious writer has become profoundly attentive to this illusion, Christendom, and has resolved to attack it with all the might at his disposal (with God's aid, be it noted)—what then is he to do? First and foremost, no impatience. . . . A direct attack only strengthens a person in his illusion, and at the same time embitters him. . . . (The illusion is destroyed) by the indirect method, which, loving and serving the truth, arranges everything dialectically for the prospective captive, and then shyly withdraws (for love is always shy), so as not to witness the admission which he makes to himself alone before God—that he has lived hitherto in an

illusion. . . . All true effort to help begins with self-humiliation: the helper must first humble himself under him he would help, and therewith must understand that to help does not mean to be a sovereign but to be a servant . . . that to help means to endure for the time being the imputation that one is wrong and does not understand what the other understands.'

[13] Cf. *Unscientific Postscript*, p. 457: "As far as I am concerned, I know only too well that I am not religious." P. 528—"regarded as a humorist I am not so bad, but bad enough to regard this in as humorous a light as possible in comparison with being a Christian, which I am not." The following passage from *Stages on Life's Way* is written in the same spirit: "Neither am I a religious soul. The religious interests me as a phenomenon, as the most interesting of phenomena. And if I am vexed to see Christianity disappear, it is not for man's sake, but my own, for I want to have material for my observations."

[14] *Journal*, 1849 (Haecker, p. 90).

[15] Cf. *The Sickness unto Death*, p. 123–5 where Kierkegaard wonders if he has not been simply a "poet" in the direction of the religious, who has only "the first prerequisite" of faith, despair, and only "an ardent longing" for the religion he loves like "an unhappy lover". Similarly, *Journal*, XII A 82 (Wahl, p. 730): "For the weak man, this thought is terrible, fatal, almost superhumanly difficult. I know this is so by twofold experience; first of all I must admit that I cannot endure it myself, and I can foresee only remotely this authentically Christian idea of Christianity. . . . That is why I do not regard myself as a Christian—I am still far from it."

[16] P. 13.

[17] *Journal*, 1849 (Haecker, p. 42)—cf. (p. 70): "It is true in several senses that my whole production is my education—but that means that instead of devoting myself seriously to becoming a true Christian I have become a phenomenon in the world."

[18] *The Point of View*, p. 133–4.

[19] Cf. *The Present Age*, p. 126–8: When a man believes he is justified in regarding his generation as evil, he finds himself faced with this alternative: "Either yield a little or let them (other men) become guilty of a murder" by provoking them to hatred and vengeance by his objurgations. "*In the one case the guilt is* that a man by yielding a little modifies somewhat or accommodates the truth which he has understood. Now, if it were possible for a man to be in absolute possession of the truth, this behaviour would be absolutely unjustifiable. But surely no man is in this situation. . . . *In the other case the guilt is this*: of letting others become guilty of murder. . . . Most people will doubtless not agree with me as to how this question is to be regarded. They think perhaps that, with respect to being in possession of the truth, this heterogeneity is most presumptuously shown by supposing that one has the truth, and so wanting to put another person to death for the sake of compelling him if possible to accept the truth. No, it is a still greater presumption to suppose that one is so thoroughly in possession of the truth that it is for the truth that one is put to death, that one lets another become guilty of putting one to death."

[20] Cf. *Journal*, 1852, X^4 A 560 (Dru 1252): "My life has already expressed far more than being a poet and expresses more if I remain different."

[21] *Journal*, 25 April 1849, X^1 A 281 (Tisseau, *L'Ecole du Christianisme*, p. xx).

Cf. Ibid. X¹ A 641 (Tisseau, Ibid. p. xxiii): "In my dying hour I shall continually repeat, if I can, what every word I have written bears witness to: I have never, never by a single word, given grounds for being myself mistakenly confused with the ideal, but I have been given confidence that my effort was useful in throwing light upon the nature of Christianity."

[22] Cf. *Journal*, 1845, VI A 107 (F. & G., p. 241): "Would it be possible to imagine someone capable of living all his life in the unending torture of not possessing faith, of whom it could be said—to whom, indeed, one would say: 'But, my dear fellow, you had faith really; your trouble was nothing but the suffering of inwardness' ".

[23] P. H. Tisseau has made a collection of a large number of the finest of them, taken from the *Journal*, under the title of *Prières*.

[24] Cf. *The Point of View*, p. 66–70: "As for the fact that I have needed God's love, and how constantly I have needed it, day after day, year after year—to recall this to my mind and to report it exactly, I did not need the aid of memory or recollection . . . so vividly, so feelingly do I live it over again in this very instant. . . . And now that I am able to talk about my God-relationship, about what every day is repeated in my prayer of thanksgiving for the indescribable things He has done for me, so infinitely much more than ever I could have expected, about the experience which has taught me to be amazed, amazed at God, at His love and at what a man's impotence is capable of with His aid . . . there awakens in my soul a poetic impatience. . . . But in still another sense I have needed God's aid, time and again, day after day, year after year, in the whole course of my activity as a writer. For He has been my one confidant, and only in reliance upon His cognizance have I dared to venture what I have ventured, and to endure what I have endured, and have found bliss in the experience."

[25] *The Point of View*, p. 103.

[26] Moreover Kierkegaard himself points out the fundamental difference between his own position and the unbeliever's: "The free-thinker wants to suppress the parson because in his lack of foresight and his blindness he thinks 'then we shall be rid of Christianity'. I want to suppress the parson so that Christianity may be able to develop." Cf. also *Journal*, X² A 163, where he compares his own position with Feuerbach's. The latter, "the devil's traitor", attacks Christians to bring about their downfall and cut them off from Christianity; Kierkegaard, "God's traitor", attacks the established Church and Christians in order to persuade them to become Christians.

PART THREE

KIERKEGAARD'S THOUGHT

THE STRUGGLE
AGAINST THE "THE SYSTEM"

Kierkegaard and Pascal.—After an essay in psycho-analysis, the object of which was in some sense to define the psychological climate in which Kierkegaard's work originated and developed, we shall now try to sketch the outlines of what may be called Kierkegaard's philosophy. But this term must first itself be qualified and explained.

Can one, in fact, speak of Kierkegaard's *philosophy* at all? Neither more nor less than one can speak of Pascal's philosophy. In reality what is to be found in him as in Pascal is above all a method. Both had reflected deeply upon the problem of religion, and what they wished to put forward were the most general conditions for an exact statement of the problem and for an authentically Christian life. They both insisted upon the absolute necessity of a choice between the world and God, upon the moral value of self-committal and of risk. Both are troubled souls, working, in Kierkegaard's phrase, to produce "disquietude in the direction of inwardness".[1] Their disquietude, however, it must be admitted, was perhaps not of the same kind. Kierkegaard suffered from a certain lack of psycho-nervous equilibrium, while Pascal was physically ailing but magnificently balanced. Nevertheless, in their disquietude they have many elements in common, which result from the resemblances and affinities to be found between Lutheranism and Jansenism. Thus they both, but Kierkegaard far more than Pascal, insist upon the irrational character of faith and the necessity of the "leap" (Pascal's three orders), upon the anguish which the consciousness of sin and the uncertainty of salvation are bound to produce. They both reveal a deep conviction that religion must be lived dramatically and almost tragically, in "fear and trembling". In another field, the parallel and the analogy between Pascal's relation to Descartes and Kierkegaard's relation to Hegel has often been pointed out. In both cases a marked anti-intellectualism and voluntarism comes into conflict with rationalism.

The Critique of "Systems".—Hence in the proper sense of the word, equivalent here to "system", Kierkegaard has no philosophy, any more than has Pascal. All systems, indeed, are radically criticized by him. "The systematic tendency," he writes, "promises everything and keeps nothing",[2] for all systems involve presuppositions, postulates, intuitions incapable of demonstration. All this indeed is excellent and necessary, but the system pretends to rest solely upon demonstration, to replace fact and hypothesis in every case by absolute authority and rigorous proof. Furthermore, the attempt to systematize, that is, scholarly, critical striving after logical perfection, eventually leads one to forget the meaning of the problem, and even the problem itself which occasioned the system: the frame has devoured the picture, dialectic has emptied the mystery of all content. Thus for Kierkegaard "system" and "closed" are identical, as remote as possible from existence and from life. For existence is *par excellence* the open. From the abstract point of view, system and existence cannot be thought of together, because systematic thought in order to conceive existence must conceive it as abolished and therefore not existent. Existence is what acts as an interval, what keeps things apart; the systematic is closing up, perfect linking together.[3]

One ought even perhaps to go further and say that Kierkegaard does not merely not believe in systems, but does not believe in philosophy. A whole section of his work, his anti-Hegelian, that is, anti-rationalist, polemic, is devoted to contesting the possibility of rational metaphysics and, *a fortiori*, of a religion confined, in Kant's phrase, within the limits of reason. The atmosphere of his thought, steeped in Lutheranism, is profoundly fideistic.

The dominant themes in Kierkegaard, relating primarily to questions of method, methods of thought and methods of living, thus form as such a kind of introduction to a philosophy which amounts, as he conceives it, to a propædutic to the Christian life, or even, by the total absorption of the possible within the actual, to an experiential consciousness of Christianity's all-embracing demands. At the very outset of his career Kierkegaard had laid down principles on this subject which he never ceased to propound as the basis of his whole doctrine: "Philosophy and Christianity," he writes, "can never be united. For if, however little it may be, I am to maintain what is the very essence of Christianity, namely the redemption, it must naturally extend, if it is real, over the whole life of man. I might be able to imagine a philosophy after Christianity, or after a man has become a Christian. But that will be a Christian philosophy. In its highest accomplishment, philosophy would involve its own total ruin, that is, it would make plain that it cannot fulfil its original intention".[4] Such, in fact, is the most general sense which can be given to the word "existentialism", which is used in the attempt to characterize Kierkegaard's method and doctrine. But there are many confusions to be avoided here, if one wishes to remain faithful to Kierkegaard's thought, without allowing it to be contaminated, or at least distorted, by contemporary forms of existentialism.

NOTES TO CHAPTER ONE

[1] *For Self-Examination*, p. 46.
[2] *Unscientific Postscript*, p. 18.
[3] *Unscientific Postscript*, p. 112.
[4] *Journal*, 1835, I A 94 (Wahl, p. 585).

II

EXISTENTIALISM

The Necessity of Self-Committal.—Kierkegaard observes that "pure ideality" makes the capital error of not envisaging "the real individual man".[1] The sense of this criticism must be rightly understood; it would be wrong to believe that all that is here involved is a claim on behalf of the concrete and the individual.[2] Kierkegaard maintains, no doubt, that there is truth for man only in "subjectivity"; that is to say, philosophy, far from dissolving the ego in the timelessness of objective and abstract thought, must furnish me with a truth in which my own individual being can play a part; understanding truth must lead to acting it, it is in no way sufficient to *know* the truth, what matters above all is to *be* in the truth. There is no truth for the individual except in so far as he creates it himself in his actions. In fact, "Truth in its very being is not the duplication of being in terms of thought. . . . No, truth in its very being is the reduplication in me, in thee, in him, so that my, that thy, that his life, approximately, in the striving to attain it . . . is the very being of truth, is a *life*, as the truth was in Christ, for He was the truth. In other words, I know the truth only when it becomes life in me". And this, too, is why Christ compares it to a food.[3] Hence the necessity for *self-committal.* "Truth has always had many loud preachers, but the question is whether a man is willing in the deepest sense to recognize truth, to let it permeate his whole being, to assume all the consequences of it, and not to keep in case of need a hiding place for himself, and a Judas-kiss as the consequence".[4] Thus Bossuet warned us that knowledge which does not lead to love is a wretched thing, and Pascal assured us that if it failed in this practical achievement all philosophy was not worth an hour's trouble.

The general reason which Kierkegaard adduces here is a re-

markable one, and it is in agreement with a view which is fundamental to existential philosophies. He observes that reality as a
thought (that is, an abstraction) is never more than a *possibility*,
whereas the ethical, and, *a fortiori*, the religious are concerned
only with the instant, which is reality itself. This point of view
would allow the abstract constructions of the intelligence to be
compared to the æsthetical, for "the æsthetic and intellectual
principle is that no reality is thought or understood until its
esse has been resolved into its *posse*. The ethical principle is that
no possibility is understood until each *posse* has really become
an *esse*".[5]

The Primacy of Subjectivity.—In reality, Kierkegaard's observations go much further than the preceding remarks, with which,
after all, rationalists like Kant or even Hegel might hope to make
common cause, at least in principle.[6] For him, indeed, the primacy
of existence coincides exactly with the primacy of passion and of
subjectivity. "Subjectivity," he writes, "culminates in passion,
Christianity is the paradox, paradox and passion are a mutual fit,
and the paradox is altogether suited to one whose situation is, to
be in the extremity of existence".[7] Objective uncertainty, then,
is the very condition of existential truth in general. "*An objective
uncertainty held fast in an appropriation-process of the most passionate
inwardness is the truth*, the highest truth obtainable for an *existing*
individual". Truth consists "in this bold stroke which chooses objective uncertainty with the passion of the infinite". This definition of truth, Kierkegaard specifies at once, "is an equivalent
expression for faith. . . . Faith is precisely the contradiction
between the infinite passion of the individual's inwardness and
the objective uncertainty. If I am capable of grasping God objectively, I do not believe, but precisely because I cannot do this
I must believe".[8]

It must be observed, moreover, that "objectivity", whose idola-
trous worship has been propagated by the modern rationalists,
might equally well be defined as "positivity". Now the positive,
Kierkegaard writes, in the sphere of thought comes under the
head of certainty in the following three cases: sense-perception,

historical knowledge, speculative results. But this positiveness is "sheer falsity". In fact, the certainty afforded by sense-perception is a deception, as the errors of the senses show; historical knowledge is approximation-knowledge, and leaves one in ignorance of oneself; as for the speculative result, it is "a delusion", because the existing subject proposes *qua* thinker to abstract from the fact that he is occupied in existing in order to be *sub specie aeterni*. When all is considered, the "positive (or objective) thinker who has found the answer" is a sort of town-crier and public auctioneer.[9]

In this connection, Kierkegaard observes[10] that the extreme attention which has been given in modern times to Bible-reading has produced a scholar's religiosity which is a mere diversion, and propagated a professorial Christianity. It may well be the case, he adds, that henceforth Christendom will need a hero who will prevent people from reading the Bible. What is necessary, in fact, is not to read the Bible as a critic and a savant, as an admirer and a connoisseur, but to read it "before God", as a man will read a letter from his betrothed.[11]

These observations are related to those Kierkegaard makes in *The Sickness unto Death* concerning the demoniacal. The modern age, he says, has succeeded in making *truth* grow enormously in extent, in mass, and even, if one will, in abstract clarity. But at the same time it has shut itself off from certainty. The philosophy of our time is like the rich man who on a dark but starry night goes out in his comfortable carriage with its brilliant headlamps and carries his own light and darkness with him. He enjoys his security and the light which is cast upon his immediate surroundings, but he does not understand that this strong glare dazzles him and prevents him from seeing the stars which the poor peasant, on foot or in his lampless cart, can observe to perfection in the vastness of the sky.[12] History shows that *certainty* has always been decreasing, so that its force and depth seem to be in inverse ratio to the weight and quantity of *truth*. Truth, then, is no proof. Or rather the proof is not to be found in the logical abstractions or metaphysical demonstrations which are commonly adorned with the name of truth.[13] It is in the ordeal of life and of action, because it is not pure reason which believes, but the real and concrete individual, the existent.[14]

The Transition from Understanding to Action.—The important point here is to understand clearly that for Kierkegaard "the real individual" is properly speaking the individual of faith and of grace, as opposed to the individual of pure nature, the abstract (rational) individual. Speculations about the latter alone are incapable of passing from theory into practice, from understanding to action, because they are in the domain of the unreal. Speculation tolerates the unreal, but action does not.[15] Christianity alone is capable of propounding a practical doctrine, of furnishing a rule of conduct, because it alone is capable of teaching man what is his real and fundamental nature, of making him understand his relation to eternity.[16]

This can be clearly realized if one considers how foreign was the notion of sin to Greek thought (Socratism). For Socrates "sin is ignorance". Sin, then, resides in the intelligence and not in the will; it is a lack of enlightenment and not a perversion of the will and, in the last resort, defiance. Christianity alone can gain acceptance for this latter view, because it knows the real nature of man, the man of original sin.

It is true that this too is what so greatly complicates the transition from understanding to action. For Socratism, and for rationalism, the transition is easy (and wholly fictitious, since it is not on the plane of reality), for "everything is 'at once' ".[17] The rationalist's game is like a game of chess; he manœuvres concepts which he keeps continually in view, no accident is conceivable in such a game. As soon as the will intervenes, however, with all its irrationality (and history, too, results from it), things are no longer so simple, nor is it possible to maintain the sang-froid and the sovereign calm of speculation cut off from reality and from life. In fact, Kierkegaard writes, all the problems of existence are impassioned, for existence, when one becomes aware of it, produces passion. In relation to action, passionate comprehension is like the spring-board from which one makes a leap: the clearer thought is, the more distinct, in the best sense of the word more passionate, the easier it makes the transition to action, as a bird about to take flight finds in the flexibility of the branch on which it perches, the supplest transition into soaring, and as it were already a presentiment of it.[18] Thus it can be seen that to reflect upon problems without taking passion into account is not to reflect upon them at all, it is to forget the main point, namely that one is oneself an existent being.[19] At the same time, it is to deny oneself choice, which cannot be made without passion and is the hall-mark of existence. To exist is to choose.[20]

Kierkegaard's doctrine of freedom of choice will help to make this point clear, Faithful to his dialectical method, Kierkegaard observes that liberty and necessity are bound up together, in such a way that *liberty* to choose culminates in the *necessity* of the choice. Common-sense has grasped this, as language reveals: "I have no choice," one says, "I choose this." It is Christianity, however, which casts the greatest light on the matter, by its simultaneous assertion of liberty (the power to choose) and necessity (in that it imposes the choice of the one thing necessary). One must therefore freely choose what one cannot not choose, what one must necessarily choose. It is this that explains how fear and trembling may help a man towards liberty, for they dominate him and force him to choose what is right, what must be chosen. The fact, then, that there is no choice expresses the immense passion or intensity with which one chooses. And so, Kierkegaard adds, at the moment of death the majority of men choose what must be chosen. But evil and illusion are here born of the fact that man is only partly spirit. He interprets the faculty of choice in a quantitative and extensive sense, as though it involved an uncertainty as to the limits of choice or consisted in allowing time or delay in making the choice, when in fact it has a qualitative and intensive value, acts within the instant and consists in opting for what it is necessary to choose.[21]

This is why no logic, however rigorous, can realize the transition from understanding to action. Christianity alone can do so, because it alone knows that evil resides in the will, that the will is capable, by delay, procrastination, compromise and deceit, of obscuring the moral and religious judgement and escaping from the necessity of choice. Its starting-point is the doctrine of sin, "the category of sin is the category of the individual". "Here," Kierkegaard declares, "Christianity is in place. It marks a cross before speculation. It is as impossible for Speculation to get out of this difficulty as for a sailing vessel to sail directly against a contrary wind. The seriousness of sin is its reality in the individual, whether it be thou or I. Speculatively one has to look away from the individual. So it is only frivolously one can talk speculatively about sin. The dialectic of sin is directly contrary to that of Speculation. Here Christianity begins with the doctrine of sin, and therefore with the individual".[22] From this it also follows that Christianity begins by positing the necessity of a divine revelation, to teach man about sin and show him that it does not consist in not understanding righteousness, but in not *wanting* to understand it, in not *wanting* righteousness.[23]

Existing before God.—At this point the sense of the existential method may be clearly grasped. It is certainly, if one likes, an appeal to the concrete and the individual, which alone *exists*, even in Aristotles' sense.[24] But above all it is the affirmation that the self can rest only upon God, and can discover itself in its eternal qualities only through God. The only authentic existence, then, is that which is "before God", and from this it follows that all the human sciences, philosophy, morals and politics must include the human destiny in all its amplitude within their range, and consequently must take into consideration all the historical conditions of that destiny—original sin, Incarnation and Redemption; further, that speculative thought, even when centred upon the real and concrete problem of human destiny, must always end, and in this sense abandon itself, in an attitude of perfect obedience to God, of experiential conformity with Christ. In this connection then existential philosophy would appear to signify primarily a Christian philosophy of action, and to comprise, like Fichte's *Anweisung*, though in a very different sense, (for Fichte leads only to a certainty and an inner life which are wholly abstract),[25] an introduction and an invitation to the Christian life.

An introduction of this sort will assume all the characteristics of a paradox, which finds its culminating point in Christian religiosity. For existence, and especially Christian existence, unites contradictories. It blossoms in eternity, but is accomplished in the instant; it is choice and expectation, dispersion and concentration, extension and tension, ecstasy and reflection, risk and gain, life and death, the future returning as the past, the past declaring itself present; it is sin breaking into the immanence of the individual and the condition of salvation; it is the intimate union of the infinite and the finite, or rather a permanent tension between them, contact and conflict. The existent being lives in a state where the extreme points of opposition are given always together, given in their very opposition: he unites within himself the pathetic and the comic, which both come from the same contradictory feeling, the feeling of absolute difference between eternity and becoming, the infinite and the finite. For the existent being, ten thousand years are nothing; a second contains infinity; perfect health is a raging fever and total drunkenness is extreme sobriety. The existent being knows at once both disquietude and peace, infinite terror and infinite confidence: the peace within him is compounded of disquietude itself and the terror of confidence. It is thus that the existent being reaches the summit of existence, by the effect of the extreme tension which the paradox produces in him. Paradox and passion are bound up together. "There are not two lovers in the world who are as well suited to each other as paradox and passion, and the struggle which goes on between them is like that between the two lovers, each striving to make the other's passion keener".[26]

"PAIN" & PLEASURE.

Socrates as an Existential Thinker.—It can be seen by now that an existential philosophy cannot assume the form of a system. That would be pure "repetition", a return to the common point of view which turns its back upon reality. The only conceivable procedure here is that of maieutics, on the model furnished by Socrates. Kierkegaard had a great admiration for Socrates' art, which for him was the perfect model of the qualitative dialectic of the living instant, that is, of a method of inducing consciences to awaken, *hic et nunc*, to what they had in them of profundity and eternity, to become themselves. Socrates had no system, no doctrine even. He aimed only at provoking in his interlocutors that return within the self which is the condition and the very definition of "conversion". His irony was the very opposite of dogmatism: he used it to insinuate doubt into minds too sure of themselves, to break up conformism, to disturb facile tranquility, to trouble consciences too comfortably at home in their temporal situation. His secret, accessible to all but mysterious by virtue of its very simplicity, consisted not in teaching but in *existing* and making men learn, not to think this or that, but to be themselves, to *exist* as individuals. He was not a professor, but, as he himself put it, a "midwife for souls".

It is in this way that whoever has the sense of living reality should proceed.[27] Aristotle, no doubt, pays tribute to Socrates for his invention of the art of definition. But where existential realities were concerned Socrates preferred example to proof, and living to defining. Aristotle moreover himself admits that in the matter of virtue the example of the wise and prudent man is better than all talking. It is in this same sense that Kierkegaard notes, with reference to the concept of the "serious", that concepts relating to existence are generally lacking in definition, and that one reveals an indisputable acuity of mind in refusing to define them. "The man who really loves," he says, "can hardly find pleasure and satisfaction, not to say increase of love, by busying himself with a definition of what love really is. The man who lives in daily and yet solemn familiarity with the thought that there is a God could hardly wish to spoil this thought for himself or to see it spoiled by piecing together a definition of what God is".[28]

A philosophy culminating in speculation, by means of concepts linked closely together by the interplay of subtle mediations, would try in vain to adapt itself to action, it would fail to be either practical or effective. For practice mocks at concepts; it consists of alternatives, of crises and leaps: its essence is to be dialectical, to include the *pro* and the *contra*, to call for choices which cannot be reduced to pure logic. As for effectiveness, how is it to be expected from words which touch only the mind, while the problem is not merely existence, but *my* existence, in all its particularity and uniqueness. The true philosophy, if it is to remain, in the Socratic sense, a search for wisdom—and for us it will be a search for Christian wisdom—must therefore approximate to the doctor's art, for each individual is concerned, not with being a "thinker", but with being someone, and everyone who aspires to communicate wisdom is concerned not with being a clever talker but a practitioner trying to summon or to recall to life.[29]

Kierkegaard reflected at length on the means of becoming that "quickener of souls" which contemporary Christianity claims to be, and of which Socrates furnished a sketch, though an ever admirable one, in Greek antiquity. The surest means, in his opinion, was unceasingly to recall the necessity of becoming and of being not only an individual (for it will readily be understood that man, unlike the animals, is not fulfilled within his species),[30] but "the Individual". To succeed in this it is necessary to make the dialectic of the "Individual" "ambiguous by its duplex movement", that is to say, one must so arrange matters that the term "individual" designates both the man who is unique among men (the extraordinary, the exceptional), and each man, everybody (taken one by one of course, not in the mass!) It is impossible to retain interest without employing the category of the Individual in this double sense: "The pride in the one thought incites some, the humility in the second thought deters others, but the confusion involved in the double meaning provokes attention dialectically".[31]

It must be noted that all influence is a relation between two selves or two subjects. Between two objects there can be only a mechanical relationship: iron which is attracted by a magnet has no choice in the matter, any more than the magnet which attracts the iron. The self is truly a subject only by "reduplication", that is, in so far as it takes possession of itself by reflection and at the same time conquers and affirms its liberty. What is it then for the self to attract another self? It is to propose a double choice: firstly in that the self which attracts has itself chosen and stands before the other as a living choice, secondly in that this self in offering the choice to another self demands of the latter the necessary reduplication and the liberty it implies.[32] If it presented itself only as an object, or if the other self was before it only as though it were before an object, there would be no movement from the one to the other, neither appeal nor attraction; for a subject before an object becomes that object; it passes into the object and becomes objective; it goes out of and away from its self and ceases to be subjective. Every influential relationship is therefore of the type "thou and I".[33]

In order to give this existentialism its full meaning one must add that the *object* with which the believer finds himself confronted, and of which Kierkegaard has asserted so insistently that from the standpoint of reason it is paradox and absurdity, this object is not a concept as the idealists think, nor a thing, as the pantheists and materialists believe; but a Person and a Subject, Someone, a Thee, facing me—which allows us to understand that "existence generates passion, but existence paradoxically accentuated generates the maximum of passion".[34] This infinite subject, no doubt, is the Transcendental. But the gulf which consequently interposes itself between Him and me can be closed by love.[35] Existentialism, then, is indeed a realism, but a realism of Love.

NOTES TO CHAPTER TWO

[1] *The Sickness unto Death*, p. 151.

[2] From this point of view Kierkegaard has sometimes been compared to Bergson. This comparison, however, is very superficial and inexact if the fundamentals of their doctrines are taken into consideration. It reduces Kierkegaard's existentialism to a level which it transcends by far, and endows Bergson's views with a scope they never possessed. It remains true, however, that Bergsonism is in part an appeal to themes with which Kierkegaard was familiar. The superior status granted to intuition rather than abstract dialectic, to quality rather than quantity, to the mystery of the incommunicable and the unique rather than the completed whole, to the individual and concrete rather than the general, to time and the instant rather than space and the homogeneous continuum: these are undoubtedly ways of thinking which meet the clearest demands of Kierkegaard's thought.

[3] *Training in Christianity*, p. 201-2.

[4] *The Concept of Dread*, p. 123.

[5] *Unscientific Postscript*, p. 288. Cf. ibid., p. 422: "While it is the specific criterion of the ethical that it is so easy to understand in its abstract expression, it is correspondingly difficult to understand *in concreto*". Similarly, *Journal*, 1837 I C 125 (Wahl, p. 589): "What does not enter into the idea is the contingent and the inessential; this results from its having received a foreign accretion, in that it is expounded within a determinate personality."

[6] Kierkegaard remarks upon the fact himself, in connection with Kant, *Journal*, 1849, X^2 A 328 (Dru 1027): "Kant is evidently thinking honestly of existence as irreducible to a concept, empirical existence".

[7] *Unscientific Postscript*, p. 206.

[8] *Unscientific Postscript*, p. 182.

[9] *Unscientific Postscript*, p. 75-8.

[10] *Journal*, 1848, IX A 442 (Dru 847).

[11] *For Self-Examination*, p. 51, 58: "Imagine a country. A royal command is issued to all office-bearers and subjects, in short, to the whole population. A remarkable change comes over them all; they all become interpreters, the office-bearers become authors, every blessed day there comes out an interpretation more learned than the last, more acute, more elegant, more profound, more ingenious, more wonderful, more charming, and more wonderfully charming. . . . Everything became interpretation—but no one read the royal command with a view to acting in accordance with it. And it was not only that everything became interpretation, but at the same time the point of view for determining what seriousness is was altered, and to be busy about interpretation became real seriousness."

[12] *The Gospel of Suffering*, p. 141.

[13] Cf. *Training in Christianity*, p. 143-4.

[14] Cf. *The Concept of Dread*, p. 124: "What extraordinary metaphysical and logical efforts have been made to furnish a new and exhaustive proof of the immortality of the soul, an unimpeachable proof which would combine all other proofs; and curiously enough while this is going on certitude decreases! The thought of immortality has a power and a pith in its consequences, an implication of responsibility in the acceptance of it, which perhaps would transform the whole of life in a way which one fears. . . . Every such individuality which knows how to produce a new proof of the immortality of the soul, but is not itself convinced, will always be in dread of every phenomenon which forces upon it a penetrating understanding of what is meant by saying that a man is immortal."

[15] Cf. *The Concept of Dread*, p. 123-4: "Certitude, inwardness, which can only be attained by and exist in action, determines whether the individual is demoniacal or not."

[16] Cf. Pascal, *Pensées*, fr. 442: "The true nature of man, his true good, and true virtue and true religion, are things which cannot be known apart from each other."

[17] *The Sickness unto Death*, p. 152.

[18] Cf. *Training in Christianity*, p. 158.

[19] Cf. *Unscientific Postscript*, p. 345: "The problem is pathetic-dialectic . . . (it) demands an existential inwardness adequate to an apprehension of its pathos, passion of thought sufficient to grasp the dialectical difficulty, and concentrated passion, because the task is to exist in it".

[20] For this reason too the existent is naturally polemical, in that it is creative. It demands room. Cf. *Works of Love*, IX, 259 (Geismar, p. 84): "The producer and the creator always want room, and this is why they are at least implicitly polemical. The demolisher wants none, for the principle of demolition is emptiness: what need has he for room?"

[21] *Journal*, 1850, X² A 428 (Dru 1051).

[22] *The Sickness unto Death*, p. 195, 197. Cf. p. 196: "Speculation does not take heed of the fact that in relation to sin the ethical has its place, which employs an emphasis which is the converse of that of Speculation and accomplishes the opposite development; for the ethical does not abstract from reality but goes deeper into reality, operating essentially by the aid of the category of the individual, which is the category overlooked and despised by Speculation. Sin is a characteristic of the individual; it is frivolity and a new sin to act as if it were nothing to be an individual sinner."

[23] Cf. *The Sickness unto Death*, p. 154: "With respect to the distinction between not being *able* to understand and not being *willing* to understand, even Socrates furnishes no real enlightenment, whereas he is Grand Master above all ironists in operating, by means of the distinction between understanding and understanding. Socrates explains that he who does not do the right thing has not understood it; but Christianity goes a little further back and says it is because he will not understand it, and this in turn is because he does not will the right. . . . So then, Christianity understood, sin lies in the will, not in the intellect; and this corruption of the will goes well beyond the consciousness of the individual. This is the perfectly consistent declaration, for otherwise the question how sin began must arise with respect to each individual." The

Socratic definition, however, Kierkegaard adds, would be given new value by saying that sin is doubtless in ignorance, it is ignorance of what sin is.

[24] Cf. *Journal*, 1849, (Wahl, p. 646): "Existence corresponds to the individual, who is outside the sphere of the concept, according to Aristotle's teaching. An individual man has no conceptual existence."

[25] Cf. *The Concept of Dread*, p. 123—p. 126: "The abstract of subjectivity is just as uncertain and just as much lacking in inwardness as is the abstract of objectivity."

[26] Wahl, p. 333, n. 1.

[27] Kierkegaard remarks (*Training in Christianity*, p. 228) that Christian truth cannot properly be the object of "reflection", for it is not we who look at it but it which looks at us. "For Christian truth, if I may say so, has itself eyes to see with, yea, is all eye; but it would be very disquieting, rather quite impossible, to look at a painting or a piece of cloth, if when I was about to look I discovered that the painting or the cloth was looking at me—and precisely such is the case with Christian truth".

[28] *The Concept of Dread*, p. 131.

[29] Cf. *The Sickness unto Death*, p. 3: "From the Christian point of view everything, absolutely everything, should serve for edification. The sort of learning which is not in the last resort edifying is precisely for that reason unchristian. Everything that is Christian must bear some resemblance to the address which a physician makes beside the sick-bed. . . . This relation of the Christian teaching to life (in contrast with a scientific aloofness from life), or this ethical side of Christianity, is essentially the edifying, and the form in which it is presented, however strict it may be, is altogether different, qualitatively different, from that sort of learning which is 'indifferent', the lofty heroism of which is from a Christian point of view so far from being heroism that from a Christian point of view it is an inhuman sort of curiosity."

[30] Cf. *Journal*, 1850, X^2 A 426 (Dru 1050): "In the animal world 'the individual' is always less important than the race. But it is the peculiarity of the human race that just because the individual is erected in the image of God 'the individual' is above the race".

[31] *The Point of View*, p. 126.

[32] Cf. *Training in Christianity*, p. 159.

[33] *Training in Christianity*, p. 228.

[34] *Unscientific Postscript*, p. 316.

[35] Cf. *Journal*, 1854, (Haecker, p. 392–3).

III

THE PRINCIPLE OF STAGES

The Unity of Kierkegaard's Work.—We can now approach Kierkegaard's work and attempt to group its essential elements according to what seems to be both the most logical order and that most in conformity with his thought. It must be admitted that this is no easy task. Kierkegaard's work appears at first sight confused and disorderly, both as a whole and in detail. If one were looking for a finished doctrine in the numerous books it comprises, this impression would no doubt remain. The very multiplicity of the pseudonymous works, in which, so Kierkegaard affirms, there is not a single word which is properly his, would tend to aggravate this impression of confusion, by leaving us in doubt as to the exact meaning of Kierkegaard's thought. Yet again, in each of his works, and especially in those which are pseudonymous, Kierkegard reveals the movements of his thought far more than the conclusions to which those movements lead. Often indeed he draws no conclusion, and this deliberately, for it is for the reader to conclude, that is to say, to *exist*. All this is bound up for him with his argument concerning "indirect communication", which in his view was both a necessity deriving from the primacy of the subjective and a "tendency in his nature". The existential, the subjective, the individual, the spiritual, the religious, cannot be directly communicated to another person, for all experience is isolated in its individuality. The person communicating remains within himself, and so also must the recipient. Consequently what Kierkegaard writes is not written in order to reveal himself to other men, but to reveal other men to themselves. All questions, then, are ambiguous; they exclude the possibility of a reply. All replies are dialectical; they re-echo the question. The impenetrable silence of the individual is a gulf in which all words are lost.

From a more literary point of view it must be added that Kierkegaard's expositions of his own ideas are often so discursive, so
frequently interrupted by marginal observations, and indeed by
long digressions, that the reader—and no doubt the author too—
in the end forgets the original purpose of the discussion. This
style of writing may in part explain the wide diversity of the
interpretations which have been placed upon Kierkegaard's works.
It must also be remarked that the very number of these exegeses
well represents the varied possibilities of which Kierkegaard's
thought admits. As we have said above, Kierkegaard is a complete theatre in himself, in which numerous characters pursue
an existence which is at once real and fictitious. He goes fishing for
monsters, he says, in the thousand depths of his own soul, upon
which he sails and which sometimes overwhelms his tiny boat;
but now and then he succeeds in "harpooning a sea-monster".[1]

It is precisely along these lines, however, that the real unity of
Kierkegaard's work may be discovered. There is no question of
an abstract, static unity, but rather of a unity of movement, like
the continuity of flight or, better still, of an organic growth whose
stages are marked by crises which are at once necessary and un-
predictable. Kierkegaard's works are the successive reflections of
his own development and, as he himself says, "his own education". "My purpose in life", he writes, "would seem to be to
present the truth as I discover it".[2] His thought takes nourishment
from his life and expresses its various phases. It has its own logic
therefore, the living, experiential logic of a soul seeking not for an
abstract, naked truth, but for its own truth. It assumes the form
of a drama, played out within Kierkegaard's heart.

Kierkegaard repeatedly draws attention to the fundamental
unity of his work. In *The Point of View* (1848) he represents it as
the progressive realization, carefully considered at every point, of
a premeditated, detailed plan. Thus Descartes too, towards the
end of his career, flattered himself that he had found in the series of
his works a logical arrangement which it certainly possessed, but
to a far lesser extent than he said or thought. It is possible that
like Descartes, like Luther, too, in his *Table Talk*, Kierkegaard
may eventually have become to some extent a legendary figure

even for himself. However, a passage in the *Journal*[3] somewhat modifies the view presented in *The Point of View*. Reconsidering this latter work, written in the previous year, Kierkegaard remarks that it would be excessive at that point to wish to embrace the whole of his enormous production "as translating a single idea". It is true that he began with a "religious resolve", but in this sense only, that *Either/Or*, and especially *The Diary of a Seducer*, which had been written "because of her" (Regina Olsen) were incorporated by Providence into a project far vaster than that which had originally inspired them. The same is true for the *Two Edifying Discourses*, published at the same time as *Either/Or* and dedicated to "The Individual": Kierkegaard had really only one reader in view, which was still *her*. But gradually this idea of the *Individual* assumed as it were an absolute, representative value. Hence it becomes apparent that everything has been ordered by Providence, that the general plan is the work of Providence and not of Kierkegaard. Even in *The Point of View*, certain remarks point in this direction. Thus Kierkegaard writes—and this, he says, seems to contradict any explanation which concedes a little too much to conscious intention—that he would be "guilty of denying God and being disloyal to Him" if he claimed to have had from the start a conception of the dialectical structure of his work as a whole, or to have exhausted all its possibilities in advance, continuously and step by step. "No, I must say truly that I cannot understand the whole, just because to the merest insignificant detail I understand the whole, but what I cannot understand is that now I can understand it and yet cannot by any means say that at the instant of commencing it I understood it so precisely—though it is I that have carried it out and made every step with reflection."[4]

Whatever the outcome of this discussion of Kierkegaard's within himself, the fact remains that his works form a series governed by a kind of law of progression making everything converge, by successive steps each called forth by another, towards the primacy of the religious, of Christianity.[5] This is what he meant when he observed that in each of his works he left a goad to prick the reader on towards the following one.

Moreover, one could perhaps succeed in finding at the very outset of his career the starting-point of all the themes he later develops in his works, when the progress of his thought and the events of his life lead him to elicit clearly what had at first been merely a foreboding, a confused glimpse, or something deeply felt indeed, but not yet grasped reflectively. If Kierkegaard's work were to be considered from this point of view, which is not historical but rather logical or doctrinal, it is in these themes that there could be found, without too much artifice, a unifying principle, a fundamental idea, which constantly reappears in different forms and gives Kierkegaard's thought its most general direction. Kierkegaard emphasises now one theme, now another, stressing perhaps the "category of the Individual". But he has also provided, in his work on the *Stages in Life's Way*, and also in *Either/Or*, a plan which enables us to form all these doctrinal themes into groups in a comparatively rigorous and logical manner. This, then, is the plan we shall adopt, acting on Kierkegaard's view that life's various possibilities can be arranged to form three distinct stages or spheres—the æsthetic stage, the ethical stage, and the religious stage.

The Category of the Leap and the Dialectic of Life. In order to grasp the exact meaning and scope of this division, it is first necessary to definite Kierkegaard's notion of the *stage* or sphere of existence. It is not to be imagined as a moment in an evolutionary process, necessarily linked to the moments preceding and following it. Such a conception would be of a rationalistic kind. On the contrary, Kierkegaard conceives the stages as exclusive and enclosed worlds. The stage is an independent sphere of life, a definitive, isolated state. All men are of necessity in one stage or another, and the problem each must solve, in order to know himself socratically, is to determine which stage he is in. KNOW THYSELF

Each stage, therefore, since it is isolated, is a kind of infinity; that is to say, it is impossible to reach the next stage by mere *development* from the state in which one is. Wholehearted devotion to the æsthetic will never lead to the ethical, nor will exasperation with the ethical effect initiation into the religious.[6] Nevertheless, isolated though they are, the stages have a positive relation to each other, in that they are successive steps on the way towards a more perfect and a richer life. They form the halting-places in life's upward climb, but in such a way that one can pass from one to another only by means of a leap.

Some stress must be laid upon this category of the *leap*, for without it Kierkegaard's thought is unintelligible. The leap is opposed to mediation, which is the category of the continuous, the homogeneous and the identical. To mediatize, in the manner of Hegel and the rationalists, is to make opposites identical, to suppress what is irreducibly original, to volatilize the concrete and the existential in favour of the abstract, to destroy quality for the sake of mere quantity. Understood in this sense, the dialectic turns its back on life and breaks down in immobility. Comparing Kant and Hegel, Kierkegaard very forcefully points out the grave errors of the idealist method and the complete contradiction in which rationalist idealism involves itself. "A scepticism," he says, "which attacks thought itself cannot be vanquished by thinking it through, since the very instrument by which this would have to be done is in revolt. There is only one thing to do with such a scepticism, and that is to break with it. To answer Kant within the fantastic shadow-play of pure thought is precisely not to answer him. The only thing-in-itself which cannot be thought is existence, and this does not come within the province of thought to think". Existence cannot be conceptualized without ceasing to be existence. "But how could pure thought possibly vanquish this difficulty, when it is abstract? And what does pure thought abstract from? Why from existence, to be sure, and hence from that which it purports to explain."[7]

This is why whenever Hegel or the idealists consent to consider existence it immediately becomes a concept like everything else, with an inevitability which is anything but mysterious. But this too is what allows us, if we enjoy the game (as the idealists do), to "create" existence. On paper, of course, for "existence is even produced, on paper, with the assistance of mediation".[8] Hegel's fundamental theme consists in fact in supposing that speculation is a continual movement whereby one passes from a given term to its opposite (thesis and antithesis), then, by means of the necessary internal changes, to a synthesis which comprehends them both in a higher unity, and which itself will in its turn become, by being set against its own opposite, an element in a further progression. Monism is thus at once presupposed and necessitated by this system; in it diversity is always merely provisional, opposition merely relative, conflict merely apparent. The motionless and the homogeneous triumph over the fluid and the diverse, the universal over the individual and unity over multiplicity.

How can it be pretended that existence is ever to be reached along this path? Existence is what serves as an interval, what keeps things apart, what distinguishes them and opposes them to each other, while the systematical is identity and continuity.[9] Thus the demands of mediation force Hegel to overcome the duality of spirit and reality, of subject and object, of internal and external. The individual consciousness is henceforth no more than an aspect or a moment of the universal evolutionary process, and it is to be found again, in more exalted shape, in the living totality formed by society and especially by the State, which is the highest form of the objective spirit, the spiritual universe in which Divine reason is made real, the means whereby the individual is finally absorbed into the universal. It could not be made clearer that existence—which is individual, personal reality—has no place in the system except as an episode. For the individual, the ideal will be to become a concept! All this, Kierkegaard notes, "makes as droll an impression on the mind as if a man were to show a letter purporting to have come from heaven, but having a blotter enclosed which only too clearly reveals its mundane origin."[10]

In opposition to it, Kierkegaard proposes a *dialectic of life*, which is a continual passage from the similar to the different, polemic and conflict and at the same time contact,[11] an act which bridges gulfs, a leap. The dialectic of life, as opposed to that of the concept, is to be defined, then, by ambiguity in succession, contradiction in time, triumph arising from defeat, absurdity victorious over reason. Hence, for example, one will never become a Christian by reasoning, but only by conversion, which is both a rupture and a radical renewal; faith is a leap into the absurd; confidence a jump into a void empty of reasons for hope. In short, Kierkegaard says, the positive can be conquered only by the negative. To the mediacy of reason, then, must be opposed the immediacy of faith; to continual reasoning, the passionate and pathetic lyricism of affirmation and intuition; to the reasonableness of logical thought and objective reflection, the paradox of the irrationality of life itself.

It can now be seen how the passage from one stage to another is to be effected: it involves a leap, that is to say, an absolute choice which is not a continuation of the preceding state but a negation of it. Psychologically this means that at the fateful moment of the leap a man is bound to be in the dark about himself. He is not following on a movement already begun. He is determining a movement and producing an act which is under no jurisdiction save that of the free decision pronounced by himself upon its essential value. It must be noted, however, that each stage contains something precious, which is its justification; it is, of one will, an aspect of life, which as such is to be found again in the higher stages, but transformed and transfigured.

A Norm for the Stages: Pathos.—The problem now is to determine what is the norm which fixes the order of the stages. Why do we say that there is an ascent, progress (non-mediatized), from the æsthetic to the ethical stage, from the ethical stage to the religious? Here, it appears, Kierkegaard conforms to the essential demands of ethics. He observes that the norm for the stages must be related to man in the most general terms; that is, it must aim at what is highest in humanity. Thus we say that man's sovereign good consists in the greatest possible harmony with the purposes of nature. But this is still extremely abstract. The exact nature of human perfection must be defined.

Kierkegaard begins with the observation that the natural man is made up of feeling and passion. Passion, he writes, is in the last analysis what is essential: "Passion . . . is the real measure of man's power. And the age in which we live is wretched, because it is without passion".[12] This point must be stressed, in order to indicate the direction which Kierkegaard is to take.

Humanity is defined by sensibility and not by reason. "By 'purely human' I mean passion",[13] he says. It is already clear that on this basis he can erect only an ethics of feeling, and that we are already moving in a "voluntarist" atmosphere. If humanity, then, Kierkegaard says, is feeling and passion, human perfection will consist in the possession of the greatest possible energy. Passion is the culminating point of subjectivity, and consequently the most perfect expression of existence.[14]

Passion, however, is in reality ambiguous, for it can mean the dissolution as well as the perfection of the individual. To be fertile, natural passion must become *ideal* passion, and must be at the service of some absolute value. Let there be no mistake, Kierkegaard writes, if I speak so much of the heart's impulses and of passion, "let no one misunderstand all my talk about passion and pathos to mean that I am proclaiming any and every uncircumcized immediacy, all manner of unshaven passion".[15] Passion must be baptized in the waters of reflection and transfigured thereby. The "pathos of ideality" alone will lead man towards full humanity.

But again, what is the "pathos of ideality"? It is a partaking of the eternal, says Kierkegaard, which alone can give human life a prodigious intensity, by making it coincide with the spiritual, that is with the life of God Himself, by means of faith, which is the highest passion in man, and every man's highest passion.[16]

Now this can only be realized by the Christian religion, not poetically or oratorically conceived in the mind, but experienced profoundly, that is to say, dramatically. The pathos of ideality is therefore properly speaking dialectical, decision and choice.

Inwardness.—Kierkegaard summed all this up in the word *inwardness*. For him religious feeling is essentially inwardness, which can be defined as "the relationship of the individual to himself before God, his reflection into himself".[17] There is a series of equations here which he sums up in these words: "Christianity is spirit, spirit is inwardness, inwardness is subjectivity, subjectivity is essentially passion, and in its maximum an infinite, personal, passionate interest in one's eternal happiness. As soon as subjectivity is eliminated, and passion eliminated from subjectivity, and the infinite interest eliminated from passion, there is in general no decision at all".[18]

Interiorization, which is the norm for the stages, and by which man realizes himself to the full by living intensively, is therefore the vital condition of personality. It must not be regarded as of peaceable organic growth. In reality, interiorization is a struggle, an interrupted becoming, marked by qualitative leaps and crises. To be born a man is to be put into a fighting position for the whole of one's life, to be established in a state of painful tension, to be given over to the serious and to suffering. Complete inwardness, which is the mark of the religious stage, therefore has suffering as its criterion. This is why Kierkegaard, in *Stages on Life's Way*, presents the religious sphere as a story of suffering.[19] Because religious feeling is inwardness, that is, the relationship of the individual to himself before God and his reflection into himself, it follows that suffering must essentially accompany it, "so that the absence of it signifies the absence of religiosity".[20]

Kierkegaard stressed this view progressively more and more, pointing out that the more a man is rooted in the specifically Christian (namely in what constitutes the true essence of Christianity), the deeper he is also involved in suffering, because the true imitation of Christ cannot but bring the believer into conflict with the world and call down upon him the tribulations which the world reserves for Christ's true witnesses.

Thus, just as Epicurean hedonism reached its culmination in an austere and serene theory of virtue, so also in Kierkegaard the ethics of pathos leads towards a state where passion submits to an aim which both judges it and completes it. The remarks set down in the fragments of the *Book on Adler* are very clear on this point. Kierkegaard observes, indeed, that tension and effort are not infallible signs of truth and virtue. It is also necessary that the individual's development should have a different end from that of pure pathos. Feeling, in itself, is not sufficient. Its value is the value of its object. Its degree of intensity will never be enough to differentiate it. It is in this way, finally, that Kierkegaard finds an escape from the dangers of the dialectic of pathos, by defining ideal passion as passion ennobled by the Christian life, that is to say, as love, but as a love which is self-forgetful in its upward flight towards Him who is its inspiration. Thus, by a strange detour, Kierkegaard would appear to return to the inspiration of an existentialist, Christian philosophy which defined man's highest perfection in terms of harmony and union with God. As with Duns Scotus, however, it is not the mind but the heart which is the motive force behind this union; and, above all, it is the repose of the will—a repose which is the culminating point of tension—which marks the summit of such a prodigious climb, punctuated as it has been by dramatic leaps beyond the categories of the reason and the mediocre joys of the visible universe.

Distinction Between the three Stages.—Now that we have a more exact idea of the notion of spheres of life and their relation to each other, we can proceed to a concrete definition of each of the stages. To sum up the whole matter in advance, it may be said that æsthetic existence is essentially pleasure, ethical existence combat and victory, and religious existence suffering, not of a momentary kind, but as an enduring state. Indeed, religious faith —faith in the strictest sense, faith which is related to something historical, namely the Incarnation of the Son of God—consists in inquiring with infinite interest into a reality which is not the believer's; and this expresses "the paradoxal relation to the Paradox (Christ)", whence suffering necessarily results. Æsthetically it is impossible to inquire in this way, except through thoughtlessness, for in æsthetics the possible takes precedence over the existing, pure forms come before concrete reality, just as (as we have seen) in the purely rational sphere possibility stands higher than reality. Neither is such an inquiry ethically conceivable, because the ethicist is infinitely interested to the highest degree only in his own reality. Thus "faith resembles æsthetics by the infinite interest which absolutely differentiates the believer from an æsthetician or a thinker", but "the believer differs from the ethicist in being infinitely interested in the reality of another", in the fact, for example, that God has really existed in time.[21] The æsthetician knows only the instant; he lives in things. The ethicist knows only himself; he lives in immanence. The Christian believer knows only the Paradox, and it is this relation to time which allows him to find eternity.

The relationship between the stages of life can be defined, again, by reference to the pathos which each involves. There is an æsthetic pathos. Its characteristic is that it does not transform the individual's existence. It is a "pathos in words". The æsthetician may possess an exact reproduction even of the religious sphere, and may derive intense pleasure from such a reproduction; but everything remains upon the plane of possibility; as an existing being he is not interested in his reproduction. The pathos of the ethical consists in action. "Wherever the ethical is present, attention is directed entirely to the individual himself and his mode of life." Its special character is to bestow immense interest upon the subject and in a sense to make him an absolute. Here, then, we already have an *existential* pathos, for this latter is present "whenever the Idea is brought into relation with the existence of the individual so as to transform it". The existential pathos *par excellence* however, is that of paradoxal religiosity (Christianity). Indeed, when eternal bliss conceived as the absolute good is in question, the pathos no longer consists of words, but in the fact that such a conception of it fundamentally transforms the individual's whole existence.[22]

Finally, one may distinguish between the stages by considering them from the point of view of their respective results. The æsthetic result is externally produced: it must be visible and tangible (the hero triumphs; success favours the ambitious man, etc.) The ethical result is much less apparent, because it is instantaneous and, already, internal: the question is merely to know whether one is guilty or innocent. But the ethical experiences the need to show this externally, that is, in a dialectic which allows the result to be described as a reward or a punishment. There is an error here, for this is to appeal to æsthetic categories and in a sense to dilute the ethical in time. The ethical result, therefore is ambiguous. In order to satisfy its own absolute demands, it ought rather to join forces with the religious.

In the religious, the external and the visible—the glory or the wretchedness of this world—count for absolutely nothing, and if they intervene in any way it is always only to tempt faith, that is to say, in order that the soul may apply itself to regarding them as indifferent and may rid itself of them. The religious result, then, has only an internal reality, that is, in faith. This is why, setting aside all externals, "the religious is commensurable, for the greatest man that ever lived, and for the most abject, and equally commensurable; commensurable for the wealth of nations and for a farthing, and equally commensurable. The religious is simply and solely qualitatively dialectic".[23]

Such are the different criteria which enable the stages to be distinguished. But we must now go into details.

NOTES TO CHAPTER THREE

[1] *Journal*, 28 June 1838.

[2] *Journal*, 1843, IV A 87 (Dru 432). Cf. *The Point of View*, p. 139: "So it seems, in a sense, that I force the ideality of the individual even higher than they (the disciples of Jesus Christ and Socrates) did. How do I understand that? In part I understand it as an imperfection in me, and in part as connected with the singularity of my task. I understand it as my imperfection, for my whole activity as a writer, as I have often said, was at the same time my own education, in the course of which I have learnt to reflect more and more deeply upon my idea, my task."

[3] April, 1849.

[4] *The Point of View*, p. 72.

[5] Cf. *The Point of View*, p. 5-6: "The contents of this little book affirm, then, what I truly am as an author, that I am and was a religious author, that the whole of my work as an author is related to Christianity, to the problem of 'becoming a Christian', with a direct or indirect polemic against the monstrous illusion we call Christendom or against the illusion that in such a land as ours all are Christians of a sort. . . . Supposing that . . . a reader understands perfectly and appraises critically the individual æsthetic productions, he will nevertheless totally misunderstand me, inasmuch as he does not understand the religious totality of my whole work as an author. Suppose, then, that another understands my works in the totality of their religious reference, but does not understand a single one of the æsthetic productions contained in them—I would say that this lack of understanding is not an essential lack."

[6] Kierkegaard notes, however (*Unscientific Postscript*, p. 144) that "the religious sphere . . . lies so close to the ethical that they are in constant communication with one another".

[7] *Unscientific Postscript*, p. 292.

[8] *Unscientific Postscript*, p. 376. Kierkegaard refers to Hegel's *Logic*, Section 2, chapter 1—cf. *The Concept of Dread*, p. 10-12.

[9] *Unscientific Postscript*, p. 112.

[10] *Unscientific Postscript*, p. 297; cf. *Journal*, 1838, II A 301 (Tisseau, p. 38): "The development of *a priori* concepts resembles prayer, in the Christian sphere . . . there is no deduction, no development of a concept or of that which has a certain constitutive form; whatever one may call it; man can merely become aware of it, and the fact of willing it, when the desire is not a mere empty, sterile, idle whim, is what corresponds to the uniqueness of prayer, and, like prayer, is worked in us."

[11] *Journal*, 1837, I A 125 and 126 (Wahl, p. 592): "Like all becoming, life is a polemical struggle." "The self is not given but only the possibility of self, and in this sense there is a conflict."

[12] *Journal*, 1842, III A 185 (Dru 396). Cf. *Fear and Trembling*, p. 55 note 1.

[13] *Fear and Trembling*, p. 184. In this sphere, in contrast with the sphere of

knowledge, where each generation receives what has been acquired by those preceding it, there is nothing to be learnt from the past. No "tradition" is conceivable here. "In this respect, every generation begins again from the beginning, possessing no other tasks but those of preceding generations and going no further." Thus, where love is concerned, no generation has learnt from another how to love.

[14] *Unscientific Postscript*, p. 176. Cf. *Fear and Trembling*, p. 150: "The conclusions of passion alone are trustworthy; they alone are convincing".

[15] *Journal*, 1844, V A 44 (Dru 488).

[16] Cf. *Fear and Trembling*, p. 185-6.

[17] *Unscientific Postscript*, p. 391.

[18] *Unscientific Postscript*, p. 33.

[19] Cf. *Stages on Life's Way*, p. 415-6.

[20] *Unscientific Postscript*, p. 391. Cf. ibid., p. 398: "The reality of the suffering signifies its essential persistence, and is its essential relation to the religious life. Æsthetically, suffering stands in an accidental relation to existence."

[21] *Unscientific Postscript*, p. 288.

[22] *Unscientific Postscript*, p. 347-50.

[23] *Stages on Life's Way*, p. 401.

IV

THE ÆSTHETIC STAGE

The Primacy of Pleasure.—The æsthetic stage is that of hedonism or of pleasure.[1] It is that of the romantic, as Kierkegaard conceived him after Schlegel, who admits of no restraint, who dissolves all reality into possibility, obeys the changing human imperatives, the call of pleasure, and moves unceasingly towards new desires. Observe the æsthetician, Kierkegaard writes: "See him in his season of pleasure: did he not crave for one pleasure after another, variety his watchword? Is variety, then, the willing of one thing that abides the same? Nay, rather it is the willing of something that must never be the same. But that is just to will the manifold, and a man with such a will is not only double-minded but all at variance with himself, for he wills one thing and immediately after the opposite, because oneness of pleasure is disappointment and illusion, and it is the variety of pleasures that he wills. Change was what he was crying out for when pleasure pandered to him, change, change!"[2] In general then it could be said that the æsthetician is the person who does not achieve reaffirmation, by reason of the fact that continual change is necessary to him since only that which has the freshness of immediacy can procure him pleasure.

The æsthetician sometimes demands this pleasure from things by becoming absorbed in them, sometimes, by a supreme refinement, he finds it within himself by reflecting upon his own situation, that is, upon the act of enjoying, which is thus an enjoyment of enjoyment.[3] It should be noted that the æsthetical tendency must not be reduced to mere sensualism. In fact it includes every attitude whose sole aim is pleasure, even if it is "noble" and purely intellectual. Thus in the *Banquet* Kierkegaard can describe, in the form of discourses upon woman, five different æsthetics, ranging from the tranquil and charming, but also some-

124

what frigid, idealism of the anonymous "young man" who is one of the speakers at the *Banquet* to the sensualism of Johannes the Seducer. To enjoy ideas, to be charmed by intellectual landscapes without one's own life's being involved, is at bottom nothing more than the pursuit of carnal pleasures, for enjoyment is still taken as the final aim. This, too, is the point of view which Judge William, in *Either/Or*, expounds to the young æsthetician to whom his discourse is addressed. "You perhaps have a presentiment," he says, "that in this deliberation of mine you will be yoked with the sort of people whom you especially abhor. You think perhaps that I ought to be gallant enough to treat you as an artist and to pass over in silence the bunglers you have trouble enough with in life and with whom you would not have anything in common if you could help it. I cannot help you, however, for you have something in common with them, nevertheless, and something very essential at that, namely your way of life, and in my eyes that matter in which you differ from them is something unessential. . . . I do not deny that it must be disagreeable to possess a view of life in common with drunken revellers and penny-sportsmen."[4]

The Failure of the Æsthetic.—To simplify matters, moreover, and to leave the æsthetic in possession of all the lustre with which it loves to adorn itself, Kierkegaard considers it only in its higher forms. Even at this level, however, the æsthetic attitude is revealed as essentially sterile. In fact, the fundamental æsthetic proposition is that the moment is everything. *Carpe diem, carpe horam.* But to say that the moment is everything amounts to saying that it is nothing, exactly as the sophistical proposition according to which "everything is true" means that nothing is true and vice versa.[5] For if the moment is everything, that is to say, if in the moment there is only the moment, it is as much as to say there is nothing in it, since as an atom of time it is perpetually vanishing. It can be understood only as a reflection of eternity in time, as a sort of conjunction of time and eternity, for the eternal is the present. Thus it is by means of the element of eternity which it includes that the moment acquires stability and reality. But it is precisely

the eternal which the æsthetician leaves out of account, and this
is why his desire to live in the moment, in the sensible—the terms
are here synonymous—is both sin and illusion, and reduces his
whole life to nothingness.[6]

Experience brings full confirmation of these abstract analyses,
for it shows that the æsthetician's life is anarchic and disordered.
Kierkegaard compares it to a pebble skimming over the waves
and suddenly sinking. Far from being fullness and intensity,
which it becomes through the eternal, the moment is merely a
superficial and passing thrill for the æsthetician. Kierkegaard
notes that the æsthetician's soul "makes chaotic, jerky movements, like a galvanized frog".[7] It is that *mens momentanea* which
Leibniz gave as a definition of matter and all connected with it;
it could be given the nickname which Barrès gave Bérénice in the
Garden (which is a very breviary for æstheticians), "little jerk".
"You are an epitome of every possibility," declared Judge
William to his æsthetic friend, "and so at one time I can see in
you the possibility of perdition, at another of salvation. Every
mood, every thought, good or bad, cheerful or sad, you pursue
to its utmost limit, yet in such a way that this come to pass rather
in abstracto than *in concreto*; in such a way that this pursuit itself is
little more than a mood from which nothing results but a knowledge of it, not even so much that the next time it becomes
harder or easier for you to indulge in the same mood, for you
constantly retain a possibility of it. Hence, one can reproach you
almost for everything and for nothing, because it is and is not
chargeable to you. According to circumstances you acknowledge or do not acknowledge that you have had such a mood;
but you are inaccessible to any calculation; what you care
about is to have had the mood, completely and pathetically
true."[8]

From this it follows, in spite of appearances, that the æsthetician
is unhappy. He is vowed to despair. In seeking pleasure, the
hedonist finds only suffering. Here Kierkegaard, with admirable
profundity, renews a theme which Plato's subtle analyses (*Phile-
bius*) might have seemed to have exhausted. The æsthetician, he
says, aims necessarily at the immediate, that is, he loses himself in

its successive sensations. Indeed, in the very bosom of pleasure the individual cannot escape the law of enjoyment, in spite of the most subtle and studied refinements: enjoyment delivers him up to the moment, and vary how he will he remains perpetually and inevitably immediate, because he is always in the moment.[9] Now this pure immediacy is a limit impossible to attain, because pleasure grows worn and faded and denies itself in its own exasperation. By dint of wishing to make reality intensive the æsthetician ends by being gorged and, so to speak, stifled with it. "Everything is cut out except the present—what wonder then that from the constant dread of forfeiting this, one forfeits it".[10] Thus boredom overwhelms the æsthetician. Disgust gnaws at the pleasure-seeker. Enjoyment has a taste of death. Every æsthetician eventually longs for death.[11] It is this which explains why although he is given up to a passionate search after the passing moment, which always deceives his hopes if only because it passes, the æsthetician lives really only in the past, by cherishing his memories. But for him memory is sadness and melancholy—the only element of inwardness which the æsthetic includes—for it consists of a past which is abolished and incapable of repetition. Hope is closed to him. This is because the two categories of recollection and hope, when they are separated, "both have a wrong relation to time. The healthy individual lives at once both in hope and in recollection, and only thereby does his life acquire true and substantial continuity".[12]

It is, therefore, in despair that the failure of the æsthetic stage declares itself: whoever lives on this plane is in despair, whether he knows it or not. This notion of despair, however, so important for Kierkegaard, must be examined more closely.

The Category of Despair.—Despair has many forms, which Kierkegaard analyses in *The Sickness unto Death*. It is important to note from the start that despair is not to be confused with doubt. It can be said, it is true, that doubt is the despair of thought. But despair in this case is only partial and relative. It does not attain the depth and breadth of a despair which is the expression of a complete personality and relates to the absolute.[13]

The lowest, and commonest, form of this despair is *weakness-despair*, which consists in the absence of despair. It is characteristic of the man who is unconscious of his spiritual destiny, of his share in eternity. This in fact is a case of a despair which is unknown to itself, of desperate ignorance of possessing a self, an eternal self, of being a spirit, of being that absolute which man can and should become. This is the state of all those who are given up to sensuality, who know only the categories of the agreeable and the disagreeable, without any concern for spirit, truth, goodness. This kind of desperate individual is, so to speak, guaranteed, though to his own hurt, against consciousness of despair; that is to say, he is within despair's sure grasp. His disease is at its height at the precise moment when he thinks he is in good health.

In another form, despair can be a self-conscious state, but in such a way that the desperate person buries his despair within himself like a secret and hides it from view beneath an apparent detachment. It may be despair of a temporal thing or despair of the temporal, that is, partial or total. But it is always related to eternity: the desperate person acquiesces in the loss of eternity and of his own self—although this abandonment can never be truly realised, for no one can ever rid himself of his eternal self. However, hermetism can take two very different directions here. In the first case, it is still only weakness-despair which is involved: the desperate person notes his weakness in attaching so much importance to the temporal and in despairing for himself; but instead of turning frankly aside from his despair towards faith and humbling himself before God for his weakness, he sinks deeper into despair and despairs of tearing himself away from his weakness. At bottom this resembles the first form, except in that it is conscious and that it is no longer merely passive but involves an act.

In another form hermetism can also include *defiance-despair*, which is despair concerning eternity, in which the desperate person abuses the eternity inherent in the self in order to be himself. It appears as a Lucifer-like defiance of truth and goodness, as a will to slavery.[14] It is pure refusal and negation, preferring, though it be with all the torments of hell, to be itself rather than call for help: this is what Kierkegaard calls *demoniacal despair*.[15]

The truly desperate are not necessarily those who say they are desperate, but those who are ignorant of their despair—those who hide their despair from themselves—those who choose despair, that is, who desperately wish to be their own masters. Despair which knows and admits its own existence leaves the door open for deliverance. The very depth of despair preserves it from oblivion; by never being healed it continually retains a chance of salvation. On the other hand, despair is "the sickness unto death" when it has the effect of fastening a man down to his desperate self, that is, of making him despair of himself with regard to eternity. Death itself cannot deliver him, because death is an unending end: death, precisely, is the inability to die, to be at one with the desperate self, from which it is forever impossible to be detached.

There is no salvation, then, except by passing through this despair, which is the universal lot because it is bound up with the nothingness of the finite and of sin. "I counsel you to despair . . . not as a comfort, not as a condition in which you are to remain, but as a deed which requires all the power and seriousness and concentration of the soul, just as surely as it is my conviction, my victory over the world, that every man who has not tasted the bitterness of despair has missed the significance of life, however beautiful and joyous his life might be".[16] Even at the ethical level despair appears as the gateway to greatness when it is the absolute and definitive negation of the finite, that is, of all the pleasures which the æsthetic proposes. For here whoever chooses despair necessarily chooses himself, not in immediacy and as a contingent individual—which is proper to the æsthetic—but in his eternal validity.[17] All the more then is this true of a despair born of the feeling of the total sinfulness constituted by nature: it is an introduction to complete submission to Christ and thence to the certainty of forgiveness. In the assurance of salvation despair remains as something abolished. Faith is absolute confidence, because it is absolute despair.

Despair grows in depth with consciousness, as consciousness

grows in intensity with despair. This explains why defiance-despair, which is despair at its most intense and the absolute form of sin, is rare in this world, as rare as an acute consciousness of the self and of the element of eternity there is in man. But it must not be concluded from this that men for the most part are not desperate, nor that sin, so to speak, does not exist. In reality the vast majority is in despair, but to a lesser degree, which is scarcely felt; and we know that this state is in a sense the gravest of all. Similarly with sin: for the majority, life is so far removed from the good, that is, from faith, that it is almost too "spiritless" to be called sin. But in this case the sin consists precisely in having allowed oneself voluntarily to slip into such a life, so devoid of spirituality and Christianity, not to say external and mechanical, so wholly wrapped up in the temporal that it seems as though the Christian categories are inapplicable to it. Is this a fate which one suffers in spite of oneself? By no means, it is man's own doing, for "no man is born with spiritlessness, and however many there be who in death bring with them this as the only acquisition of their lives—this is not the fault of life".[18]

One might well say that, just as the despair of the majority consists in the absence of despair, sin here consists in the very absence of sin. Not that there is any merit, far from it, in being a real sinner, any more than there is in raising despair to the intensity of defiance. But is it not a real evil to reduce oneself, by drunkenness for example, to such a state of unreason that one is no longer aware of one's actions and their moral value, and in general to sink little by little below the level of humanity into a situation where one can no longer distinguish between right and wrong?

Despair, then, is dialectical; it opens up divergent paths. Its value is not wholly negative, it may have some virtue. It embraces salvation and perdition, demoniacal pride and Christian humility, abandonment and choice, truth and untruth, time and eternity. It marks a frontier. Here all depends upon how one despairs. If one despairs "from the point of view of the finite", that is, if the despair fails to produce a rupture within the depths of the soul and leads on the contrary to a spiritual hardening, one is lost. If despair forces the soul to gather up its last resources, to "despair in truth", absolutely, it awakens the soul to consciousness of its eternal validity and breaks the magic circle of the finite.

What matters then is to despair in truth. For this, one must truly wish to do so. But as soon as one truly wishes it, at once and the same time one is free from despair, because "when one has willed despair one has truly chosen that which despair chooses, i.e., oneself in one's eternal validity."[19]

NOTES TO CHAPTER FOUR

[1] The æsthetic point of view is expounded in the first part of *Either/Or*, which includes aphorisms, essays and discourses and in conclusion, the *Diary of the Seducer*—and also in the first part of *Stages on Life's Way* (*The Banquet*), and finally in *Repetition*.

[2] *Purify your Hearts*, p. 43–4.

[3] Cf. *Either/Or*, I 253 (*The Diary of the Seducer*). "His whole life was motivated by enjoyment. In the first instance he enjoyed the æsthetic personally, in the second instance he enjoyed his own æsthetic personality. In the first instance the point was that he enjoyed egoistically and personally that which reality in part gave him, partly that with which he had impregnated reality; in the second instance his personality was effaced, and he enjoyed the situation and himself in the situation."

[4] *Either/Or*, I 152.

[5] *Unscientific Postscript*, p. 265.

[6] *The Concept of Dread*, p. 83.

[7] *The Concept of Irony*, (p. 238).

[8] *Either/Or*, II 15.

[9] Cf. *Either/Or*, II 193: "The most adequate expression for the æsthetic existence . . . is in the moment."

[10] *Either/Or*, II 21.

[11] Cf. *Either/Or*, II 194. The æsthetician finally realizes that the temporal is his ruin. "He demands a more perfect form of existence, and at this point there comes to evidence a fatigue, an apathy, which resembles the languor which is the attendant of pleasure. This apathy may rest so broodingly upon a man that suicide appears to him the only way of escape. . . . He has not chosen himself, like Narcissus he has fallen in love with himself. Such a situation has certainly ended not infrequently in suicide". Cf. the admirable portrait of Nero, the typical æsthetician, II 156–9.

[12] *Either/Or*, II 119.

[13] *Either/Or*, II 178.

[14] *Journal*, 1854 (Haecker, p. 360).

[15] Kierkegaard defines the general category of the *demoniacal* as follows (*Stages on Life's Way*, p. 219): "Every individual is demoniacal who through himself alone, without any middle term (implying in this instance silence towards all others), stands in relation to the ideas; if the idea is God, the individual is religious, if the idea is evil, the individual is in the stricter sense demoniacal." It is the demoniacal in the strict sense which Kierkegaard studies at length in *The Concept of Dread*, p. 105 ff, characterizing it as "Dread of the good", dread of the evil, on the other hand, being a modality which is within the sphere of the good. The demoniacal, Kierkegaard further observes (*Fear and Trembling*, p. 159), can sometimes not be the individual's fault, at least in so far as its beginnings and original conditions are concerned. Such is the case if one is

"placed outside the universal either because it is one's nature, or because the circumstances of life have led one to it".

16 *Either/Or*, II 175.
17 *Either/Or*, II 177.
18 *The Sickness unto Death*, p. 165.
19 *Either/Or*, II 179.

V

THE ETHICAL STAGE

The Primacy of Duty.—Let us then suppose that, by the efforts of a true despair, the leap has been accomplished which effects an introduction into the ethical stage. This is an absolutely new sphere of life,[1] The æsthetician pursued sensations and aimed only at pleasure. The ethicist, that is, the man who has morality as the chief principle of his conduct and the ultimate end of his activity, aims above all at obedience to duty. For him "the chief thing is, not whether one can count on one's fingers how many duties one has, but that a man has once felt the intensity of duty in such a way that the consciousness of it is for him that assurance of the eternal validity of his being".[2] In this way, the ethicist reckons upon and obtains, on the one hand, inner coherence and clarity, while the æsthetician is given up to anarchy and instability, while on the other hand by obeying the absolute of duty, which becomes *his* own personal duty, he can hope to realize in his own person "the synthesis of the universal and the particular".[3]

It is by this synthesis that the individual's personal vocation is accomplished. One cannot stress too much the importance of the idea of *vocation* from the ethical point of view. It means in fact that there is a rational order of things in which everyone, if he wishes, has his place, so that he represents both humanity in general and the individual. Talent, in which the æsthetician egotistically sees only a superior means to enjoyment and the source of all rights, for the ethicist itself becomes a vocation, a responsibility and a duty.[4] It is by vocation, too, that moral unity can be created between individuals; however different from each other they may be, and even, truth to tell, incommensurable with each other, yet they are equally subject to the universal law of duty, and consequently, in this sense, to the same duties. From this it can be understood how social ethics, that is, perfect conformity to the laws governing social behaviour, has been able to appear as a constant principle of conduct, and how community life, and especially marriage as a typical case of it in general, has been considered as the most favourable means towards morality.

The Category of the General.—In short, the ethical stage involves categories which are purely general: it is a question of doing, if not as everybody does, at any rate as everybody can do, for if talent is needed to be a wretched creature, anyone who wishes can be an honest man.[5] What could be more monotonous, the æsthetician objects, fearing to see life lose the bewitching multiplicity it possesses as long as it remains subject to the variety of the æsthetic categories. But Kierkegaard protests, from the ethical point of view. Ethical repetition, he says, is not mechanical. For the individual, the force of the moral life consists in the repetition with ever renewed spontaneity of gestures which from the outside appear uniform and impersonal. The ethicist is established upon the plane of generality, it is clear. But he must in some sense individualize the general, renew the common, personalize repetition, and hence as it were stabilize the present. It is a question of seriousness, not of a seriousness bestowed (or withheld) by one's temperament, but one which everyone can and must acquire, and which substitutes the peaceful and solid continuity of duration for the punctual, staccato time of the æsthetic. In reality, much courage is needed to live not in differences but in the general. "When the ethical individual has completed his task, has fought the good fight, he has then reached the point where he has become the one man, that is to say, that there is no other man altogether like him; and at the same he has become the universal man. To be the one man is not in itself anything so great, for that everybody has in common with every product of nature; but to be that in such a way that he is also the universal man is the true art of living".[6]

The ethical stage is evidently superior to the æsthetic stage, whose real values it saves and transforms—those, at least, which the æsthetician pursues with passion but without solid and lasting success, beauty and harmonious equilibrium in life. Indeed, if

absolute choice posits the ethical, it in no way results in an exclusion of the æsthetic. "In the ethical the personality is concentrated in itself, so the æsthetical is absolutely excluded or is excluded as the absolute, but relatively it is still left".[7] For Kierkegaard, however, the ethical considered in itself is the object of
increasingly sharp criticism, which we may briefly resume as
follows.

The ethical, as is shown by its motto, *cum pietate felicitas*, is an
attitude which finds the meaning of life in the joy of action, in
the conviction that open-hearted obedience to duty must bring
happiness. But it follows precisely from this that the ethical cannot
subsist when happiness has departed; if he cannot see his moral
activity blossom forth into joy the pure ethicist despairs. He cannot breathe in an atmosphere of unhappiness and suffering. Job's
friends (and in the first instance his wife) acted as consistent
ethicists.

There is another aspect in which the ethical becomes deficient.
Morality, which ensures a wisdom compounded of good sense
and moderation, suffices, it is said, for the solution of the ordinary
problems of life; that is, for everything which is to be defined as
"the general". But, Kierkegaard objects, it also by that very fact
involves the grave danger of making man forget that he is and
must be an Individual, subject to his own personal duties and
endowed with a responsibility which is inalienably his own. The
ethical, which is the law of the general, favours the tendency we
all have to lose ourselves in the crowd, to become a passive
element in the multitude. At the same time, it compromises its
own principles, for the crowd perverts everything, and *its* morality, which it passes on to the Individual, has nothing to do with
true Morality.[8] Its judgement has nothing of the moral in it: it is
purely æsthetic. It "admires everything that has power, cunning,
selfishness—and luck, *i.e.*, so that it wins money, honour, and
respect".[9]

It must be remarked here, however, that when Kierkegaard
educes the ethical to the general, it is possibly the facts rather
than the rights of the matter which he has in mind. For by its
very essence, as we have seen, the ethical is directed towards

the individual. Kierkegaard draws attention to this himself: "Nevertheless," he writes, "ethics and the ethical . . . have an indefeasible claim upon every existing individual; so indefeasible a claim, that whatever a man may accomplish in the world, even to the most astonishing of achievements, it is none the less quite dubious in its significance, unless the individual has been ethically clear when he has made his choice, has ethically clarified his choice to himself. The ethical quality is jealous for its own integrity, and is quite unimpressed by the most astounding quantity".[10] Further on, Kierkegaard declares in even stronger terms: "The ethical is and remains the highest task for every human being. The ethical is the very breath of the eternal".[11] It is the only certainty: to concentrate oneself within it is the only duty which is not at the last moment transformed into hypocrisy; to be in it is the only knowledge which is assured and guaranteed by something outside itself. In the common run of things, however, the ethical norm tends more and more to coincide with public opinion or, to be more precise, with custom. "Through an absorption," Kierkegaard says, "in constant contemplation of the accidental, of that *accessorium* through which historical figures become historical, one may easily be misled into confusing this with the ethical, one may existentially be betrayed into developing an unwholesome, frivolous and cowardly concern for the accidental".[12] On the other hand, even when it is directed towards the individual the ethical would still be unable to provide a solution in cases where the exceptional is involved. It resolves individual problems only by general methods. In ethics, the individual always keeps at least the generality of what is called in law a "case".

The Conflict of the General and the Exception.—There are cases, then, where the ethical is wholly powerless, and even cases in which it is quite impossible to find a rule for conduct. It is then that the ethical, embraced and followed with the apparent firmness of duty, may become a great temptation. "Whoever has had inwardness enough," Kierkegaard writes, "to lay hold of the ethical with infinite passion, and to understand the eternal validity of duty and the universal, for him there can neither in heaven or on earth or in hell be found so fearful a plight, as when he faces a collision where the ethical becomes temptation".[13] Here, as in *Repetition*, Kierkegaard is alluding to his own case. He believed in good faith that he loved Regina Olsen, and for her part she was ready to marry him. Yet in fact he was forced to admit that in her he loved something other than herself, namely the Idea or God. Hence the drama which no recourse to the universal could resolve. Repetition, that is to say, in this case, the universal, counselled him to follow the custom and marry. But in his eyes this was impossible, for he could not marry Regina without deceiving her concerning the nature of his feelings. What was to be done? Reason or morality are defeated, and so the moralist too in his turn is led into despair and death.

Let us take another case, which Kierkegaard meditated at great length and which he regarded as typical. It is that of Abraham called upon by God to sacrifice his son Isaac. From the ethical point of view, Abraham is confronted with the absurd and the monstrous. Does the universal offer any means of resolving so dramatic a situation? Surely not. The ethical would condemn both God's command, declaring it to be impossible, unreal, illusory ("God's wisdom demands that . . ."), and the patriarch's obedience. And yet Abraham obeys, and sets off with the knife and the wood for the sacrifice. He chooses the absurd. He denies the universal. In this way he passes from the ethical to the religious sphere. But if he has been obliged to make the transition, or rather the leap, it is precisely because within the ethical realm the problem he had to solve admitted of no solution.

The Ethical Before Repentance and Sin.—Criticism of the moral, however , can be taken much further. Kierkegaard observes that the ethical, even at the universal level, is contradictory, and as such it can only be a temporary abode. Its highest expression, it must be noted, is the repentance which accompanies guilt. Repentance is the sole condition which allows the individual to choose himself absolutely. "He repents himself back into himself, back into the family, back into the race, until he finds himself in God". Repentance is the necessary form of love for God: if I do not love God thus, I do not love Him absolutely from the depths of my being; every other way of loving the absolute is an error. The reason for this is that the individual's self is as it were external to him: "It has to be acquired, and repentance is his love for this self, because he chooses it absolutely out of the hand of the living God".[14] Now what is repentance but an affirmation of one's self, in so far as one is responsible for one's action, and at the same time negation of the self, in that one is guilty? Thus I become a person, I acquire and strengthen awareness of my personality, only at the cost of a negation of my self, since "it is only when I choose myself as guilty that I choose myself absolutely". Abstraction makes existence indifferent, but guilt "is the expression for the strongest self-assertion of existence, and after all it is an *exister* who is to relate himself to an eternal happiness".[15] It is impossible, then, to remain within the ethical sphere, both because the ethical ends in an impasse, and because, being devoted to the universal, it leaves no place for the religious exception, and forces the religious hero to regard himself as an abnormal and eccentric creature.

Now if there is an ideal for life in which life can attain its maximum intensity and harmonize with the eternal, the "abnormal" and the "eccentric" elements in the religious must clearly take precedence over the normal and the universal of the ethical. The exception will have to be put forward as an example for all, and the universal will have to beg its pardon for existing. From this it can be seen that ethics can be "a dangerous science".[16]

Finally, the very fact of sin is an invincible obstacle for the ethical, and in two ways. On the one hand, the ethical is situated in the ideal, and consequently in the abstract and the unreal: it is concerned only with a concept, that of man *in genere*, capable of practising virtue without backsliding and attaining the highest perfection. But the real involves sin, and sin deprives the ethical of its ideality. For sin does not occur merely accidentally within the individual; it imposes itself as a more and more remote presupposition, which far exceeds the limits of the individual and eludes analysis, and indeed grows into the sin of the whole species. On the other hand, sin places the sinner outside the universal: it relates him, though negatively, with the absolute. From this it follows that salvation is henceforth possible only if the sinner, who has no further relation to the universal, enters into a positive relation with the absolute. What does this mean, however, but that he must leave the ethical in order to enter the religious? The ethical, then, is powerless before sin: repentance, to which it leads and which is its completion, is at the same time its denial. It can thus be understood how the category comes to be situated wholly outside the realm of the ethical.[17]

Not only does the ethical come into collision with sin, with a fact, that is, which it is quite incapable of assimilating; it is not even able to distinguish between good and evil, although these categories are so necessary and so familiar to it. How could it distinguish between them from its ideal, abstract point of view— as though good and evil were definable apart from liberty, which is the essential element and the very pre-condition of the real and the concrete? The only effective ethics, then, is that which is founded upon dogmatics. The ethical can fulfil itself only by denying itself, that is, by summoning the intervention of sin, which demands the dialectical leap and appeals to the transcendency of the religious.[18]

NOTES TO CHAPTER FIVE

[1] The ethical conception of life is systematically expounded in three treatises. One consists of Judge William's manuscript, published by Victor Eremita (a pseudonym of Kierkegaard's) and forming the second part of *Stages on Life's Way*. It is entitled: *Various Observations about Marriage, in reply to Objections, by a married man*. Further, in *Either/Or*, (vol. II) there are two other memoirs by Judge William, *Æsthetic Validity of Marriage* and *Equilibrium between the Æsthetical and the Ethical in the composition of Personality*.

[2] *Either/Or*, II 223.

[3] Cf. *Either/Or*, II 220-1: "Duty, (it is said) is the universal; what is required of me is the universal; what I am able to do is the particular. . . . But this must be more closely defined. . . . I never say of a man that he does duty or duties, but I say that he does *his* duty, I say, 'I am doing *my* duty, do *yours*.' This shows that the individual is at once the universal and the particular. Duty is the universal which is required of me; so if I am not the universal, I am unable to perform duty. On the other hand, my duty is the particular, something for me alone, and yet it is duty and hence the universal. Here personality is displayed in its highest validity. . . . (It) reveals itself as the unity of the universal and the particular."

[4] *Either/Or*, II 242.

[5] Cf. *Fear and Trembling*, p. 75: "Ethics is as such the universal, and as the universal it is valid for all, which may be expressed in another way by saying that it is valid at every moment. It rests immanent in itself, having nothing outside itself which is its τελος, being itself the τελος of everything outside itself, and once this has been integrated in ethics, it goes no further Defined as a being, immediate, physical, and spiritual, the Individual is the Individual who has his τελος in the universal and his ethical task is to express himself continually in the universal, to strip himself of his individuality in order to become the universal. As soon as the Individual desires to assert his individuality over against the universal, he sins and he can only become reconciled with the universal again by recognizing it."

[6] *Either/Or*, II 191, 215.

[7] *Either/Or*, II 150.

[8] Cf. *The Point of View*, p. 153-4. (*On my Work as an Author*): "And this is my faith, that however much there may be that is confused and evil and detestable in men who have become that irresponsible thing without possibility of repentance which we call the 'public', the 'crowd', there is just as much truth and goodness and loveliness in them when one can get hold of the individual. Oh! and in what high degree would men become—men, and lovable men, if they would become individuals before God!"

[9] *Journal*, 1850, X^2 568 (Dru 1081). Cf. *Purify your Hearts*, p. 160: "The judgement of the masses has its significance, and none ought proudly to ignore it or refuse to heed it—for if only a man see to it that he does the opposite,

then most likely he does what is right; or if from the first he does what is opposite, and then it happens that the verdict of the masses is expressed against him,
he may be sure enough that he has apprehended what is right. And then he
has not only in his own mind pondered deeply and tested his conviction, but he
has this added advantage, that again he puts it to the test by means of that scorn,
which may inflict a wound, but by that very wound shows that he is on the
right way, the way of honour and victory."

[10] *Unscientific Postscript*, p. 119–120.

[11] *Unscientific Postscript*, p. 135–6.

[12] *Unscientific Postscript*, p. 120.

[13] *Unscientific Postscript*, p. 231.

[14] *Either/Or*, II, 181–2

[15] *Unscientific Postscript*, p. 470.

[16] *Fear and Trembling*, p. 162 (note).

[17] *Fear and Trembling*, p. 147 (note): "As soon as sin enters the discussion,
ethics fails over repentance, for repentance is the supreme expression of ethics,
but as such contains the most profound ethical contradiction."

[18] Cf. *The Concept of Dread*, p. 13–21.

VI

THE RELIGIOUS STAGE

A.—*The Religious Categories*

The Ethico-Religious.—From *The Concept of Dread* onwards Kierkegaard progressively diminished the value of the ethical as compared with the religious life.[1] In the *Unscientific Postscript* he even shows that the religious attitude alone corresponds to the real life of man. Here above all it is impossible to pass by any continuous path from one stage to another, from the ethical to the religious. This, however, does not signify that the ethical is excluded from the religious domain. On the contrary, as Chestov has well observed,[2] the ethical elements become more and more numerous, and more important, at the heart of the religious. But it would appear that Chestov is wrong in inferring from this that Kierkegaard thereby contradicts himself. In reality, just as the ethical embodied in a higher sense everything that was just and healthy in the demands of the æsthetic, so also the religious gives birth to a new ethic which perfects and fulfils all the demands which the ethical could never satisfy alone. In contrast to the ethical of the pre-religious stage, which made religion subordinate to itself as one of its own elements, the religious takes the ethical into its service and gives it new validity. The fact remains that the religious realm cannot be reduced to the moral, for it is the realm of the infinite, of the "prodigious", to which one can attain only by virtue of the "absurd", outside all rational principles. "The "absurd" here defines faith not only as belief in mysteries which are above reason—and even, according to Kierkegaard, *contrary* to reason—but also as hope justified by no tangible or rational reason.

Irony and Humour.—The leap, however, does not prevent the existence of a kind of intermediate or transitional position con-

stituted by humour; its rôle is parallel to that played by irony as a
boundary region between the æsthetic and the ethical. *Irony*, indeed appears whenever the details of finite life are continuously
brought into relation with the element of infinity in the demands
of the ethical, and the contradiction between them thus made
apparent.[3] The ethical, then, is expressed in irony, but so to speak
incognito, for the ironist "grasps the contradiction there is between the manner in which he exists inwardly, and the fact that he
does not outwardly express it". Often irony is even a sort of
protection for the ethical. The ironist "sets the comical between
himself and them (other men), in order to be able to hold fast to
the ethical in himself with still greater inwardness". In this case,
irony is the form assumed by ethical inwardness on the defensive.[4] Perhaps in the majority of cases however it is egoism, that
is, a state of superior indifference, because it lacks the ability to be
ironical about itself, to destroy itself by self-observation.[5]

The boundary region between the ethical and the religious,
humour, is lyrical, unlike irony. It is by humour that the serious
in life is taken to its furthest point.[6] It can in fact be defined as
awareness of the nothingness and the temporality of the self. By
its help, then, we can achieve some consciousness of the conflict
between time and eternity, and have as it were a presentiment of
the value of the paradox and the absurd. This is because humour
does not absorb the suffering side of the paradox, nor the ethical
side of faith, but merely the amusing aspect.[7] The humorist has a
keen sense of the contradictions which exist between, for example,
the behaviour or the talk of a (self-confessed) believer and the
demands of a faith which he himself may perhaps not possess. A
merchant, grown wealthy in business, declares: "Once, at the
start of my career, I had no faith, no religious life, and nothing
went right with my business. I was on the point of going bankrupt. Then I was converted to God and never afterwards missed
going to Church on Sunday. From that day on my business
prospered wonderfully and I was able to build up a large fortune.
By that I saw clearly that God had blessed my conversion". To
this speech the humorist will reply: "Nothing is more certain,
and that shows that Jesus, Mary and Joseph must have been a

mighty long way from God and could never have been converted, since they clung so obstinately to their poverty".[8] The humorist's reply does not necessarily presuppose faith, but only a sense of the contradiction between the merchant who has made a fortune and been "converted", and the reality of Christian life. Humour grasps the paradox, but, so to speak, from outside. Thus it is "the last stage of existential inwardness before faith".

It can thus be seen, Kierkegaard notes, that "the humorist constantly sets the God-idea into conjunction with other things and evokes the contradiction—but he does not maintain a relationship to God in terms of religious passion *stricte sic dictus*, he transforms himself instead into a jesting and yet profound exchange-centre for all these transactions, but he does not himself stand related to God".[9] The fact remains that humour has the effect of accentuating discord with the world. If it has the grave defect of not realizing that time has a decisive value for eternity, of seeing its nothingness and not its greatness, yet it contains an urge to go still further, and it can be said that "the Christian humorist is like a plant whose roots are invisible but which flowers for the sun on high".[10]

None the less, the leap remains necessary, and it is always brought about by the feeling that man cannot balance himself—in short, that is, by despair, but by true despair, which is absolute and leads man to abandon himself wholly to God. In this way it can be understood how the religious transcends the ethical. In the latter, indeed, there is something of the religious: the moral man—according to the Kantian canon—connects duty with God, at least as a postulate, and believes in post-terrestrial sanctions. But is it not plain that in this case the religious is subordinated to the ethical, as Kant indeed expressly indicated? It is a consequence or a result: it is not a principle, nor even an absolute value.

The category of "before God" and sin.—The religious alone establishes a relation to the absolute and, better still, an absolute relation to the absolute; that is, where the Christian religious is concerned, for one can also be relatively related to the absolute.

This is achieved, from different viewpoints, by the ethical and by the pagan religious, which conceive the absolute only from the angle of interest, and immanently. Now the paradox which is encountered as soon as one approaches the religious absolute is that of sin, which is bound up with the consciousness of being "before God" and which conditions the position of the self, since the individual becomes a self only by and in sin. The consideration of sin is therefore in some sense the necessary preliminary to the transition to the religious, and as it were an introduction to it.

We have noted above that the ethical is incapable of assimilating the category of sin, whose possibility it cannot even envisage. Psychology is no more competent to do so, for if it can explain the possibility of sin as a function of human nature, it can give no account of its reality: one cannot move simply and immediately from the possible to the real; if psychology explained adequately that sin *existed*, then sin would be necessary and ethics and religion would be at an end. Neither has metaphysics any greater value in this sphere, for on the one hand it conflicts with the essentially individual and concrete content of sin, and on the other hand, for this very reason, with what is inconceivable in its essence: no metaphysical reduction of the problem is in place here. Dogmatics alone remains competent.

Here we may begin from the consciousness of the self. From the religious point of view, indeed, various degrees of self-awareness can be distinguished. First of all, at the lowest and commonest level, there is the man who knows nothing of his eternal self and is absorbed, as it were, by the world, as if his destiny were absolutely and totally fulfilled in it. Then there is the man who is conscious of the eternal element in his self. Such a man is "before God", that is, he has all that is necessary to enter into the realm of the religious. But for that it is necessary that he should be "before God" in the right way.

There is, in fact, a way of being before God which, far from being in conformity with the truth of faith, is the very model of sin. It consists in this, that the despairing man, before God, does not wish to be himself—or that he wishes to be. To refuse to be oneself is to refuse the eternal element in man. To wish to be oneself amounts to the same thing: it is to claim to be content with the purely human. In either case despair becomes a state, a choice. As such it is the sickness unto death, and sin.[11]

This helps us to understand the nature of sin. For it must be considered in relation to God, and not simply in itself. For the man taught by Revelation about the nature of sin, it always signifies a refusal to raise the human self up to God's measure. "The measure for the self always is that in the face of which it is a self".[12] To be before God, then, is properly to accept that God should become my measure, that I should become qualitatively identical with my measure, that it should be both my moral rule and the universal rule. Now man, who knows he is before God and who thus understands everything eternal that is in himself, man refuses this eternal and objects to the infinite measure. In this he sins, and it will even be said, with "the earlier dogmatic", that "the fact that the sin was before God infinitely potentiated it". Indeed, "despair is potentiated in the ratio of the measure proposed for the self, and infinitely potentiated when God is the measure. The more conception of God, the more self; the more self, the more conception of God. Only when the self as this definite individual is conscious of existing before God, only then is it the infinite self: and then this self sins before God".[13]

This refusal, which is sin itself, is the state of man, not only in that he is a particular sinner who has committed such and such actual sins, but of man as such, that is, as a son of Adam. This is why every man must confess himself a sinner and be aware of his guilt, as Kierkegaard says "as a totality"—not only of his guilt which is accidental and personal, but of sin, which is valid for the whole of existence and the whole of the human race, so that to be born means to become a sinner.[14] Suffering and anguish are bound up with this consciousness; within the religious, it is the highest form of existential pathos.[15]

It can thus be understood that it is never possible to define sin without the intervention of "before God", or even more precisely of "before Christ", for the self increases in proportion as the idea of Christ grows. The quality of the self, we have said, depends upon its measure. "That Christ is the measure is on God's part attested as the expression for the immense reality a self possesses; for it is true for the first time in Christ that God is man's goal and measure, or measure and goal".[16] Sin is the refusal to take Christ as the measure of the self. This is why there is no sin except in relation to God. Any other conception leaves us at the æsthetic level; wrongdoing will be, if one will, an aberration or an accident, but not a "disobedience defying God's commandments". In short then it can be said that in its very essence sin is "against God". That is the fundamental teaching of Christianity, and of Christianity alone. This is why "the consciousness of sin is the *conditio sine qua non* of Christianity; if one could be exempted from it, one could no longer become a Christian. And the proof that it is the supreme religion is precisely that no other has expressed with such profundity and such elevation the significance which the fact of being a sinner has for man. Yes, consciousness of this is what paganism lacks".[17]

Thus one can measure the gravity of the act whereby someone who is "before God" turns this "before God" into an "against God". Conversely, however, if one were to reduce wrongdoing to its pure essence, one would in a sense make sin disappear. It cannot be forgotten that up to a certain point one can be perfectly in the right with mankind, one can be, as the saying goes, a good father and a good husband, a devoted friend and a respectable citizen, without one's whole life being any the less sin, and known to be sin: our glittering vices, our wilfulness, "which either spiritlessly or impudently continues to be or wills to be unaware in what an infinitely deeper sense a human self is morally under obligation to God with respect to every most secret wish and thought".[18]

Kierkegaard concludes by affirming that the opposite of sin is not virtue, but faith. This, for him, is "for the whole of Christianity . . . one of the most decisive definitions". In reality, in its form at least, it is pure Lutheranism. If faith is belief in revealed truths, the opposite of faith is not sin, but unbelief or the refusal to believe. If sin is disobedience to God's law, the opposite of sin is not faith, but obedience to God's law. However, what Kierkegaard means to say is quite right, for he defines the "virtue" which he will not accept as the opposite of sin as virtue in the purely human, that is, ethical or pagan, sense of the term. He has just shown that such a virtue is reconcilable with sin. If sin is relative to God, so must also be its opposite. Now this opposite, he says, is faith and faith alone, for "faith is: that the self in being itself and in willing to be itself is grounded transparently in God".[19] It should be said, more precisely, that the opposite of sin is *charity*, that is, the virtue proceeding from God's grace. This is what Kierkegaard is trying to express by means of formulas which derive directly from Luther.[20]

Sin as a State.—If sin is now envisaged, no longer simply as an act, but as a state, that is, as the "continuation of sin" or conscious perseverance in sin, three successive stages can be distinguished whereby sin grows in gravity and depth, simultaneously with the despair which accompanies and characterizes it.[21]

There is first of all sin (and despair) which consists in despairing over one's sin. This state is realized when sin shuts itself within its own result or decides to remain there. The sinner claims that he alone is concerned, and wants to insure himself, through despair, against any surprise attack from goodness. He is conscious of having burnt his bridges behind him, of having freed himself from goodness, just as goodness has freed itself from him, in such a way that even in a moment of weakness no turning back is possible for him.

A further stage consists in despairing over the remission of sins, which amounts to deliberately choosing offence. Offence, no doubt, is necessary, for it is within faith. "What a sad dose of dullness is needed, if one is not a believer (a believer being one who believes in the divinity of Christ), not to be offended that a man should claim to forgive sins". But the offence is overcome by faith, in which Christ is God. None the less, offence can go so far as to come into a kind of hand-to-hand conflict with God. This occurs when the sinner, in touch with God, who could and would forgive him his sins, protests: "No, no, sins are not remitted, it is impossible."

Such a state is near to the supreme sin, the sin against the Holy Ghost, which consists, Kierkegaard asserts, in not merely abandoning Christianity but also treating it as a lie and a myth. From this point on there is war between man and God. Man here changes tactics, for from the defensive position he has hitherto adopted, he passes to the offensive. Henceforth it is sin which attacks, by formally denying Christianity.[22]

The Movement of Faith.—All the above observations concerning sin show clearly that the essential category of the religious stage is faith. As we have already noticed repeatedly, the term *faith* must be understood in a strongly Lutheran sense; we must understand that Kierkegaard's personal experiences add moving overtones to the pathos which a genuinely Lutheran faith inevitably involves. Indeed, we may discern here both the dramatic inability of the reason to enter into categories not intended for it and which abuse it singularly, and also the tragic inability of confidence to found itself upon something human and resistant. "There is nothing to be said of an eternal happiness except that it is the good which is attained by venturing everything absolutely".[23] Faith always brings us face to face with the paradoxical and the absurd, and involves us in risking everything, like a man far out at sea, alone in a frail skiff with seventy thousand fathoms beneath him, miles and miles away from all human help.

The perfect example of "movement according to faith" is offered by Abraham. Abraham accomplished the movement of absurdity by agreeing to sacrifice his dearest possession, and thereby agreeing to suspend ethics and abandon the universal; yet at the same time he remained firmly convinced that he would receive Isaac back again. He thus achieved the highest form of existence; he entered into an infinite relationship with the Infinite, into an absolute relationship with the Absolute, which is the very essence of the religious. "Whenever I try to think about Abraham, I am as it were annihilated. At every moment I am aware of the enormous paradox which forms the content of Abraham's life, at every moment I am repulsed by him, and in spite of all its passion, my thought cannot penetrate the paradox, even by a hair's-breadth . . . a paradox which can transform a murder into a holy act pleasing to God, a paradox by which Isaac is returned to Abraham, a paradox which no thought can encompass because faith begins where thought leaves off".[24]

The story of Job might provide another striking example, though of rather different bearing and significance.[25] In reality, Job is not a "hero of faith" for Kierkegaard. His case belongs to the category of the ordeal, which is not in itself of an æsthetical, moral or dogmatic order, for it must first be known, for example, that the ordeal is an ordeal before it can be admitted dogmatically. Once this knowledge exists, the ordeal "loses its elasticity" and forms an introduction to a decisively transcendental category, that of the religious or of faith, for it brings man into a strictly personal relationship with God. Job, however, in a sense, does not take us so far. The meaning of his story is that it depicts in dramatic form the conflicts which arise at the frontiers of faith. But it must be regarded as an analogy, for the ordeal here is a *temporary* category; it has a temporal ending, and in fact it ends for Job in repetition (or the twofold restitution of his possessions). The religious, on the contrary, cannot look forward to this kind of repetition; faith establishes itself upon the plane of the absolute and the eternal. It is a state, not an ordeal—even though it includes the ordeal in the form of offence. That is why "Job does not tranquilize like a hero of faith".[26]

Religious Suffering.—The religious, then, inevitably involves suffering, for it means the defeat of the reason and its natural clearness, passionate hope in the total absence of reasons for hope, conflict, sometimes bloody conflict, with the world. The consequence is that suffering belongs *essentially*, not simply by accident, to the paradoxically, that is, authentically, religious. "In connection with æsthetic or ethical existence", Kierkegaard writes, "suffering plays an accidental rôle; it may be absent, and the mode of existence may still be æsthetic or ethical, or if it gains here a deeper significance, it is as a transitional phase. Not so here, where suffering is posited as something decisive for a religious existence, and precisely as a characteristic of the religious

inwardness: the more the suffering, the more the religious existence—and the suffering persists".[27]

In the case of the religious-paradoxical *par excellence*, that is,
Christianity, suffering, Kierkegaard notes, is necessarily at its
maximum. Here, however, he comes into conflict with the
passage in the Gospels where Christ declares that His yoke is easy
and His burden light.[28] But on this point, rather than admit that
the Christian life, according to the point of view from which it is
regarded, may be both arduous and easy, smooth and harsh, Kierkegaard, in his usual manner, puts forward an original interpretation, according to which the easiness of Christianity consists
precisely in its difficulty.[29] This, moreover, is the general law of
the religious, in which the positive is recognizable by its negative.
"A revelation is signalized by mystery, happiness by suffering,
the certainty of faith by uncertainty, the ease of the paradoxical-
religious life by its difficulty, the truth by absurdity".[30] If this is
not firmly upheld, Kierkegaard adds, the religious is confused
with the æsthetic, for the religious address must be directed,
resolutely and powerfully, towards profundity. "As soon as the
religious address squints in the direction of fortune, as soon as it
seeks to give comfort by recourse to probabilities, as soon as it
seeks to strengthen by means that fall short of a radical remedy,
then it is a false doctrine, constitutes a regress to the realm of the
æsthetic, and is therefore a bungling patchwork."[31]

It is certain, then, that it is only in suffering that the religious
begins to breathe freely. Moreover, how can one enter into a relationship with God's holiness without being distressed by awareness of one's own selfishness and sin, and thus being plunged into
grief? But this suffering, it is sometimes said, is precisely what
earns us forgiveness, and with forgiveness, peace. By no means,
Kierkegaard objects, for forgiveness does not mean that the feeling of sin disappears from the believer's life. The deeper communion with God becomes, the clearer also becomes both the
sense of responsibility and the passion and inward trembling of the
religious life. Pascal then, Kierkegaard observes, was right in
saying that "suffering is the natural state of the Christian".[32]

Infinite Resignation and Faith.—To enter into the religious sphere, with all the suffering and the wrenching away which it entails, is thus, properly speaking, to renounce everything finite. Admittedly, this point of view is that propounded in Kierkegaard's last works. But he had earlier thought that "repetition" might be envisaged upon the religious plane. This is one of the themes of *Repetition* and of *Fear and Trembling*, which were written at the same time (1843). "The movement of faith," he says, "must always be performed by virtue of the absurd, and—this is important—in such a way that the things of the world are not lost but entirely regained".[33] By resignation I renounce all: this movement I accomplish by myself, and if I fail to accomplish it it is the fault of my cowardliness, my flabbiness, my lack of enthusiasm. "I perform this movement by myself, and the reward is therefore myself in my eternal consciousness, in a sacred understanding with my love for the eternal being. By faith I renounce nothing; on the contrary, by faith I receive everything, in precisely the sense in which it is said that he who has faith as a grain of mustard-seed shall remove mountains. . . . It needs the paradox and the most humble courage to seize upon the whole of temporality by virtue of the absurd, and this courage is the courage of faith. It was not by faith that Abraham renounced Isaac, but by faith that Abraham obtained Isaac".[34] Thus, just as Abraham recovers Isaac after having consented, by virtue of the movement of the absurd, to the suspension of the ethical, so also Kierkegaard might have found Regina again if he had had more faith. The knight of faith can hope, then, to return into the world he has left and be reconciled with both the universal and the ethical, which are henceforth transformed for him by religion. If there is a religious sphere, Kierkegaard writes, "that which is suspended is not lost, but remains preserved".[35] "The justified exception is reconciled with the universal",[36] to the extent of having nothing to distinguish him externally, for "those who bear the jewel of faith are not so easily recognizable, because in their outward appearance they bear a striking resemblance to a class of people which is bitterly despised by faith and infinite resignation alike— they bear a close resemblance to the narrow *bourgeoisie*".[37]

Kierkegaard, however, was unable to abide by this conception; and it may well have expressed only one of those "possibilities" which he heeded for a time. The fact is that even as early as in *Fear and Trembling* he declares that he has failed to accomplish the movement of faith. "I cannot perform the movement of faith, I cannot close my eyes and confidently plunge into the absurd, to me an impossible thing, but neither do I boast about it".[38] Perhaps he could not even accomplish the preliminary movement of "infinite resignation" which is man's own handiwork and consists in renouncing the object of one's desire as a worldly reality, in order to possess it subjectively in a sort of immanent eternity: thus Kierkegaard, having lost Regina, continues always to love her, and Regina lives within him. But infinite resignation is terribly dialectical. It postulates an eternity subject to the hazards of contingency: if Regina marries her former fiancé, all is lost, unless Kierkegaard is strong enough to ignore this marriage and keep Regina's image unchanged in his heart: but is this really possible? It demands a reciprocity, too, which is of the most hazardous order: will Regina also want to join "the order of knighthood of infinite resignation", thanks to which the lovers will be in harmony to all eternity?[39] Looking deeper, moreover, Kierkegaard abandons the point of view expressed in *Fear and Trembling*. He admits that neither infinite resignation, which does not imply faith, but only a purely philosophical sense of eternal consciousness, nor the movement of faith, which consists in discounting the victory of the absurd, can justify the hope of being able to welcome the finite anew. In reality, the movement of faith necessarily establishes one in another sphere, which implies the radical denial of the æsthetic and the ethical worlds envisaged from the aspect of the universal. In any case, the repetition is not to be expected on this earth. The hope one may have of it is included in the total risk of faith.

Kierkegaard's Asceticism.—In characterizing Kierkegaard's point of view, is it possible to speak, as does C. Koch, of an "anti-vital asceticism"? Koch quotes numerous texts, drawn from his latter writings and from the *Scattered Papers*, which might seem to justify such an expression. "Christianity exists," Kierkegaard writes, "because there is hatred between God and men". "God hates all existence". "To be a Christian means that you will be tortured in every way. The best thing is that you should have an inexhaustible fund of inventions for torturing yourself; but if you are not strong enough, you can always hope that God will have pity on you and help you to reach the state of suffering". "If the most terrible of terrible sufferings, the perpetual grinding of the soul, fills you with horror, well then, be sincere enough to admit you have no true relation to Christianity". "It is a frightful thing, the moment when God gets out his instruments for the operation no human strength can carry out: cutting away from a man his desire to live, killing him so that he can live like a dead man. The object of this life is to give us the highest possible degree of distaste for living. Like a man who would be ready to travel anywhere in the world to hear a singer with a perfect voice, so does God listen in heaven; and whenever He hears rising up to Him the worship of a man He has led to the uttermost point of disgust with life, God says quietly to Himself: 'That is the note.' "[40] The theme which Kierkegaard unceasingly resumes and amplifies towards the end of his life could thus be summarized in the words: "God is your mortal enemy".

It would be unjust, however, to forget that Kierkegaard, whenever he speaks of "God's cruelty", does not fail to add that this cruelty is the necessary condition of man's perfection and happiness, so that his happiness and perfection are in a sense within the cruelty, that is, within suffering. "It is my firm conviction," he writes, ("and I have never understood Christianity differently) that severe as it is, it is equally gentle".[41] The cruelty is real only from the human standpoint; in actual fact it is a form of love, and man ceases to be offended by it as soon as he understands what it means to be a Christian and as soon as he is one himself, truly and profoundly. "This is the test: to become and to remain a Christian, through sufferings with which no other human sufferings can compare in painfulness and anguish. Yet it is not Christianity that is cruel, nor is it Christ. No, Christ in Himself is gentleness and love. He is gentleness and love itself; the cruelty consists in the fact that the Christian has to live in this world and express in the environment of this world what it is to be a Christian—for Christ is not so gentle, i.e., so weak, that He would take the Christian out of the world. In a passionate mood prompted by the possibility of offence it will seem to one as if Christianity were cruel; but this is not so, it is the world which is cruel, Christianity is gentleness and love".[42]

This observation is constantly repeated in the latter years of the *Journal*,[43] and Kierkegaard is clearly concerned with combating a lax and feeble conception of Christian religiosity, consisting, in its most vulgar form, of making God an indulgent and innocently sentimental old uncle, whose essential function is to distribute gifts and sweets;[44] in another aspect, it consists in supposing that suffering, struggle and temptation in this life are only a bad period, to be lived through as quickly as possible, and that they ought in the end to give place to the joy and peace of a life without tears, the natural reward of the Christian who "does his duty". The "frightful verity . . . that severity is the only thing that can help"[45] is either misunderstood or forgotten—that suffering is of one flesh with Christianity so that to cease to suffer and to be tortured is to cease to be a Christian, and if there is indeed joy, the ineffable joy of the Christian, it can consist only in accepting (if not in understanding, for in a sense to understand would abolish suffering) that it should be so, and that this fact in itself expresses the fatherhood of God, who can love creation only by torturing it. Here as elsewhere, the positive is revealed in the negative: love in severity, gentleness in harshness, peace in war. Oh infinite Love! Kierkegaard cries repeatedly, every time he returns to the subject of the terrible sufferings which assail him. Just as the nearer one approaches God, the further one moves away from Him as one sinks into unknowing,[46] so also the more deeply one is in agreement with Christianity, the further one descends into the abyss of suffering.[47]

From this it can be seen how, starting from a correct idea of the Christian's indispensable asceticism, Kierkegaard eventually yields to his fundamental tendency to depreciate *en bloc* everything that is human, to condemn it radically and irremissibly.

It may here be observed that Kierkegaard felt the burden of his melancholy as increasingly overwhelming, and also that the incidents of the latter years of his life gave his thought a polemical form which tends to distort its expression: in the end he admitted that Christianity was almost too polemical for him.[48] Above all, however, it must be noticed that it is both Kierkegaard's conception of God and the Lutheran notion of the relationship between nature and grace which are here at stake. On the one hand, indeed, Kierkegaard always insisted on the "absolute qualitative difference" existing between God and man. Would it be to attribute too much systematic precision to his thought to discern in this idea the influence of an exacerbated nominalism? This is implied moreover in all his work, and led him to deny all rational communication between the Infinite and the finite. In any case, the analogical point of view, so essential, nevertheless, to anyone who wishes to give some meaning to even the simplest pronouncement concerning the "divine names" (however negative theology may be), clearly has no intelligible significance for Kierkegaard. As a result of this, the "absolute qualitative difference" between man and God for him assumes a metaphysical aspect which eventually has severe repercussions upon the ethical aspect, by transforming the opposition between finite and Infinite into a radical negation of the temporal (or the finite) considered as evil. The material world, as in Plotinus, incurs a sort of all embracing, mass reprobation, which at bottom is merely the transposition into ethical terms of an opposition rendered abyssal and irremediable by the equivocal nature of metaphysics. This is why a certain Manicheism hovers about Kierkegard's religion.

On the other hand, this very tendency is strongly reinforced (and indeed perhaps inspired) by Kierkegaard's Lutheranism. It seems, indeed, that Kierkegaard's asceticism is the logical outcome of a conception which refuses to see in man, or even in nature, anything not fundamentally corrupted by sin. Going to extremes in this direction, Kierkegaard in the end even condemns marriage as incompatible with the Christian state.[49] He bases this conclusion on a doctrine which expresses a kind of contempt for woman; according to him, she is egoism personified, and her destiny is to ruin the spiritual in man. Thus man degrades himself by being associated with the life of the other sex; marriage becomes an absolute obstacle for whoever wishes to serve God. "It is an abominable lie," he writes, "to say that marriage is pleasing to God. From the Christian point of view it is a crime, and what is odious about it is that by this very crime the innocent individual is introduced into that community of criminals which is human life".[50]

These are hard words, and they justify one in speaking of a certain "hostility to life". But this hostility to life which can be discerned in Kierkegaard's last works is less an accident in his career than the imprint of the twofold heritage which weighs upon his thought and his life: that of his father, the taciturn old hosier, melancholy and sombre, and that of Luther, that is, of both nominalist philosophy and the Lutheran theology of nature and grace. It depicts before our eyes the dramatic nature of the dispute, inconclusive as long as it remained within the confines of Lutheranism, which racked Sören Kierkegaard's great soul.

The Category of Dread.—Care must be taken to distinguish dread from despair. The latter is bound up with defeat and is its result, whether it be a question of sin or of the contradiction of the paradox and the absurd, which is the defeat of reason. Dread on the other hand precedes sin, and is bound up with possibility and freedom. It arises from the very possibility of freedom: it is the state which precedes sin, which approaches as closely as possible to it, though it does not explain sin, which can result only from the "qualitative leap". "The relation of freedom to guilt," Kierkegaard writes, "is dread, because freedom and guilt are still a possibility. But when freedom is thus with all its wishful passion, and would keep guilt at a distance so that not a jot of it might be found in freedom, it is not able to refrain from staring at guilt, and this staring is the ambiguity of dread, just as the very act of renunciation within possibility is a yearning".[51] Dread is giddiness in the face of nothingness, that is, in the face of what is not, but which might be, by the action of a freedom which does not yet know itself; just as physical giddiness is simultaneously the fear and the attraction of emptiness. Dread is the first reflex of possibility, a glimmer and yet a terrible spell.[52]

In this way, Kierkegaard observes, one can see the importance of this category, which is really central to the explanation of the nature of original sin, and indeed of all sin. "Vigilius Haufniensis (the pseudonymous author of *The Concept of Dread*) has quite rightly drawn attention to 'Dread' as a middle term in relation to temptation. That is really the dialectic of temptation. If a man could be entirely without dread, then temptation could get no grip upon him. And that again is what I understand by the snake having tempted Adam and Eve; for the snake's power is none other but 'dread', it is not so much shrewdness and cunning as the shrewdness which knows how to make people afraid. And dread (as Anti-Climacus [the pseudonymous author of *The Sickness unto Death*] quite rightly observes in relation to immediateness) is greatest of all before nothing. In that way the tempter and temptation insinuate that the one who succumbs to temptation has himself discovered the temptation; for, says the tempter and temptation: I really said nothing at all, what you dreaded was nothing".[53] A kind of sympathetic antipathy or antipathetic sympathy, dread is desire for what one fears; it is a strange force, which seizes the individual without his being able, or wishing, to escape, for he is afraid, but his fear is itself a desire. "Dread renders the individual powerless, and the first sin always happens in a moment of weakness; it therefore lacks any apparent accountableness, but that want is the real snare".[54]

These abstract notions become clear in the light of Kierkegaard's early experiences, when his father filled his soul with a dreadful fear of sin, in order to keep him far removed from it; in this, however, he also ran the risk of giving rise to temptation as soon as the boy acquired the notion of a sort of fatality whereby he saw himself as it were led towards something by a series of consequences over which he felt he had no control. "One must thus be very careful with children, and never stimulate that anxious consciousness, whereby innocent but weak souls might perhaps be fatally tempted to believe themselves guilty, might despair and thus take the first step towards the goal their anxious presentiment announced to them, an announcement whereby the kingdom of Evil finds an opportunity, with its hypnotic serpent's glance, to reduce weak creatures to a kind of spiritual impotence".[55]

Dread is the inevitable lot of all human life. Every man is in dread, as he is in despair. But dread is in some sense analogical and ambiguous: it has something in common with the three stages and something which cannot be reduced to any of them. Its general character consists in its ambiguity; it prepares and foretells a rupture, in that it indicates both an untenable position and a leap to be performed. It is at the junction of possibility and reality. This applies, Kierkegaard notes, both individually and historically, and there is a parallel between the three historical stages and the three spheres of existence. The dread of paganism corresponds to that of the æsthetic. Kierkegaard, however, always made an exception of Socrates, whose sayings and behaviour he never ceased to meditate upon. Socrates represents for him the greatest existential thinker of Greek antiquity. The Socratic ignorance, he writes, is something analogous to the movement of faith, with this difference, however, that the offence of the absurd, that is, of faith, involving only the certainty that it is absurd, assumes an infinitely greater tension in the corresponding inwardness.[56] "The Socratic ignorance is as a witty jest in comparison with the earnestness of facing the absurd; and the Socratic existential inwardness is as Greek light-mindedness in comparison with the grave strenuosity of faith".[57] In all, in spite of Socrates, an obscure and deep sadness hovers over the whole of Greece, established as she was upon the immanence of the human, deprived of consciousness of sin. Her dread, it might be said, has its roots in her lack of dread, since this exists only in the form of anxiety before destiny; for the pagan's dread finds its object, its nothingness, in destiny, with which he cannot enter into any relationship, for "one instant it is necessity, the next instant it is chance".[58] Here then dread is commonly dread of the finite and the enclosed, of which Greece made the very model of perfection.

From another point of view, closely bound up with the foregoing, paganism might be defined as "the life of man in God's abscence".[59] Thus in paganism man conforms to nature, and "his inability to worship constitutes the most overwhelming charge which can be brought against him: the simple and noble sage himself could remain silent in wonder, but he could not adore". This power, Kierkegaard adds, is not of the order of visible glory; it is not exerted upon things apparent to the eye; yet nature in her visible glory sighs, she implores the sovereign power, she reminds man unceasingly that he must not ultimately forget—to "adore".[60]

In Judaism dread becomes inward: through consciousness of sin, it assumes the ethical form. Man experiences the incalculable bitterness of being unable ever to find rest and peace in the rites and purifications of the law. Dread expresses the twofold anxiety of a purity which the law cannot make assured, and a weakness it can neither prevent nor redeem. Judaism, then, is confronted with a mystery which it is powerless to explore, and the fullness of this nothingness, that is, of this mystery, at once overwhelms and sustains it.

In the religious, dread increases still further, and assumes the dual aspect of the demoniacal and the religious. The demoniacal is the soul—here a form of dread—which shuts itself up within itself, which buries itself in its lies and barricades itself behind its secret. It takes the shape now of hypocrisy, now of pride and weakness, which are one and the same thing. In short, in the form of "spiritual insensibility" it is a flight from goodness and true eternity and the will to substitute for it the pseudo-eternity of art and metaphysics.[61] As we have seen, it then coincides with despair, which in this case is not an aspect of dread but, on the contrary, the exclusion of dread, abandonment of the possibility of the leap and refusal to make it. Dread still remains within despair, but, as it were, refused and denied.

As for religious genius, that is, the specifically Christian life, so far from allaying dread, it carries it to unheard-of depths.[62] Indeed, it inevitably involves extreme anxiety concerning guilt and sin. The greater the religious genius, the more it measures the extent of guilt and is filled with dread at it. Further, it is even filled with dread at the paradox of forgiveness and the remission of sins. Thus understood, dread foretells perfection, for by means

of it the individual encounters his own limitations. It destroys all
finiteness, it heightens awareness of possibilities and opens up
perspectives of infinity; it is allayed through worship, for "the
supreme glory is to be nothing and to adore".[63] Dread is thus the
remedy for dread, as despair is the remedy for despair. It summons up infinite faith, which is hope against all hope. It compels
one to make the desperate leap, which is the essence of the religious and the condition for salvation.

Dread Saves through Faith.—If dread, through faith, has an educa-
tive value, in that it "eats away all the things of the finite world
and lays bare all illusions", it is also true that it is the most overwhelming of the categories; it means that "terror, perdition,
annihilation dwell next door to every man". It is these vague
and confused possibilities, the reflection of freedom in the midst
of the realm which is open to it, which define and universalize
dread.

In order to become the disciple of possibility, in the sense of
the infinite, one must be sincere with possibility, and have faith;
that is, one must have "the inward certainty which anticipates
infinity", as Kierkegaard here defines it according to Hegel's
admirable formula. If one declines to learn from possibility, in
order to avoid dread, one will never have anything more than a
faith contained within the limits of finite widsom, and one will
fall victim to the aggravated dread of the demoniacal, that is, to
dread of the good (the demoniacal proper).[64] This in particular is
emptiness and boredom, the absence or exclusion of the inner life,
the lack of that seriousness whose object is the individual himself
in his eternal aspect. Possibility imposes a dread which takes the
individual for its victim, but in order to save him and introduce or
restore him to faith. In nothing else is repose to be found.
Through faith one receives all things anew, as no one can in
reality, "one receives the infinite".

The important thing, then, is not to mistake the significance of
dread and not to allow oneself to be turned away from faith by it,
when it should lead one to it. Otherwise one is lost. The true
disciple welcomes dread as the instrument of his salvation. "The

dread enters his soul and searches it thoroughly, constraining out of him all the finite and the petty, and leading him hence whither he would go". Through faith, dread teaches man to trust in Providence, for it is not a renunciation of the finite to calculate the disappointments it will involve, any more than it is a renunciation of gambling to stop because one has lost a great deal.

The same is true of guilt, which is "the other" that dread lays bare. To know one's guilt only in the finite, that is, by its finite effects (a fine, imprisonment, dishonour, etc.) is really to lose all, for one does not know one is guilty if one does not know one is infinitely guilty. This, Kierkegaard concludes, is why "he who with respect to guilt is educated by dread will therefore repose only in atonement".[65]

It can thus be understood how Kierkegaard could write: "Abolish awareness of dread and you can shut the churches and make dance-halls of them." At the same time, however, it can be seen that awareness of dread, although it is raised to its highest point by Christianity, can be allayed only by Christianity. This, at least, is the direction taken, after some hesitation, by Kierkegaard's thought. Thus he writes in the *Journal* in 1847, contrasting his old madness with the state in which everything is possible to God through faith, and in which man is transformed to his very depths: "It is then that one finds peace in the forgiveness of sins, when the thought of God does not remind us of sin, but of forgiveness, so that the past does not recall to us the full extent of our guilt, but the full extent of our pardon". A little further on (August 1847) one can read this prayer: "Heavenly Father! Do not side with our sins against us, but with us against our sins, so that the thought of Thee when it arises in our souls, and every time that it arises, may not remind us of our transgressions, but of Thy forgiveness, and not of how we have gone astray, but of how Thou hast saved us!"[66]

It is very evident nevertheless that faith in forgiveness cannot abolish the sense of sin and the suffering which accompanies it for the hero of faith, since by definition the sense of forgiveness is also the sense of sin. To feel and to believe that one is forgiven is at the same time to know and to feel that one is a sinner.[67] But the anguish of sin is as it were dissipated by the joy of forgiveness and the peace it brings. Or rather, the sense of sin only increases the joy and the peace of the forgiveness, in the absolute conviction that God is love. "Here is the reason for joy: at every moment both present and future it is eternally certain that nothing has happened or can ever happen, not even the most fearful horror invented by the most morbid imagination and translated into fact, which can shake the belief that God is love. And again, the reason for joy is that if man will not understand this willingly, he will yet be brought to understanding by guilt. From the moment when a man continually suffers before God because of his guilt, he is assured all the time and whatever may happen, that God is love; or rather, he is continually kept from falling into doubt, because awareness of guilt thrusts itself upon him."[68]

[1] The religious stage is principally described in the following works: *Fear and Trembling*, *The Repetition* and the *Edifying Discourses*, *Philosophical Fragments* and the *Postscript to the Philosophical Fragments*, *The Concept of Dread*, *Three Discourses on imagined Occasions*, *Stages on Life's Way*, Part III, and *Training in Christianity*.

[2] L. Chestov: *Kierkegaard et la philosophie existentielle*, Paris, 1936, p. 77.

[3] *Unscientific Postscript*, p. 450.

[4] *Unscientific Postscript*, p. 450–1.

[5] *Journal*, 1837, II A 102 (F. & G. p. 68.—Cf. ibid., p. 62, 67).

[6] *Journal*, 1837, II A 102 (F. & G. p. 68).

[7] *Unscientific Postscript*, p. 259.

[8] Cf. *The Instant*, 217 (Geismar, p. 245): "Did the apostle Paul have an official post? No, the apostle Paul did not have an official post. Did he make a lot of money in some other way?—No, he made no money at all.—Was he married, at least?—No, he was not married.—Then Paul is not a serious-minded man?—No, Paul is not a serious-minded man."

[9] *Unscientific Postscript*, p. 451.

[10] *Journal*, 1837, II A 102 (F. & G. p. 68). Kierkegaard remarks (II A 114, Dru 141) that there was certainly humour in the Middle Ages too; but it was in a totality, in the Church, partly at its own expense, partly at the expense of the world, and that was why there was less of the unhealthiness about it which, he believes, belongs to that concept. That also was the reason why a section of the modern humorists became Catholics, "desired once again to have a community, a foot-hold, which they could not find within themselves." Concerning humour, cf. also the notes in the *Journal* for 26 August and 15 November 1837, II A 138–42 and 195. (F. & G. p. 73–5, 76–7. For II A 140, see Dru 153).

[11] Cf. *The Sickness unto Death*, p. 126–32.

[12] *The Sickness unto Death*, p. 127.

[13] *The Sickness unto Death*, p. 128–9.

[14] *Unscientific Postscript*, p. 517

[15] *Unscientific Postscript*, p. 471: "The consciousness of guilt is the decisive expression for the relationship to an eternal happiness."

[16] *The Sickness unto Death*, p. 186.

[17] *Journal*, 1844, V A 10 (Dru 479, in part.)

[18] *The Sickness unto Death*, p. 131.

[19] *The Sickness unto Death*, p. 132.

[20] Kierkegaard bases his doctrine on a text of St. Paul, often invoked by Luther, namely *Romans* xiv, 23: "For whatsoever is not of faith, is sin." Kierkegaard also deduces from this, or rather from the Lutheran interpretation of this text, that "the state of being in sin is the new sin . . . every unrepented sin is a new sin." (*The Sickness unto Death*, p. 171). In actual fact, all this rests upon a misunderstanding, for, as the context clearly shows, the word "faith" here

means not theological faith, but simply the conviction of the conscience
with regard to the moral quality of an action. St. Paul observes that one must
always act in accordance with one's conscience (or conviction: fides, πιϛτις);
to act against one's conscience is always sin.

[21] In *The Concept of Dread*, p. 14, Kierkegaard had written that sin is not a
state, for "its idea is that its concept is constantly annulled", that is, it is an act
and renewed activation. "As a state (*de potentia*) it is not, whereas *de actu* or *in
actu* it is and is again." However, this does not contradict the doctrine Kierkegaard propounds in *The Sickness unto Death*, for by the word "state" he there
no longer understands merely potentiality or possibility, but the deliberate and
renewed wish to remain in sin. And such a wish is *par excellence* an action.

[22] *The Sickness unto Death*, p. 205: "Sin is despair: here one fights by evading.
Then came despair over one's sin: here one is still fighting by evasion or by
fortifying oneself in the position to which one has retired. . . . Now the tactic
is changed: notwithstanding that sin becomes more and more absorbed in itself, and so withdraws, yet in another sense it comes nearer, becomes more and
more decisively itself. Despair of the forgiveness of sins is a definite position
directly in the face of the offer of God's compassion; sin is now not entirely in
flight, not on the defensive. But the sin of abandoning Christianity as a false-
hood and a lie is offensive warfare."

[23] *Unscientific Postscript*, p. 382.

[24] *Fear and Trembling*, p. 39 and 74.

[25] Cf. *Repetition*, p. 112–3: "Speak, therefore, O Job of imperishable memory!
Rehearse everything thou didst say, thou mighty advocate who dost confront
the highest tribunal, no more daunted than a roaring lion! There is faith in thy
speech, in thy heart there is godly fear, even when thou dost complain, when
thou wouldst justify thy despair against thy friends who rise up like robbers to
assault thee with their speeches, and even when incited by thy friends thou dost
tread their wisdom underfoot and despise their defence of the Lord, accounting
it the finite shrewdness of a veteran courtier or a worldly-wise minister of state.
Thee I have need of, a man who knows how to complain aloud, so that his
complaint echoes in heaven where God confers with Satan in devising schemes
against a man. Complain! The Lord is not afraid, He is well able to defend
himself, but how might He be able to speak in His defence if no one ventures
to complain as it is seemly for a man to do? Speak, lift up thy voice, speak
aloud, God surely can speak louder, he possesses the thunder—but that too is
an answer, an explanation, reliable, trustworthy, genuine, an answer from God
Himself, an answer which even if it crush a man is more glorious than gossip
and rumour about the righteousness of providence which are invented by
human wisdom and circulated by effeminate creatures and eunuchs."

[26] *Repetition*, p. 130.

[27] *Unscientific Postscript*, p. 256. Cf. ibid., p. 259: "For it is a species of suffering, a martyrdom even in peaceful times, to have the happiness of the soul tied
to that which the understanding despairs about."

[28] *Matthew* xi, 30.

[29] Cf. *Unscientific Postscript*, p. 385: "No, the help in solving the problem of
life which Christianity has brought to the individual is marked by only one
distinguishing feature, namely the difficulty which it has introduced. It is in this

fashion that its yoke is easy and its burden light—for him who has thrown all burdens away, those of hope, of fear, of despondency, and of despair; but this is a very difficult thing to do. And the difficulty again is absolute, not subject to a comparative dialectic (as if easier for one human being than another); the difficulty is proportioned absolutely to each individual separately, absolutely requiring his absolute exertion."

[30] *Unscientific Postscript*, p. 387, note.

[31] *Unscientific Postscript*, p. 390.

[32] *Stages on Life's Way*, p. 416. Pascal says: "*Sickness* is the natural state of the Christian."

[33] *Fear and Trembling*, p. 47.

[34] *Fear and Trembling*, p. 66.

[35] *Fear and Trembling*, p. 76.

[36] *Repetition*, p. 153.

[37] *Fear and Trembling*, p. 48.

[38] *Fear and Trembling*, p. 40. Cf. p. 71: "The last movement, the paradoxical movement of faith, I cannot perform, whether it is my duty or no, although there is nothing I would sooner do".

[39] Cf. *Fear and Trembling*, p. 59–60.

[40] C. Koch, *Sören Kierkegaard*, p. 201–17.

[41] *Journal*, 1850, X^3 A 187, (Dru 1113).

[42] *Training in Christianity*, p. 194.

[43] Cf. 1852, X^4 A 624 (Dru 1266): "It is necessary to die, in order to be able to love God. If you do not desire to die then neither can you love God, you talk of quite different things from him. Thus we see that in Christianity it is not even the law which commands you to die; it is love which says: do you not love me? And if the answer is yes, then it follows of itself that you must die."

[44] *Journal*, 1849, (Haecker, p. 112).—Cf. *Training in Christianity*, p. 222–3: "Although I was living in Christendom, where indeed all are Christians . . . I have never heard any discourse or sermon about which, if before God the question was put to me, I could dare to say unconditionally that it was Christian —for even the most Christian sermons I have heard had ever about them a suspicious admixture of reasons, a smack of human whimper and compassion, a dissonant note of ingratiation."

[45] *Training in Christianity*, p. 223.

[46] *Journal*, 28 September, 1849 (Haecker, p. 95)—1851 (p. 255).

[47] Cf. *The Instant*, XIV, 195 (Geismar, p. 122): "Those who do not abandon themselves at all to God enjoy the happiness of not being tormented by God in this life, which is a terrifying piece of irony. No, it is only for those whom he loves and who give themselves up to him that, humanly speaking, he can be called a mortal enemy, but through love."

[48] *Journal*, 1854, XI^1 A 275 (Dru 1333).

[49] In contradiction to the views developed in *Either/Or*, where marriage appeared as the natural state of the majority of men and the means of achieving the fullest ethical life, celibacy being admitted only as an exceptional case, and as rarely realizable. To this, however, it must be added that Judge William's point of view was valid only for a pre-religious or pre-Christian stage.

[50] E. P. IX, p. 503—cf. *Journal*, 13 December 1854, E. P. IX p. 363, (Dru

1400), a note in which Kierkegaard thanks God for three things, of which the first is "that no living being owes its existence to me".

51 *The Concept of Dread*, p. 97.

52 *Journal*, 1849, X² A 22 (Dru 967).

53 *Journal*, 1849, X² A 22 (967).

54 *Journal*, 1842, II A 233 (Dru 402).

55 *Journal*, 1837, II A 38 (F. & G. p. 59).—Cf. similarly ibid., 1846, VII A 91 (F. & G. p. 260): "With the best of intentions, one can depict evil so movingly that dread may be thereby introduced into a young man's soul".

56 *Unscientific Postscript*, p. 183.

57 *Unscientific Postscript*, p. 188.

58 *The Concept of Dread*, p. 87.

59 *The Lilies of the Field* (French translation, p. 92).

60 *The Lilies of the Field* (French translation, p. 92–3). Kierkegaard concludes with the words: "How magnificent it is, then, to be a man!" which are strangely reminiscent of Shakespeare's exclamation, epitomizing his humanistic optimism: "How beauteous mankind is!" (*The Tempest*, Act v. Sc. 1, l. 182.)

61 *The Concept of Dread*, p. 85–6.

62 According to Kierkegaard (*The Instant*, XIV 192, Geismar, p. 85), the genius, in the purely human sense of the word, is "the extraordinary in the realm of nature; no one can become such by himself". The Christian, and *a fortiori* the religious, genius, "is the extraordinary in the realm of freedom or, to be even more exact, the ordinary in the realm of freedom, which is met with only in an extraordinarily rare way, but which we all ought to be."

63 *The Liles of the Field*, (French translation, p. 93).

64 *The Concept of Dread*, p. 105 ff.

65 *The Concept of Dread*, p. 139–45.

66 VII A 247 (Tisseau, p. 18.)

67 Cf. *The Gospel of Suffering*, (p. 54): "Forgiveness, reconciliation with God is a light burden to bear, just because it is a burden of gentleness, for, for flesh and blood it is the heaviest of all, heavier than consciousness of sin, for it is offence. . . . Faith says: all is forgotten, remember thy pardon. One can forget in many ways, from foolishness or light-mindedness; one can think all is forgotten because one has forgotten oneself. But eternal justice cannot and will not forget, save in one way, by forgiveness; but then the believer must not forget either, on the contrary he must constantly remember that he has been forgiven."

68 *The Gospel of Suffering*, p. 84.

THE RELIGIOUS STAGE

B.—*The Christian Life*

For Kierkegaard the religious is *par excellence* Christianity, the Christian life as such, that is, lived in accordance with all its breadth, with all its demands. For there is a non-Christian religious, which is "pure dialectic, not paradoxo-dialectic". It involves inwardness indeed, since this is essential to the religious in general, but not an inwardness ordered by paradox (or faith) and which, as such, leads in the direction of a new pathos. Thus understood, in so far as it consists in expressing its relation to an eternal blessedness outside Christianity, and therefore presupposes only human nature in general, the religious can exist in paganism. Even within Christianity it is met with in those who are not decisively Christian.[1]

As against this non-Christian religious, Kierkegaard attempts to define the essential conditions of the genuinely Christian life. These conditions may be summed up as subjectivity—as contemporaneity with Christ—as the imitation of Christ or Christian witness.[2]

Subjectivity.—The Christian life is first of all subjectivity. Kierkegaard is unwilling to admit that the Christian life may be achieved to the full by external obedience to a system of thought or a body of doctrine sanctioned by the Church. That is "the objective". Admittedly he does not claim to exclude this "objective" element. But the question arises in this form—should the accent be placed upon the doctrinal content of the religious life as such, or rather upon the personal assimilation of the religious life, that is, upon subjectivity? Kierkegaard replies that absolute and final truth is objectivity in the corresponding subjectivity. "The subjectivity which I think must first of all supervene in regard to the Church . . . is already typified in the fact that the most objective section of the creed begins: *I* believe".[3] The ideal, then, would be that Christianity should be taught as constituting the objective, and that the hearer should assimilate its content in such a way as to establish himself in a personal relationship to God.[4]

Subjectivity and Subjectivism

Kierkegaard, there is no doubt whatever, is very far from subjectivism such as it is expressed by Schleiermacher—whom Kierkegaard frequently criticises—and the liberal Protestants. "One must insist upon the fact", he writes, "that Christian monotheism cannot ever possibly be explained on the basis of pagan monotheism, and one must do so even more forcibly, in order that the concept of revelation may not disappear and vanish away for us under the influence of such witticisms. Not only does it express something which man has not given to himself, but something which would never have entered any man's mind even as a wish or an idea, or under any other name one likes to give it".[5] "Philosophers," Kierkegaard again observes, "think that all knowledge, and even God's existence, is something humanity produces itself, and that it is only improperly that one can speak of revelation. I have expressed the opposite of this thesis in another of my notebooks, by saying that all knowledge is breathing".[6] It is in this sense that he states that subjectivity does not signify immanence, that the subjective, on the contrary, brings one into contact with transcendency, and that belief is absolute dependence with regard to its object, which is the paradox and the absurd. There is an indissoluble bond between the idea of transcendency and the idea of the paradox, because the paradox is a protest against immanence. Revelation cannot be conceived purely as the determination of subjectivity; it postulates both subject and object, and this object is a subject and even the Subject, or absolute Existent. This is why when subjectivity reaches its maximum it is once more objectivity. "And this," Kierkegaard observes, "is an aspect of the principle of subjectivity which, so far as I know, has never before been presented or worked out".[7]

Thus the faith and trust of an upright heart can never be deceived concerning the true God, and necessarily look to the Father of Jesus Christ, as He is revealed in the Gospels.[8] There is therefore no question of denying the existence of a determinate object of faith. "From the Christian point of view," Kierkegaard writes, "truth does not reside in the subject, but in a revelation, which must be proclaimed".[9] We must note in passing that this point of view, if he had pursued it, would have led Kierkegaard straight to Catholicism: if the faith is to be "proclaimed", that is, announced, preserved and transmitted, taught and made certain, how is this possible save through an authority which has received from Christ Himself both its visible titles and a promise of infallibility?[10] But Kierkegaard wishes above all to emphasize that *true* faith must establish the believer in a relationship of personal intimacy with God: the religious life will result from this permanent tension between objective and subjective. The Christian is not a speculative thinker, concerned with *objectively* defining Christianity, its history and its doctrines. He is essentially an *existent* being, for whom Christianity is above all action and life, inwardness and passion. To exist subjectively with passion (and objectively one can exist only in distraction) is an absolute condition for having some idea of Christianity.[11] The misfortune of our age is that it has had too much learning, to the point of forgetting what it is to exist and what inwardness means.[12]

However, it must be admitted that Kierkegaard's thought lacks precision on this point. When he writes that "Christianity is not a doctrine",[13] what he undoubtedly means is that Christianity is not a doctrine of the philosophical kind, that is, pure speculation capable (allegedly) of explanation and rational demonstration,[14] but that on the contrary it is essentially paradox, and as such an offence to reason,[15] and that it is also, and primarily a life; the doctrine being the means to the life, and the life the end of the doctrine. "Christianity is no doctrine concerning the unity of the divine and the human, or concerning the identity of the subject and object; nor is it any other of the logical transcriptions of Christianity. If Christianity were a doctrine, the relationship to it would not be one of faith, for only an intellectual type of relationship can correspond to a doctrine. Christianity is therefore not a doctrine, but the fact that God has existed".[16] Thus Kierkegaard would have Christianity defined simply as "an existential communication", with regard to which the highest is not to understand it but "to exist in it", for Christianity is "a doctrine that proposes to be realized in existence", and not "a philosophical doctrine which desires to be intellectually grasped and speculatively understood".[17]

All this is easily understood. But the fact remains that Kierkegaard incontestably has a tendency to depreciate the "objective" for the sake of the purely subjective, and to misunderstand the function of the Church. In general, as we have already remarked, his doctrine of faith has markedly Lutheran characteristics, and the rôle of the Church as the mistress of faith seems comparatively uncertain. On this point there is a very revealing passage in the *Unscientific Postscript*, where Kierkegaard encounters the objection that Christianity, if it is not a doctrine, is "contentless". He refuses to allow this, but instead of insisting (as in the passages we have quoted above) upon the difference between a philosophical doctrine and "an existential communication," he declares, in terms which betray the imprecision of his thought, that "when the believer exists in his faith, his existence acquires tremendous content, but not in the sense of paragraph-material".[18] To which it is only too easy to reply that what is in question is not the content of the *believer's* existence, but the content of Christianity or of *faith*. In other words, the objection related to the "objective" and Kierkegaard replies by the "subjective"; this involuntary diversion of the argument is a function of the species of uneasiness he feels with regard to the idea of the "objective" and of the Church in general.

The Idea of the Church.

The great truth which Luther brought into the world, in Kierkegaard's view, is that Christianity consists essentially in establishing man in a personal relationship with God. However, the truth here, as in general with Luther, who is so lacking in dialectics and never sees more than one side to anything,[19] must also admit the contrary truth. Inwardness, which is necessary, must also leave room for outwardness, that is, for the intermediaries between man and God, for ritual and the Church. Otherwise pure inwardness will lead to the strange result of making belief disappear and Christianity more external than ever.[20]

It seems that these views, scattered about the *Journal*, ought to have inclined Kierkegaard towards a conception of the Church very different from that of Protestantism. In actual fact he bases authority upon the apostles. Now authority must be expressed in the realm of the tangible; it must have the visible appearance of an institution and the power of a hierarchical society. The Church then, Kierkegaard admits, is a Christian conception. Without it Christianity falls apart. The Church in fact is the necessary support for belief; it is the means whereby every individual can acquire faith; it is through the Church alone that the objective truth of God can become subjective truth.

In reality, these remarks remain very far removed from the Catholic conception of the Church, and Kierkegaard, it appears, was concerned only to exclude sectarianism and illuminism. On the three major questions of authority, the priesthood, and the function of the Church he does not seem to have broken away from Protestantism, in spite of his reservations and rebelliousness. *Authority*, for him, results from the direct relationship which the religious apostle has with God, and of which he can furnish no proof apart from himself. This relationship indeed, Kierkegaard notes, is of a dialectical nature, that is, ambiguous for everyone but the apostle himself, and paradoxical, that is, not rationally demonstrable. The *Journal* states, more precisely, that this "paradoxical authority" must be carefully distinguished from moral authority, which consists of "being ready, by a single, self-conscious and firm decision, to sacrifice one's life for a cause, to give expression to the cause in such a way that one is united with it, without any fear whatever".[21] Moral authority itself depends upon "paradoxical authority" as its source. If the latter, however, being paradoxical, offers no external justification for itself, nor tangible proof of its reality, what difference can one make between it and moral authority, which depends only upon the free decision of each individual? Here we return once more to subjectivism.[22]

Concerning the *priesthood* too, Kierkegaard is far from the

Catholic view. This point, moreover is bound up with the previous one, and it is not surprising that Kierkegaard appeared
sometimes to envisage the possibility of a religion without priests
and without ministers.

As for the concept of the *Church*, Kierkegaard notes that in its
perfect form the Church can exist only in eternity, where it will
reunite all who have emerged triumphantly from the trials of this
earthly pilgrimage. A Church which is a "congregation" is
necessary, however, even in this world. But Kierkegaard seems to
admit it only reluctantly, as a kind of *pis aller* necessitated by
human mediocrity.[23] In itself it succeeds only in reducing the
shock between the individual and God, that is, in preventing or at
least weakening that personal and direct relationship with God
without which there is no true religion.[24] The fact, however, is
precisely that men are incapable of this personal relationship,
understood in the full extent of its demands.[25] The Church suits
Christianity to their capacities; it protects them, and at the same
time maintains the need for faith which they never cease to feel.

On this subject, however, Kierkegaard had known many hesi-
tations, as the *Journal* bears witness. Thus in 1849 he alludes to the
Catholic doctrine of the Church as the mystical body of Christ.
But he does not seem to have grasped its full sense and bearing. He
observes that the Church makes Christ distant in time, whereas
Christ should be the contemporary of every soul. But is it not
through the Church, the mystical Body of Christ, that this contemporaneity can be effectively realized? Kierkegaard objects that
this would lead to the admission of indulgences.[26] The remark is
a fair one, but it protects the principle of indulgences.[27]

In connection with his meditations on original sin, moreover,
Kierkegaard had already confirmed the strictly catholic validity
of the notion of a Church. The *Journal* contains some extremely
interesting indications on this point, originating in the search for a
genuine parallel—in accordance with the Pauline doctrine of
Romans v, 13–14—between the first and the second Adam. This
parallel, Kierkegaard notes, can be real only if the Christian finds
himself in a relationship to Christ which is not individual, but
truly "social", in the same way that original sin, made possible

through the guilt of the first Adam, posits sin as a relationship to the whole human race, "for it explains nothing to say that the individual is declared a sinner only if he adapts himself to common humanity and makes the common nature his own, and to argue also that the children of the second Adam are pardoned only in so far as they participate in him; this is to forget well and truly that to be a son of the first Adam is a necessity, while being a son of the second is only a possibility repeated for each one of us". Now does not this, Kierkegaard asks more exactly, lead us to introduce "the doctrine of the rôle of the Church, of its treasure-store of good works and the charity it brings, according to the Catholics, as the sole adequate counterpoise?" It seems, then, that original sin logically entails the Catholic doctrine of the Church, otherwise "the facts of heredity no longer run parallel with the social facts", individuals lose all their roots in society and the concept of the Church is inoperative and devoid of content.[28]

Furthermore, the ordinary psychology of the believer fits in spontaneously with the social purpose of the Church, when, anxious and worried in the world of sensible reality, he feels the need of some intercessor. This, Kierkegaard adds, is "radically un-Protestant". Thus, he concludes, one can see the value of a doctrine which offers the Christian a treasure-store of good works in the bosom of the Church and as it were a christening present in his cradle, a true counterpoise to Adam's heritage. To this may also be added "the ineffable need to pray for themselves which the poor dead try to satisfy by means of the living", as is implied by the dogma and practice of the Catholic Church in offering up the sacrifice of the Mass for the souls of the departed.[29]

These views, if he had followed them out, would have brought Kierkegaard close to Catholicism upon a point of capital importance. In actual fact, *Training in Christianity* marks a return, rather, to individualism of the Lutheran kind. At all events, Kierkegaard observes, the Christian Church ought only to be an aggregate of unique entities (or Individuals), not a social body properly so called, having validity by virtue of its own reality, compelling recognition by its judicial organization. The true

Church cannot be anything other than an army of individuals each fighting for himself.[30]

This point of view, which is not a Catholic one—although Catholicism meets all those of its demands which are proper—is not in agreement either with the official Lutheranism of the established Church. It seems, however, to be in the logic of Protestantism. But Kierkegaard is far from being firm upon the point. His thought is hesitating and full of contradictions. He feels keenly both the absolute necessity of "personal relationship" with God and the dangers of subjectivism; he reacts, then, towards authority and hierarchy, but without successfully ridding himself of the erroneous opinion which makes him see the Church as a screen and an obstacle between man and God. In reality, the Church which he conceives—and rejects—is always the established Church in which he was born and grew up, the Church he has before his eyes, and which, powerless to justify itself, intervenes without titular right (for lack of authority) and without efficacity (for lack of sacramental life) between the individual conscience and God.[31]

To the foregoing remarks we may add those called forth by the manner in which Kierkegaard apprises what he calls "the monastic movement of the Middle Ages", that is, the religious and monastic institutions of the Catholic Church in general.

The Middle Ages, he writes, have a certain resemblance to Greece, and they possessed what the Greeks possessed, namely passion. "The monastic movement was the expression for a passionate decision, as is becoming in relation to the absolute *telos*, and in so far it is in loftiness far above the wretched middleman's wisdom of mediation", that is, the mediation of Hegelian rationalism. Kierkegaard objects, however, that the monastic movement of the Middle Ages was wrong to think that the inner life can be expressed externally. No doubt it wanted simply to be sure of a secluded little corner where it could effectively busy itself with the absolute. However, "this was a loss for the absolute, since it became something external". In short, by wanting to express inwardness "by means of a specific outwardness which is supposed to be inwardness" monasticism involves itself in contradiction, for "being a monk is just as truly something external as being an alderman"—and in error, for "the outwardness does not directly assume to express the inwardness".[32]

To these remarks, which frequently recur in the *Journal*, one could no doubt reply that the religious vocation and monastic life in the Middle Ages, and in Catholicism in general, involved the principle that inwardness, that is, the effective reality of the Christian life, corresponds *necessarily and immediately* to outwardness, namely to the conventual life and garb.[33] No such claim seems to have been made. In actual fact, "outwardness" is first of all a *means* before it is a *sign*, and if it is a sign of "inwardness", it is a sign of what it should be and not of what it is (of which God alone is witness and judge).

The Characteristics of Subjectivity

If subjectivity, for Kierkegaard, is not reducible to doctrinal subjectivism, it is a very real insistence upon the unique value of the *individual* from the religious and the Christian viewpoint. "It is Christianity itself," he writes, "which attaches enormous weight to the individual subject, it wants to concern itself with him, him, him alone, and so with each one in particular". Even from the ethical point of view it can be observed that the species exists for the individual; we would say to-day, in more precise terms, but in the same sense as Kierkegaard, that the species and society exist for the *human personality*, that is, are ordered so as to promote in man the development of reason and of spiritual freedom. All the more then is it true that Christianity, starting from the dogma of sin, by that very fact starts from the individual, for it is always the individual, not the crowd or the species, that commits sin.[34]

In opposition to this view, Kierkegaard notes, the idea of the sin of the species, or original sin, has often been put forward. But this is certainly a mistake, for the fact is overlooked that "sin, although common to all men, does not embrace them all in a common concept, a group, club, or company, any more than the dead in a cemetery form a club; but it scatters them as individuals and keeps each one isolated as a sinner. This dispersion, moreover, is in accordance with the perfection of existence and tends towards

it through its finality". It is because this has not been understood
that it has been said that the human race as such was redeemed
en bloc by Christ. How easy everything would be, in that case;
the individual would gain everything, without trouble, merely by
participating in the abstraction known as "the human race". But
humanity, all the same, is something different from animality,
where the species is of more value than the individual. What
distinguishes man is the natural superiority of the individual, of the
single example over the species. "And this characteristic is again
dialectical; it means that the individual is a sinner, then again that
it is perfection to be the individual".[35]

Offence, which we shall have to study as a category of the religious, will also give us further insight into subjectivity. It can
be understood only through subjectivity, for it is bound up with
the individual. Christianity makes of each man an individual, a
particular sinner, then it collects together every possibility of
offence which there is to be found, and commands each one of us
to believe. "Be offended or believe". Clearly, this has no meaning except in relation to the individual, for it is not the crowd or
the mass which believes, but the concrete single being. This, too,
is why it is never any use to take shelter behind numbers and
make the excuse of having acted "as others did", for God's judgement will not fall upon the masses.[36] One can chastize the masses,
"massacre them, drench them with hosepipes, flatter them, in
short, treat the crowd like an animal in a hundred ways—but to
judge people like animals is impossible: animals are not judged".
A judgement which did not judge people one by one would be
merely a lying farce. But this, too, is why God is the perfect
judge: it is because he knows nothing of the crowd and knows
only individuals, and because he alone is capable of penetrating
to the darkest, the most secret corners of each heart. "For what
else is eternal judgment but that the voice of conscience is eternally
established in its eternal claim to be the only voice?"[37]
Subjectivity has the further characteristic of necessarily excluding "direct communication", that is to say, every voluntary and
immediate expression of the self to another self. "Inwardness,"

Kierkegaard writes, "cannot be directly communicated, for its direct expression is precisely externality, its direction being outward, not inward. The direct expression of inwardness is no proof of its presence",[38]—as we have already remarked concerning monasticism. This is why it is of the essence of religion to isolate the individual, to separate him from the rest of men: religious experience can have only God alone for a confidant. Thus subjectivity has at its disposal only *indirect communication*, and this is effected through the testimony of life, and especially through the testimony of martyrdom.

Finally, the fundamental law of subjectivity and the essential condition for being or becoming an individual is to realize within oneself *perfect purity of heart*, for it is only through this that all danger of division can be avoided. Without purity of heart man is inevitably divided; he is no longer an individual, but a colony of incoherent desires and contradictory impulses, a public square, full of bustle; far from being a subject and a person he becomes a thing, subject to the law of things, which is to be activated and controlled from outside.

But of what does purity of heart consist? Its character, says Kierkegaard, is to will one thing, that is to say, both the only necessary thing (*unum necessarium*) and unity, which the only necessary thing, which is God, alone can make it possible to realize. For it goes without saying that neither pleasures nor the things of this world can unify the soul even if one decided to will them exclusively. Neither does willing one thing apply to great matters conceived in vanity, which take on the appearance of the one thing only by the effect of a kind of dizziness. To will one thing truly, one must will the good, for the good alone can unify the soul, and one must truly will the good. Otherwise the will is still divided. And in order to will the good truly, one must be willing to do anything and suffer anything for it.[39]

Contemporaneity and Offence.—Subjectivity, thus understood, is the only possible means of becoming contemporary with Christ. Every other means of coming into relationship with Christ amounts in fact to transforming him into an object. But to be

before Christ as a subject before an object is to be his contemporary.[40] This contemporaneity, however, must not be understood
in an immediate sense, that is, in this case, in a spatial sense. Christianity is really what might be called trans-historical, to the
extent that the "contemporary" in the historical sense of the term
has enjoyed no special privilege with regard to Christ, contrary to
what is commonly thought and to what is factually and historically the case. To become a contemporary of Christ, then, will
not mean to be or to become an "eye-witness", which would
suffice only at the historical level, but "to receive the condition",
that is to say, the grace which creates the will to make the leap
into the absurd and to possess "the autopsy of faith".[41] But "in
this autopsy every non-contemporary (in the immediate sense)
becomes a contemporary". To have faith is a relationship which
transcends space and time: it is an absolute relation to God, that
is, to God as absolute Truth, as excluding all the mediations of
reason, and to Christ as a historical reality but as such absolutely
transcending history and its conditions.[42]

The Offence of Faith

Contemporaneity will thus lead to a second immediacy, which
upon reflection involves paradox and the offence to which it
gives rise. For God puts himself forward as the Man-God, as
misunderstood and humiliated God. That is why offence is inseparable from the Christian estate. It is inseparable from the
serious, which is awareness of God's gaze directed upon the self,
inseparable from being "before God". How, indeed, could the
believer be before God, without being overcome at the mystery
of the Infinite entering into relation with the finite and with sin,
and even, through the Incarnation, coming down into the midst
of the finite? Offence here, then, is the very form assumed by
consciousness of the mystery.[43]

It is important, however, not to be mistaken on this point.
Kierkegaard knows well that Christ said: "Blessed is he whosoever is not offended in Me!" He comments on this saying as
follows: "Yea, blessed is he who is not offended in Him, blessed is
he who believes that Jesus Christ lived here on earth and was

the One He said He was, the lowly man and yet God . . .
blessed is the man who knows no other to go to, but knows in
every case that he may go to Him. And whatever a man's
condition in life may be, though he live in poverty and wretchedness—blessed is he who is not offended but believes that He fed
five thousand men with five loaves and two small fishes . . .
who . . . believes that Peter sank (when he walked upon the
lake) for the one and only cause that he did not believe fully and
firmly . . . (who) believes that He said to the man sick of the
palsy, 'Thy sins are forgiven thee,' and that this was just as
easy for Him to say as to say to the palsied man: 'Take up thy
bed and walk'—blessed is he who is not offended but believes
in the forgiveness of sinners, although they are not helped like
the palsied man to believe by the certainty of healing. . . .
Blessed is he who . . . (like a child who is taught to say these
words as it falls asleep) says, 'I believe' . . . and then sleeps; yea,
blessed is he, he is not dead, he sleepeth. And whatever sufferings
a Christian may endure here on earth on account of his faith,
though he be ridiculed, persecuted, put to death . . . blessed is
he who is not offended but believes—blessed the victory that overcometh, for faith overcometh the world by overcoming every
instant the enemy within him, the possibility of offence. Fear
not the world, neither poverty, nor wretchedness, nor . . .
men's injustice . . . but fear thyself, fear what can kill faith, and
therewith can kill for thee Jesus Christ. . . . Fear and tremble;
for faith is contained in a fragile earthen vessel, in the possibility
of offence. Blessed is he who is not offended in Him but be-
lives".[44] It can now be understood that God does not wish us to
remain permanently in the state of offence, which would then be
negation and refusal. But he cannot help the fact that his acts and
words at first offend us, that is, upset everything human, rational,
and finite that there is in us. Offence, as such, is the shock which
opens up the perspectives of faith. Thus it too is a "specifically
Christian" category.

The Object of Offence

Offence, in the strict sense of the term, says Kierkegaard, is

directed against the Man-God, and takes two forms: either it
concerns elevation: offence is taken at hearing a human individual
say he is God, act or speak in a manner which reveals God; or
else it concerns abasement: offence is taken at seeing that the
man who is God is such a lowly person, suffering like a weak
creature and powerless in the end.[45] The absurd, in which offence
has its source, Kierkegaard writes, "is—that the eternal truth has
come into being in time, that God has come into being, has been
born, has grown up, and so forth, precisely like any other individual human being, quite indistinguishable from other individuals." The Man-God is the absolute paradox.[46] Thus it is
inevitable that reason should eventually find it a stumbling-block.
"The doctrine of Christianity is the doctrine of the God-Man,
of kinship between God and men, but in such a way, be it noted,
that the possibility of offence is, if I may dare to express it thus,
the guarantee whereby God assures Himself that man cannot
come too near to Him. The possibility of offence is the dialectical
factor in everything Christian. . . . To be so near to God as
Christianity teaches that men can come to Him, and dare come
to Him, and shall come to Him in Christ, has never entered into
any man's head. If this then is to be understood bluntly, just as a
matter of course, without the least reservation, to be taken quite
unconcernedly and flippantly—then . . . Christianity might be
the invention of a crazy God; such a doctrine could only occur
to a god who had lost his wits—so a man must judge who had
kept his wits".[47]

It is the same kind of offence which awaits us when we discover that faithfulness to Christ must find its expression for us in
the hostility of the world, that joy can be had only in suffering
and death, that earthly affections must be sacrificed to God, that
Christendom slips constantly from Christianity into paganism.[48]

To sum up in conclusion, offence is inevitably born of the
impossibility of "direct communication", that is, of the fact that
the Man-God cannot be known and apprehended directly as God.
He is a sign, His miracles are signs, which is the negation of immediacy, since signs must be interpreted, their meaning must be
known. What is more, Christ is a "sign of contradiction", that is

to say, a sign which, attracting attention to itself, reveals within itself an inner contradiction. The sign is a revelation or at least a summons to attention; but the sign which is Christ is an enigma and a mystery, a sign which has meaning only on the condition that the normal criteria of meaning are abandoned. Thus to deny direct communication amounts to demanding faith, and hence to evoking the possibility of offence.[49]

This is the same point of view that Kierkegaard puts forward from another aspect when he observes that the Christian religious involves a fundamental "dialectical contradiction", consisting in the fact that eternal blessedness must be founded upon the absolute truth of historical facts which can never be more than probable.[50] The historical element is "that God, the Eternal, appeared at a particular moment in time as a human individual". Now this historical factor "is a breach with all thought", for it is contradictory that what is by nature eternal should appear in time, should be born, grow, and die. Rationalism, indeed, has tried to give an intelligible form to this appearance of God in time: it makes it an eternal appearance, that is, in the pantheistic sense, a divine eternal becoming. In this case, however, the historical—which metaphysical, abstract thought can only abolish, being unable to grasp and assimilate the elements of contingency and chance which it contains—the historical becomes a myth.[51] We thereby abandon Christianity, for which God's appearance is temporal in the strict sense of the term. But that is absurdity itself, the essence of offence, the realm of faith.[52]

Offence and Religious Pathos

Offence, then, is suffering. As we have seen, this is why Kierkegaard linked suffering essentially with the religious, and in particular with the "paradoxically religious", and consequently regarded it as a permanent state, as the state peculiar to the Christian. In actual fact, he states, suffering here results from "the dying away from immediacy".[53] Man naturally looks for the immediate, that is to say, for that which corresponds exactly and directly in every sphere to the demands of instinct: pleasure in the sensual sphere, happiness in the affective, clarity and obviousness in the intellectual. In the pursuit of this immediacy the individual transforms relative ends into absolutes: he stakes all he has and all he is upon pleasure, clarity and happiness. Now the religious, by making the individual relate himself absolutely and totally to "the absolute τελος" (the absolute goal), necessarily makes him die to immediacy, since it forces him to give up happiness, clarity and pleasure and expose himself to total risk. That is truly "self-annihilation" and "the essential form of the divine relationship".[54]

Kierkegaard uses the most forceful expressions to indicate the nature of religious pathos in Christianity. "To relinquish his understanding and his thinking, and to keep his soul fixed upon the absurd". The individual "can discover that there is something which is . . . against his understanding and way of thinking. When he stakes his life upon this absurd, he makes the motion in virtue of the absurd". "In case this absurd is Christianity, he is a believing Christian". One can thus speak without exaggeration of "the martyrdom of faith", which consists in "the crucifixion of the understanding", and which is not the martyrdom of a moment, but martyrdom for the whole of life. Suffering for the faith is "like rolling a burden up a mountain".[55]

The religious is truly pathos *par excellence*. To describe it, the term *heroism* would be misplaced and insufficient, for the hero, as Kierkegaard conceives him, derives from the ethical and not from the religious. Subject to the absolute imperative of duty, he admittedly commits himself to despair, by the sacrifice of everything he loves and possesses, including his life and his honour. But he can express himself and call the chorus and the characters in the drama to witness, and if the sacrifice earns him the satisfaction of duty done, it is in immanence that it is accomplished. By his own strength the hero renounces everything and finds peace and rest in suffering, but he does not transcend his own limitations: he loses himself at the same time, and in the same movement, that he fulfils himself.[56] This is why Greek tragedy produces the same effect as a marble statue, which lacks the power of sight.[57] The knight of faith, on the other hand, has nothing to lean upon except faith, that is to say, the absurd. All attempts at speaking are forbidden to him, for by the use of language he would enter the realm of the universal. He must therefore en-wrap himself in silence, alone in his own presence and in God's.[58] His sacrifice is a total one. Through faith, however, he knows, even in his suffering, the joy of being in perfect harmony with the element of eternity within himself. "Christianity has also a joy which comes towards us smiling out of the depths of the cup of bitterness, and which appears all the more clearly as the cup is bitterer".[59] For the knight of faith, then, despair opens the way to the transcendental. His lips are sealed, but his eyes are open. Faith has the power to transform shame into glory and defeat into victory.[60]

The Leap beyond Offence.

Such, then, is Christian offence. What we have said of it, how-ever, will allow us, if not to reduce the paradox—for it is essentially paradoxical—at least to grasp its exact meaning. Properly speak-ing, it is a possibility, which places one at a cross-roads leading either to offence, which is thus negation, or to faith. It is thus impossible to attain faith without passing through the possibility of offence, which is "the repellent force by which faith comes into existence—if one does not choose instead to be offended".[61] The victory of faith is precisely the leap beyond offence. It is offence experienced and overcome. To abolish offence, then, would be to abolish faith, and to abolish faith would be to abolish Christ—which is precisely the occupation of all the rationalists who, being unable to conquer offence, try to reduce Christ and His deeds and sayings to the level of the human and the finite. Thus Kierkegaard concludes: " 'Blessed is he whosoever is not offended in Me!' Ah, if thou couldst hear Him say that Himself, hear in thine inward man that He suffers for thee also by reason of the contradiction that, in spite of love, for very love, He cannot put it beyond peradventure whether thou wilt be offended in Him or not; that He who came from far, far away, from the glory of heaven, that He who descended far, far below, until He became the lowly man and now is ready to save thee also . . . must leave it to thee whether thou wilt be offended or not, whether thou through His salvation wilt inherit blessedness, or make thyself unblessed and Him as sorrowful as only love can be! . . . So human is His divinity!"[62]

Christian Witness and the Imitation of Christ

The Nature of the Witness

The Christian life, begun by the leap of faith, must be a *witness*, that is to say, both the act of apprehending Christian truth in its objective aspects—for Christianity is something objective which is realized in the world—and proclaiming without fear or reticence what one has seen and learnt; and at the same time the act of welcoming Christianity within oneself, of making it one's own as something personal, and of bearing witness to this, above all by one's life.[63] All this could be summed up by saying that the true witness is the imitator of Christ. Modern Christendom, says Kierkegaard, produces more admirers of Christ than imitators of Him. Imitation implies self-renunciation, self-denial, facing the "double danger".[64] Admiration, on the other hand, is often a form of self-satisfaction. It always involves at least some degree of such complacency. The admirer is comfortably ensconced in his theatre stall. He approves of the play. He enjoys it. He feels pleased with himself for admiring, for to admire (or understand), as Goethe says, is to equal. For him the hero's life is a matter for enthusiasm, moderated, of course, by the prudence necessary to avoid all contact with the danger. But if the man who is admired were to ask such people "whether they should not now decide to do as he did, instead of playing at warfare in the parlour—then everything is changed, they cautiously withdraw from the admired man, they even become angry with him".[65]

In reality it is impossible to avoid admiration at the very first. It is a mistake, but in a sense it is necessary in order that we may be carried away. However, it cannot last. As it takes effect it must necessarily become intolerable to the admirer, because it operates upon the æsthetic plane. It is enjoyment of a spectacle, while the Christian life is participation. It is not a question of admiring truth, but of living in it, otherwise one becomes entangled in a mass of lies and contradictions. The imitator alone is the true Christian. The admirer's attitude to Christianity is strictly speaking a pagan one.

What is it, then, to be an imitator of Christ? It consists in understanding his words as addressed directly to oneself, in taking care to "live entirely in the same way",[66] in identifying oneself with Christ in thought and action, and consequently in accepting suffering and death, which is the absolute paradox of the Christian life, for the sake of forgiveness of sins. Forgiveness, indeed, is the all-embracing category of the Christian life, the term which sums up faith, just as redemption sums up Christ's work. "Infinite humiliation, then grace, then an effort to be grateful: such is Christianity"[67]

Prayer [68]

At the same time the meaning and value of prayer may be defined. It is really the breath of the soul. Does anyone ask me why I breathe? I reply: "Because otherwise I would die."[69] Prayer has the wonderful effect of transforming, little by little, the soul of the person who prays. We ask God, indeed, to grant us this or that favour, to make us understand this or that; but God triumphs over us by substituting Himself for our interested ends, by substituting for our own self another self which is in an absolute relation to the Absolute which He is from our standpoint. "He who truly prays is involved in conflict in his prayer; and he triumphs, because God triumphs in him".[70]

It must be clearly understood, moreover, that this triumph extends to the depths of the soul, to the very roots of the will, for the will is of one piece with true prayer, and like prayer it is operated passively within us.[71] Little by little we cease to speak to God in order to present our wishes and desires to Him: they fade one after another in the light to which prayer admits us. Prayer becomes the act of listening to the word of God; in its highest form it is silence and admiration before God, who from being infinitely distant has come infinitely near.[72]

It can thus be seen how great an error it would be to imagine one could become an imitator of Christ by means of works and ritual conformity. Luther insisted on this point, and there is no doubt, Kierkegaard notes, that he attached too little value to works and thus played into the hands of secularism.[73] But it is true that works are of value only in so far as they emanate from faith. Without faith, works are barren, just as faith would be dead without the works of love. Genuine Christianity demands reciprocity: he alone can receive love who himself gives love. Love—and the works which it inspires and strengthens with its ardour—is the vital and necessary manifestion of faith.

The Mystery of Love

Indeed, it is by love alone that the true relation to God is established, because love is the only means whereby God is revealed to the soul, and the soul to God. "Christ says: I will manifest myself to him who loves me. But that is true everywhere, the thing one loves manifests itself to one . . . one too easily thinks of the recipient as inactive and that which manifests itself as actively communicating, but the relationship is that the recipient is the lover and so the thing loved is made manifest to him, for he himself is transformed into the likeness of the thing beloved, and to become what one loves is the only fundamental way of understanding. . . . Moreover one sees that in this case to love and to know are essentially synonymous; and just as to love means that the other becomes manifest, it naturally means also that one is made manifest oneself".[74]

From this one can understand what it means to become a contemporary of Christ: it is the ineffably happy assurance that God is love; it is a deep union in love.[75] But this mystery of love, which is the secret of the Christian soul, can be neither understood nor made plain. It is accessible only to God. It remains a mystery even for the one who loves: it can be related to feeling only by reducing it to the level of the æsthetic, and what is more it necessarily involves the risk of faith, the risk which is love itself. In Christian terms, "love is the work of love. The love of Christ is not an inner feeling, but the work of love, a work which was his very life".[76]

Kierkegaard's Mysticism

These remarks may help us to define Kierkegaard's mysticism; its meaning, however, cannot be understood without taking account of the forceful criticisms of the mystical life which Kierkegaard made.

On the one hand, he says, it is difficult to absolve the mystic from charges of indiscretion in his relations with God, in so far as he considers himself the object of divine favour. By this, indeed, he belittles God, whom he makes into an idol, and he also belittles himself, by reducing to chance, namely to a sort of divine favouritism, that which sets him apart from others. On the other hand, there is an element of softness and weakness in the mystic's life. He wants to be assured of his own love for God: but is it not excessive to claim to renew the experience of this love continually? Finally, the mystic's life is a sort of fraud upon the world in which he lives, and a deception of the men to whom his duty binds him. In practice, he chooses the solitary life, and thus excludes relationships which have claims upon him; in any case, he becomes such a stranger to all men that they, even those nearest to him, become indifferent to him.[77]

To this it might be added that the mystic remains upon a metaphysical, that is, an abstract, plane: he never becomes concrete, either before himself or before God; he lacks transparency. Even his repentance remains abstract, because it relates, not to his own concrete existence, but to reality in general, which is defined as vanity, illusion and sin. Thus his great care is to flee from sin, which is an abstract care; the true ethical and concrete care, on the contrary, leads one to become aware of sin, to enter into it in order to suppress it or endure it.[78]

Kierkegaard's position with regard to mysticism being such—at least if Judge William's point of view corresponds exactly with his own thought[79]—it will be easily understood that the majority of commentators refuse to admit the idea of Kierkegaard as a mystic. But there are many ways of being a mystic. Here all depends upon the way in which religious experience is defined with regard to Kierkegaard. We know that for his own part Kierkegaard never had an immediate relationship with God,[80] and that his inner life was more acquainted with barrenness than with uplifting joy and consolation. Spleen, according to the moderns, aridity and acedia, according to the mystics, or silent despair as his father put it, was the basis of his existence.[81] "He was," he says of himself, "a religious soul who could never, or only very rarely, rest confidently in grace".[82] Moreover he often laughed at those who defined mysticism in terms of oscillations from ardour to barrenness or from barrenness to exaltation. He undoubtedly experienced all the feelings which give birth to the Christian life, and in particular that joy which surpasses all feeling, and which he has spoken of in moving terms. "There is melancholy in everything in my life, but then again an indescribable happiness. . . . I have, quite literally, lived with God as one lives with one's father".[83] However, it was not in the joy of intercourse with God that he wished to place the ideal of Christian life on earth. In the first place, such joy comes only rarely, in the form of a sudden explosion and as a transitory state: it is like a ray of sunlight which touches the topmost peak of the soul in the midst of the solitude and darkness into which it is plunged by the crushing presence of God. Secondly, to seek for joy would be to return to the æsthetic, to renounce God for the finite.[84]

It must be added that mystical experience defined as a state in which, through love, the soul becomes one and the same being with God has no clear meaning in Kierkegaard's psychology, where an interval ("the infinite distance")[85] must always be maintained between the soul and God—for it is just this which is the sign of a faith which proves itself by self-trial, and at the same time it is the absolute condition for the believer's individuality and personality.

Kierkegaard speaks, no doubt, of the experience of "unknowing" in terms which recall St. John of the Cross and the mystics in general. "The difference between knowing and unknowing," he says, "is annihilated in the absolute prayer of unknowing".[86] "Man," he writes again, "has a natural dread of walking in the dark—what wonder then that he naturally has a dread of the absolute, of having to do with the absolute, of which it is true that no night and 'no deepest gloom is half so dark' as this gloom and this night, where all relative ends (the common milestones and sign-posts), where all relative considerations (the lanterns which are normally a help to us), where even the tenderest and sincerest feelings of devotion—are quenched . . . for otherwise it is not unconditionally the absolute".[87] God, in fact, is the being without predicate, and, according to the expression of St. John of Damascus, the ocean of indeterminacy, pure subjectivity of which we cannot speak, light which is darkness to our feeble eyes and is light only to itself, mystical nothingness and infinite intensity, absolute void and overflowing abundance. The mystics have accustomed us to such language. But not only the mystics, for philosophers have also spoken of God in the same terms, which come from Neo-Platonism. Negative theology is common to both, and one is not necessarily a mystic because one professes that "the most perfect knowledge of God is unknowing" (*Deus qui melius scitur nesciendo.*) Now precisely in Kierkegaard's case, it would seem, such phrases are used, not to convey ineffable personal experiences, but merely to emphasize recurring themes of Christian thought concerning the incomprehensibility of God; themes which, for him, were strengthened and ordered by a conception of faith which, as we have seen, greatly accentuated the gap between the human reason and the mysterious.

These observations are valid only with regard to a strict and in a sense technical conception of mysticism, that is to say, of the experience defined as prayer through intuitive contemplation and the state of passiveness in which the life of perpetual communion is carried on. But if the term is taken in a broader sense to mean all ardent and profound spiritual life, with longer or shorter periods of tranquil contemplation, then there is nothing to prevent us speaking of Kierkegaard as a mystic, and on the contrary every inducement to do so. The fervour of his praying is in itself evidence of a magnificent spiritual intensity. But it is above all through the experience of decision and choice that Kierkegaard's mysticism finds expression for us: the Christian life, lived in its full depth and truth, consists in the decision, constantly renewed in the midst of the contradictions which overwhelm the believer, to choose the infinite and the eternal, or to choose oneself in one's eternal aspect. It was not for nothing that Kierkegaard insisted so much upon the value of passion or pathos, which here represent the crucifying experience of doubt and offence within faith itself, of the paradox and the absurd, of the reason torn to shreds, of fear and terror. It is in this that Kierkegaard tests his faith and knows, in fear and trembling, that he is near to God. According to one of his favourite opinions, the positive is made manifest in the negative: to approach God is to move away from Him; every forward movement is a step backwards, and yet truly, and for that very reason, a step nearer.[88] No anguish is comparable to that of drawing too near to God.[89]

Thus God reveals Himself in this dramatic struggle in the same way that He is manifested in the divine darkness of the mystics. One might say that with Kierkegaard mysticism is transferred from the plane of the consciousness to that of the will. For him religious experience culminates in choice, which is the highest point of pathos, because, proceeding from faith, it is accomplished in absolute risk, which is the equivalent, on the plane of the will, of the darkness of Johannine mysticism.[90] Nor is the feeling lacking that all this is brought about under the influence of a divine movement. Here one may discern a form of the mystical experience of passiveness, that is, a state in which the soul, abandoning itself to God, feels obscurely that a higher power animates and controls it;[91] and this is the mystery, at once crucifying and uplifting, of infinite Love. Such is the essential experience with which Kierkegaard became more and more profoundly acquainted, and which he expressed in many ways, by means of indirect communication. "Father of love," he writes, "I have succeeded in nothing and yet Thou art love. And there again, I have not succeeded in maintaining that Thou art love—and yet Thou art love. Wherever I turn, the only thing I cannot avoid or leave behind is that Thou art love; and that is why, when I have not succeeded in maintaining that Thou art love, I believe that Thou in Thy love dost permit it to be so. Oh, infinite Love!"[92] If there is mysticism in Kierkegaard, both as living experience and spiritual doctrine, it is here, we believe, that it is to be found. And it is this very mysticism which best reveals to us, in its profound truth, Kierkegaard's spiritual ardour—and which thus perfectly epitomizes the whole of Christian life, consisting as it does in faith, which means trusting in the love of God, made manifest in Christ, the Saviour and the Pattern of the human race.

NOTES TO CHAPTER SIX—B.

[1] Cf. *Unscientific Postscript*, p. 495.

[2] Cf. *Journal*, IX A 413 (quoted by Tisseau, *Ecole du Christianisme*, p. xxxiii): "The victory I have won is to have succeeded in relating the categories to the fact of being a Christian, and to have riveted them to it so firmly that no dialectician will be able to break them away. Without being deceived I have seen that what must offer resistance is not Christianity but the fact of being a Christian, then the concept of contemporaneity, then the concept of offence, then, at their head, at the very top, the concept of faith."

[3] *Journal*, 1835, I A 56 (Dru 15).

[4] *Journal*, 1836, I A 152 (Wahl, p. 614): The relation between the law, as something postulated in a purely external, objective way, and the reception it receives from the individual within himself. . . . Appropriation."

[5] *Journal*, 1839, II A 517 (Wahl, p. 595).

[6] 1839, II A 523 and 524 (Wahl, p. 593). How is this point of view to be reconciled with that expressed in the following passage from the *Journal*, (1839, II A 440, Dru 283): "Dogma is nothing but the concrete expression of universal human consciousness"? It appears that Kierkegaard is here propounding not his own but the Hegelian view, which he refuses to admit.

[7] *Journal*, 1849, X^2 A 299 (Dru 1021).

[8] Cf. *Journal*, 1836-7, I A 328 (Dru 88): How has Christianity been dealt with?—"Every Christian concept has been so sublimated, so completely volatilized into a sea of fog, that it is impossible to recognize it again. To such concepts as faith, incarnation, tradition, inspiration, which in Christianity must be referred to a particular historical fact, it has seemed good to philosophers to give an entirely different general meaning . . . and still I have not mentioned the idea which has not only been reduced to nothing but even profaned, the idea of salvation. . . . We shall hope for the appearance of strongly armed men who will win back the lost power and meaning of words, just as Luther won back the concept faith for his age."

[9] *Journal*, 1848. Cf. ibid., 1839, II A 452: "Christianity is an objective act which is realized in the world."

[10] Przywara (*Das Geheimnis Kierkegaards*, Munich 1929) lays much stress upon these observations of Kierkegaard's. He strives to show that there is an implicit catholicism in Kierkegaard (or if one will, a catholic logic): by repeatedly emphasising the Christian demand for an *objective authority* and the necessity of the ordination of priests as an *objective intermediary authority* between the Christian and God, Kierkegaard was obviously leaving the paths of Lutheranism and turning towards catholicism. With this we are in agreement. It must be added, however, that in other aspects of his thought Kierkegaard contradicts these views outright, or at least creates serious obstacles to their

logical development. We shall return to this question in the conclusion to this study, when we shall attempt to judge Kierkegaard's thought *as a whole.*

[11] *Unscientific Postscript*, p. 350. Cf. *The Point of View*, p. 135-6: " 'The individual'—that is the decisive Christian category, and it will be decisive also for the future of Christianity. . . . Hence men must become single individuals in order to get the proper Christian-pathetic impression of Christianity" . . . " 'The individual'—with this category the cause of Christianity stands or falls". Kierkegaard adds that this category is not that of the missionary proclaiming Christianity to pagans, but of a missionary work within Christendom with a view to introducing Christianity into it.

[12] It must not be forgotten that subjectivity itself is dialectical. "Subjectivity or inwardness is truth: is there a more intense way of expressing that? Yes, if the discourse entitled 'subjectivity is truth' begins: 'Subjectivity is error'." Subjectivity indeed is the situation of the individual who is before God. But we know we are before God only by our consciousness of sin, which is the most profound consciousness of our existence which we have. Subjectivity, then, is conditioned by sin; in a sense indeed it is sin. This is why, like all existential reality, it implies tension and suffering. Moreover (*Journal*, 1850, Haecker, p. 155) all the things of the spirit are dialectical in this sense, that when taken to extremes they may end up as their own opposites.

[13] *Unscientific Postscript*, p. 339.

[14] Cf. *Journal*, 1848, IX A 207 (Geismar, 237-8): "There are two major misunderstandings concerning Christianity. 1° Christianity is not a doctrine. This conception is the source of all the disorders of orthodoxy, with its struggle against this and that while existence remains unchanged; in order to know what Christianity is in itself men have striven with each other exactly as they might over the meaning of the philosophy of Plato. Christianity is the communication of existence. 2° Because Christianity is not a doctrine it is not a matter of indifference, as it would be in the case of a doctrine, to know who expounds it provided he (objectively) says what is correct. If Christianity is not reproduced in the individual who expounds it, then he is not expounding Christianity, which can only be expounded by existence. 'To exist in it,' 'to express it by existing', means—to reproduce it."

[15] Cf. *Unscientific Postscript*, p. 339: "If Christianity were a doctrine it would *eo ipso* not be an opposite to speculative thought. . . . Christianity has to do with existence, with the act of existing; but existence and existing constitute precisely the opposite of speculation." This is the same idea that Kierkegaard expresses elsewhere (*Training in Christianity*, p. 123), saying that men "have simply done away with Christ, cast Him out and taken possession of His teaching, almost regarding Him at last as one does an anonymous author—the doctrine is the principal thing, is the whole thing. . . . They have nonsensically forgotten that here the Teacher is more important than His teaching."

[16] *Unscientific Postscript*, p. 291.

[17] *Unscientific Postscript*, p. 339. Cf. p. 501: "Christianity is an existence-communication which makes the thing of existing paradoxical and difficult to a degree it never was before and never can be outside of Christianity."

[18] *Unscientific Postscript*, p. 339-40.

[19] *Journal*, 1849, X² A 312.

[20] *Journal*, 1849, X² A 207.

[21] *Journal*, November 1847 (Wahl, p. 399, note 1.)

[22] Authority, whatever it may be, Kierkegaard declares (*Training in Christianity*, p. 227 ff) cannot exist in any case without "repetition" or "reproduction"; that is, all preaching and teaching must correspond exactly to the personal life of the preacher or teacher. The poet can be moving and persuasive; he does not have authority. This latter belongs to the witness, more properly to the martyr. This is why Kierkegaard, who was far from such reproduction (so at least as he thought, in his humility) hesitated so much over publishing *Training in Christianity*, in which he condemned himself by speaking of Christianity without having the authority of the witness. Eventually he attempted to solve the problem by using a new pseudonym (Anticlimacus).

[23] Cf. *Training in Christianity*, p. 217–8: "Such a conception as that of 'the congregation', about which people in these days especially have been so busy, is really, as applied to this life, an impatient anticipation of eternity. . . . 'The congregation' . . . belongs properly to eternity; 'the congregation' is at rest what 'the individual' is in unrest. But this life is precisely the time of testing, the time of unrest, hence 'the congregation' has not its abiding place in time but only in eternity, where it is the assembly at rest of all the individuals who stood the test of combat and probation".

[24] Cf. *Journal*, 1854 (Haecker, p. 339): "Nothing, nothing, nothing, no misdoing, no crime is so absolutely against God as is everything that is official. And why? because the official is the impersonal, and hence the deepest insult possible is to offer it to a person."

[25] E. P. IX p. 353 (Wahl, p. 400).

[26] *Journal*, X² A 231.

[27] Sometimes however, Kierkegaard seems to moderate the vigour of his "individualism" and admit a kind of moral communion between the members of the human family. Cf. *Purify your Hearts*, p. 138: "Even if it were denied the sufferer to work by example, even if he were cut off from all other men, yet he shares in the great common cause of mankind. At his lonely post he, as it were, defends a difficult pass, in saving his soul from the besetting snares of suffering. Though no man see him, humanity feels with him, conquers with him!"

[28] *Journal*, 1837, II A 117 (F. & G., p. 70–71).—Later, (1839—II A 446, F. & G., p. 92), Kierkegaard reproaches catholic theology with having made original sin something fundamentally foreign to the individual, like a wrong title which is put right when a book is rebound.

[29] *Journal*, 1837, II A 117 (F. & G., p. 71). Cf. Ibid., 1838, II A 233 (F. & G., p. 80): "In the last resort, few men are able to bear the *Protestant* idea of life, and if it is to be truly a force for the *populace*, it must be realized through small congregations (separatism, conventicles, etc), or else it must draw nearer to Catholicism, so that in either case, social support is given to the sharing of the burden of life, which only outstandingly gifted people can dispense with. Christ died for all, it is true, but also for me in so far as I form part of the multitude."

[30] *Training in Christianity*, p. 218.—Cf. *Journal*, 18 July 1840 (Wahl, p. 401): "Omnipresence means precisely that God is not only everywhere at all times, but also that he is wholly present in his presence, present in his absoluteness in

each Individual, completely in each one, and yet in all; He is not split up, and partially in each—that is pantheism—but he is totally in each one and yet in all, and that is theism, personality, individuality."

31 All this, moreover, did not lead Kierkegaard to demand the emancipation of the Church (disestablishment of the Church or separation of Church and State). Not that he did not think it wholly desirable in theory, for he thought, as we have seen, that the Church, which is dedicated to the future, fundamentally contradicts itself when it becomes "established", and thus assumes the static form of the State. But he feared the remedy might be worse than the disease, and that emancipation of the Church would be effected in the name of a conception of toleration which amounted to pure indifference in religious matters, and even concerning the truth (Cf. *Journal*, 1851, Haecker, p. 229). This is why he felt obliged to disavow the theologian Rudelbach, who had used his name, in a treatise on *Civil Marriage*, to advocate the twofold reform of the institution of compulsory civil marriage and of the separation of Church and State.

32 *Unscientific Postscript*, p. 360–72.

33 *Unscientific Postscript*, p. 372.

34 *The Sickness unto Death*, p. 197.

35 *The Sickness unto Death*, p. 197, note.

36 Cf. *Purify your Hearts*, p. 157–8: "Here in time . . . numbers tempt us, we are tempted to count, to count ourselves in with the crowd, and the brain is easily made to seal with good round numbers. Yea, here in time, no individual perhaps will ever succeed, not even if we could say of him that he willed the Good truly, in breaking up the crowd; but eternity can do it. Eternity lays hold of each separate one with the strong arms of conscience and enfolds him as an individual, sets him aside with his conscience, and woe to him if it only passes judgement on him, for eternity sets him aside with his conscience there, where no doubt there is pressure on people, but not as in time, where the pressure supplies an excuse, and is even counted as victory; nay, but there, where what presses on him is to be alone and without excuse, to be alone and be lost. . . . And so this sense of being an individual is the fundamental consciousness of a human being, his eternal self-consciousness."

37 *Purify your Hearts*, p. 152. Cf. *The Point of View*, p. 112–22, where Kierkegaard develops the theme that "a crowd is untruth".

38 *Unscientific Postscript*, p. 232.

39 *Purify your Hearts*, p. 41 ff—cf. p. 142–3: "Purity of heart is to will one thing. . . . The decision for the Good is the decisive *one thing*, and to God we cannot draw nigh by guile or ingratiatingly, we cannot draw nigh to him with the tongue, while the heart is far away. Nay, as God is a spirit and is truth, we can only draw nigh to him in truth, willing to be holy as he is holy, through purity of heart. Purity of heart! This is a figure of speech which compares the heart with the sea. And why with the sea in particular? Because the depth of the sea makes it pure, and its purity makes it transparent. . . . When . . . being deep and transparent, it is pure, then it is one throughout, no matter how long you keep looking at it; its purity is its consistent unity. . . . As the sea reflects the height of heaven in its pure depth, so does the heart reflect, in the calm of its transparency, the heavenly height of the Good of its pure depth".

[40] *Training in Christianity*, p. 67.

[41] *Philosophical Fragments*, p. 57.

[42] Cf. *Training in Christianity*, p. 66–72.

[43] *The Sickness unto Death*, p. 133–41.

[44] *Training in Christianity*, p. 79–80.

[45] *Training in Christianity*, p. 84.

[46] *Unscientific Postscript*, p. 188.

[47] *The Sickness unto Death*, p. 206.

[48] Cf. *Training in Christianity*, p. 113–14: "In established Christendom this and every other possibility of offence is in effect abolished—in established Christendom one becomes a Christian in the merriest possible sort of way, without in the least becoming aware of the possibility of offence. In established Christendom the natural man has managed to have his own way. There is no endless contrast between the Christian and the worldly. . . . Christianity is related directly to the world, it is movement without budging from the spot—that is to say, feigned movement."

[49] Cf. *Training in Christianity*, p. 132 ff.

[50] Cf. *Unscientific Postscript*, p. 510: The dialectical contradiction emerges when "the subject in the extremity of such subjective passion (in the concern for an eternal happiness) has to base this upon an historical knowledge which at its maximum remains an approximation."

[51] Cf. *Journal*, 1840, III A 1 (F. & G., p. 113): "History is a unity compounded of metaphysics and chance. Of metaphysics it is true that without it, without this eternal ribbon of existence, the phenomenal world would decompose; of chance, in so far as each event contains a possibility of having happened in an infinity of other ways, and this unity is from the divine point of view, *Providence*, and from the human, *history*."

[52] *Unscientific Postscript*, p. 513.

[53] *Unscientific Postscript*, p. 412.

[54] Cf. *Journal*, 1853, X⁴ A 72 (Dru 1287): "Little by little I noticed increasingly that all those whom God really loved, the examples, etc., had all had to suffer in this world. Furthermore, that that is the teaching of Christianity: to be loved by God and to love God is to suffer."

[55] *Unscientific Postscript*, p. 495–6, 502. Further on (p. 516–19), he states more precisely that the pathos of the paradoxical-religious, which is "sharpened pathos" results from the following three causes: sin-consciousness, the possibility of offence, and the smart of sympathy, in that the believer may be led to hate his father and mother. When he is separated from them—which happens whenever they do not base their blessedness upon faith—it is "as though he hated them".

[56] Cf. *Fear and Trembling*, p. 72.

[57] *Fear and Trembling*, p. 122.

[58] Cf. *Journal*, 1850 (Wahl, p. 655): "There is a relationship of silence which binds us to God, and which is broken if we discuss with someone else what is the most vital thing of all for us."

[59] *Journal*, 1839, II A 365 (Wahl, p. 608).

[60] Cf. *The Gospel of Suffering*, p. 184.

[61] *Training in Christianity*, p. 122.

[62] *Training in Christianity*, p. 80-1.

[63] *Journal*, 1839, II A 452 (Wahl, p. 631). Cf. Ibid. 1850, X^3 A 5 (Dru 1091): "What is a witness? A witness is a man who immediately supplies proof of the truth of the doctrine he is proclaiming—immediately, well, partly by there being truth in him and blessedness, partly by at once offering himself and saying: see now whether you can compel me to deny this doctrine. As a result of that fight, where the witness perhaps succombs physically—dies—the doctrine triumphs."

[64] Cf. *Training in Christianity*, p. 217: "Magister Kierkegaard has shown (in the conclusion of the Second Part of *The Works of Love*) what is to be understood by Christian self-denial, that this exists only where there is 'double danger', that the second danger, the danger of suffering because one denies oneself, is the decisive definition."

[65] *Training in Christianity*, p. 237.

[66] *Training in Christianity*, p. 13.

[67] Cf. *For Self-Examination*, p. 216: "The Pattern must be brought to the fore, for the sake at least of creating more respect for Christianity, to get it made a little bit evident what it is to be a Christian, to get Christianity transferred from learned discussion and doubt and twaddle (the objective) into the subjective sphere, where it belongs, as surely as the Saviour of the world, our Lord Jesus Christ, brought no doctrine into the world and never lectured but as the 'Pattern' required imitation—casting out, however, if possible, by His atonement all anxious dread from men's souls."

[68] Cf. the texts concerning prayer, taken from the *Journal* and translated into French by P. M. Tisseau, in: Sören Kierkegaard: *Prières*, p. 37 ff.

[69] *Journal*, 1848, IX A 462 (Tisseau, p. 56).

[70] This is the theme developed in the last of the *Four Edifying Discourses* (which is the eighteenth of the *Religious Discourses*), published in 1844: "True prayer is a struggle with God in which one triumphs through God's triumphs." This *Discourse* has been published in French translation by P. H. Tisseau as an appendix to the fragments on prayer (*Prières*, p. 94 ff), but not as yet in English.

[71] *Journal*, 1838, II A 301 (Tisseau, p. 38).

[72] Cf. *Journal*, 1846, VII A 56 (Dru 572): "The immediate person thinks and imagines that when he prays, the important thing, the thing he must concentrate upon, is that *God should hear what* HE *is praying for*. And yet, in the true, eternal sense it is just the reverse: the true relation in prayer is not when God hears what is prayed for, but when *the person praying* continues to pray until he is *the one who hears*, who hears what God wills. The immediate person, therefore, uses many words and, therefore, makes demands in his prayer; the true man of prayer *attends*."

[73] *For Self-Examination*, p. 40 ff.

[74] *Journal*, 1848, IX A 438 (Dru 846).

[75] Cf. *Journal*, 1848: "Assured, by a guarantee that is the fullness of happiness, that God is love, in spite of everything, even if I had to suffer all my life, yes, a guarantee which is the fullness of happiness, I was always sure, with a happy certainty, that God is love; nothing has been more certain for me than that." Ibid., 1848, IX A 216 (Tisseau, p. 51): "Oh, he also loves God, God loves him too, and raises him up; that is his education. . . . Oh what joy that God is also

love, that everything is possible to Love, and that He for whom everything is possible is Love."

[76] *Journal*, 1849 (Haecker, p. 68).

[77] *Either/Or*, II p. 202-207.

[78] *Either/Or*, II p. 207-10.

[79] The *Journal* frequently repeats the criticisms made in *Either/Or* insisting especially upon the two points that mysticism leads back to the æsthetic level and, above all, that it tends to dissolve the individual in the impersonal.

[80] *The Point of View*, p. 68-9.

[81] *Journal*, 1839, II A 484 (Dru 292).

[82] *Journal*, 1849, X^2 A 157.

[83] *Journal*, 1848, IX A 65 (Dru 771). Cf. *Journal*, 1850: "It is as though sweetness appeared, welled up before me, as though I breathed it in, and as though I wished, by my preaching, to lead men to a security which would almost be in danger of becoming abandon or vain carefreeness." Ibid., 1851: "Possessing this sweetness is like having a feeling. The deeper the feeling, the more one dreads letting it show." *Pap*. III, p. 94: "That is why my joy must ring out louder than the voice of a woman who has given birth, louder than the rejoicing of angels over a converted sinner, more joyful than the song of birds in the morning. For what I sought I have found, and if men took everything from me, if they exiled me from their society, I should still retain this joy."

[84] Cf. *Journal*, 1853, X^5 A 79 (Tisseau, p. 89): "The spirit of God wishes to give suffering more felicity than pleasure has. Naturally this must not be understood, and Providence will keep you from it, in the sense that the very second you freely renounce yourself you will receive felicity, and that it is much the same as what the immediate man covets. No, in that case renunciation would be a crafty deal."

[85] *Journal*, 1849, X^2 A 272.

[86] *Philosophical Fragments*, (Wahl, p. 411).

[87] *Journal*, 1854, XI^1 A 95 (Dru 1308).

[88] *Journal*, 1851, X^4 A 253 (Dru 1212).

[89] *Journal*, 1853, X^5 A 72 (Dru 1287)—cf. ibid., 1851, X^4 A 253 (Dru 1212): "How wonderfully consistent is everything divine! It is always double in its action: in taking away he also adds . . . just as in relation to the ideal where every step forward is a step back, so too in relation to God: approach, withdrawal and yet, *real* approach." This point of view is developed especially in the discourse on *The Publican*.

[90] Cf. *Judge for Yourselves!* XII, 383 (Geismar, p. 241): "Whoever does not renounce probability will never enter into relationship with God. All religious risk, all the more then all Christian risk, is beyond probability, is where probability has been renounced."

[91] Cf. *Journal*, 1838, II A 301 (Tisseau, p. 38) concerning prayer: "We might believe that man has entered into relationship with God in the freest, the most subjective manner, and yet we learn that it is the Holy Spirit who operates prayer, so that the only prayer remaining would be that of being able to pray; and yet this too, if we look closer, is operated within us."

[92] *Journal*, 1850, X^3 A 49 (Tisseau, p. 24)—Cf. ibid., 1854, XI^1 A 382 (Tisseau, p. 93): "If my contemporaries could understand how I suffer, how Providence,

if I may say so, maltreats me, I am sure they would be so profoundly moved that in their human sympathy they would try (as is sometimes done for a child maltreated by its parents) to take me away from Providence. And yet that is a mistake. For I rest in the assurance that Thou doest it for love, yes, for love. Infinite Love! I know that in Thy Love Thou sufferest with me, more than I, infinite Love—although Thou canst not be changed by that."

CONCLUSION

CONCLUSION

Such were the life, the soul and the works of Sören Aabye Kierkegaard. Among these works, whose variety and wealth is really prodigious, we in our turn must make a choice. Kierkegaard himself invites us to do so; so afraid was he of attracting groups of disciples that some of his writings were composed in order to upset any sort of agreement with his views which might, in however small a degree, take on the form of a party, of a sect, let alone of a Church.[1] Above all he wished to arouse anxiety, to provoke reflection, to make his contemporaries take notice. Uncritical adherence would be directly contrary to his aim and to his method. Let us then attempt, now that we have a general picture of Kierkegaard's work, to draw up a statement of profit and loss, to make an inventory of the magnificent riches it offers us, but also of the dangers which it seems to us to involve. To this end it is desirable that we should begin by defining Kierkegaard's attitude towards Lutheranism.

I

KIERKEGAARD AND LUTHER

The Dialogue with Luther.—There is no doubt whatever that Kierkegaard's thought was profoundly influenced by Lutheranism.[2] But Kierkegaard continually raised objections, some of them very far-reaching, to Luther's main theses. Indeed, towards the end of his life, at the time of his clash with the established Church and after his attempt to go back from Lutheranism to Luther, he seems to have developed fundamental doubts concerning the Christian value of the Lutheran religion.

For Luther, sin and faith are the twin poles of Christianity. Man is sin, says Luther: to apprehend oneself as sin is the first condition of the Christian life. One must be careful, moreover, to give the notion of sin its full significance. It is not a question simply of saying that there are in man sins which come accidentally to upset or harm a nature which is in itself healthy and good. The reality of sin goes far deeper: it affects man's very *existence*, which, for this reason, is sin and nothing but sin—to the extent that everything derived from nature, works and even "good works", rational inquiry, institutions and the hierarchy, are to be laid to the charge of sin.

The antithesis and the remedy, according to Luther, is faith, which consists in despairing absolutely of oneself and throwing oneself with abandon into the arms of Christ crucified, through whose grace comes salvation. "Luther's great discovery," Kierkegaard writes, "is that relationship to God does not belong to the sphere of the reason, but that it is an irrational, personal, spiritual relationship, which embraces two elements which are rationally altogether irreconcilable: the consciousness of being at once a sinner and justified". This is an admirably precise and accurate definition of Lutheranism, for in Luther's view, justification being only the extrinsic imputation of the merits of Christ (something like a garment covering the whole body), the Christian must recognize himself as a sinner even in the midst of justification. Strictly speaking, sin is not effaced or abolished by Christ's grace: it is merely concealed and dissimulated.

Such are the essential teachings of Lutheranism. Against them, the Catholic Church has always maintained, in accordance with tradition, on the one hand that human nature has not been totally corrupted by sin, but only impaired and disturbed, especially in the domain of the will, and consequently that man, even without justification, is capable of doing some good, honouring his parents for example, or accomplishing a religious act, but not of fulfilling the whole moral law. On the other hand it teaches that works are necessary for the personal appropriation of the merits of Christ, and that they are of value for salvation when they are informed with the supernatural virtue of charity—but that they are such only by virtue of the merits of Christ the Redeemer, which implies that God's gift is wholly gratuitous and that salvation is absolutely supernatural in character.

From this it is clear that the distance between Catholicism and Lutheranism is considerable. Kierkegaard, in so far as he is concerned, is undoubtedly on Luther's side. Faith for him, as it was for Luther, is a "leap into the absurd", that is to say a choice contrary to reason, lacking any credible motive, an act of absolute confidence in Christ's grace, without any reason whatever for hope. Furthermore, sin has the same sense for him as for Luther: it affects the whole nature and corrupts it in its very essence. Thus he reproaches bishop Mynster, who was a declared adversary of Hegelian rationalism, with thinking that Christianity consists, not in "effacing nature", but in "ennobling" it. If this is so, Kierkegaard objects, Christianity is culture and it is Hegel who is right.[3]

In reality, Mynster's point of view, un-Lutheran as it is, did not necessarily lead to the conclusion drawn by Kierkegaard, that Christianity is only culture. If it does not assume that nature is corrupt in its very substance and rotten at heart, it may present itself as a form of culture, by preserving and uplifting everything in nature that is good and healthy. But it is very different from culture, since it introduces the supernatural, which is participation in the very life of God, and which as such absolutely transcends all nature's demands. On this point, however, Kierkegaard is anxious to remain faithful to Lutheran inspiration. Consequently he asserts that the sense of sin is alone capable of opening the way to faith, without its being necessary for any human reason to intervene. Its intervention, moreover, he thinks would merely impair the "movement of faith". The opposite of sin, then, is not virtue but faith: without faith, all is sin; but faith abolishes sin. " 'But if the Christian life is something so terrible and frightful, how in the world can a person get the idea of accepting it?' Quite simply, and, if you want that too, quite in a Lutheran way," Kierkegaard replies: "only the consciousness of sin can force one into this dreadful situation—the power on the other side being grace. And in that very instant the Christian life transforms itself and is sheer gentleness, grace, loving-kindness, and compassion. Looked at from any other point of view, Christianity is and must be a sort of madness or the greatest horror. Only through the consciousness of sin is there entrance to it, and the wish to enter in by any other way is the crime of lèse-majesté against Christianity".[4]

These precise statements in *Training in Christianity* were none the less accompanied, in the earlier works, by corrective reservations which led Kierkegaard a good way from Luther. For the latter, unjustified man is incapable of recognizing his sin; he is so ill that the seriousness of his condition escapes him completely. Faith alone can bring him awareness of sin. That is why Luther declares that one must "become a sinner" and that that is something very great and very rare.[5] Sin, then, is an object of faith, not of experience. Kierkegaard on the other hand, although he asserted in *The Concept of Dread* that sin cannot be a subject for psychology, thought that psychological analysis can be applied to the *possibility* of sin, and eventually argued as though the sinner was perfectly capable of carrying out his own diagnosis. It was this same attitude which led him to think, as we have observed, that man can achieve for himself, by the path of "infinite resignation", an outline or a beginning of faith. Thus even in this sphere, fundamental though it is, Kierkegaard's Lutheranism is not free from hesitancy and reservation.

In this there is nothing astonishing. Kierkegaard does not defend theses properly so called. He avoids dogmatic teaching. His Lutheranism seems to have been reduced primarily to an influence working in secret upon his thought, by virtue of his education and the deeper tendencies of his nature, given up as it was to melancholy and dread. In actual fact, whenever he encounters Lutheran themes in their dogmatic aspect he enters strong reservations. The *Journal* furnishes valuable evidence on this point. But the works he himself published also often express lively opposition. Thus in his essay *For Self-Examination*,[6] Kierkegaard discusses incidentally the Lutheran doctrine of faith and works. It was necessary for Luther, he says, in order to preserve the complete gratuity of salvation, to set aside works—and the Epistle of St. James. But on the one hand Luther involves himself in an insoluble contradiction by excluding St. James' Epistle as apocryphal, for he thus assumes a standpoint higher than the Bible and contradicts his own Biblical theory.[7] On the other hand, the exclusion of works may lead to grave excesses, if one is to suppose that faith can dissociate itself completely from works. There is in all of us a tendency either "to make a virtue of works when one practises them, or to emancipate oneself from them as far as possible when one puts one's trust in faith and grace". Both the one and the other, then, are to be avoided. Luther, however, Kierkegaard concludes, was working in the end for secularism, which "completely suppressed merit—and works too".[8]

The following observation from the *Journal* is similar in trend to the criticisms in *For Self-Examination*: "If Luther meant that because men have grown as lecherous and sensual as they are, it is impossible to live chaste outside marriage: that is quite possible. But in that case the Reformation is . . . a concession made to lechery and sensuality".[9] If chastity is *impossible* outside marriage, then the unmarried man has a complete excuse for being sensual and depraved. Kierkegaard sums up his thought in the words: "Luther accredited mediocrity".[10] The exclusion of works, the fundamental assertion that all nature is corrupt, that justification is effected by the extrinsic imputation of the merits of Christ, favour laxity, surrender to evil tendencies, and the development of a state of passivity which is the very antithesis of Christian heroism. Kierkegaard adds: "One does not normally realize that it requires a hero to accredit mediocrity for the first time". This is because in order to effect the brutal upheaval which produces this paradoxical result, a truly extraordinary man, a hero, was needed; the dangerous consequences of Lutheran principles were to be hidden by the elements of justice and purity they contained, and by the ardour with which they were proclaimed.[11]

There is, however, a further defect in Lutheranism which is yet more fundamental, for it involves its very source. Kierkegaard draws attention to it by saying: "Luther expresses Christianity in the interest of man, is really the reaction of mankind against Christianity in God's interest".[12] In the Lutheran religion, indeed, everything is centred upon the personal salvation of the soul and not upon the coming of the Kingdom of Heaven and the glory of God. It is not in man's own interest, however, that man should act, but for the glory of God, which alone is "God's interest". For the glory of God is the universal end of all creation, the only goal which can exalt human passion by making man desire absolutely, forgetful of self, the divine Absolute.[13] Lutheran anthropomorphism is so profound that the "disinterestedness" which is such a familiar and constant feature in the mystics, and even in every soul which lives intensely in the Christian faith, here appears as nonsensical and impossible.[14] The greatness of the Middle Ages and of Catholicism on the other hand has been to have put forward the idea of Christ as a pattern, and not only as a gift as Luther does.[15] But from this point of view, Kierkegaard adds, the danger would be that of giving the imitation of Christ a purely external and legal form, of attaching merit to the mechanical observation of ritual. Luther preserves us from this danger. None the less, Kierkegaard does not hesitate to write: "Luther is the absolute opposite of an 'apostle' ",[16] for the apostle, as opposed to the genius, has the essential characteristic of never thinking, in all his actions, and even in his personal life, of anything but the glory of God, from which he derives both his mission and his power.

The essay *On the Difference between the Genius and the Apostle* (1847), and also the fragments of the book Kierkegaard planned to write on Adler, allow us to define this last point more exactly. Kierkegaard there develops his notion of the apostle, and opposes it to that of the religious genius. The latter, he says, is characterised by immanence and unity: by immanence, in that what he has to offer derives always from the human sphere, and remains within that sphere; by unity, in that the genius has nothing within him but himself. The apostle on the other hand reveals a truth which transcends the human sphere, which presupposes a duality in him, namely the duality of his own person and the message which he brings. Thus no one can become an apostle by himself: something must be added to him, and this something is *authority*. To deny that Luther was an apostle is thus to contest the view that he had authority.

There is yet another point, however, which takes the criticism of Lutheranism still further. If the Lutheran reformation is to be judged as a whole, Kierkegaard remarks that it would have attained its full value only if it had limited itself to being a "corrective to Catholicism", that is, to calling attention to various aspects of true Christianity which the fifteenth century appeared to have neglected, and especially to the necessity for personal relationship with God, and to combating the many abuses which had developed (against which, moreover, the Church itself was attempting to take action).[17] The Protestant error, then, Kierkegaard says, is not that it was a corrective, for a corrective was needed, but that it was "a corrective made into the norm, the whole", and that this "is *eo ipso* confusing in the next generation (when that which it was meant to correct no longer exists)."[18] And he adds: "Things get worse with every generation, until in the end the corrective produces the exact opposite of what was originally intended".[19]

The *Journal*, in the last years of Kierkegaard's life, bears witness more and more to his disillusionment concerning Protestantism, and abounds in criticisms of it, some of them very sharp: "Catholicism," he says, "has a conception and idea of the Christian ideal: to become nothing in this world. Protestantism is worldliness from beginning to end".[20] Finally, Kierkegaard sums up his thoughts in these lines, which receive a special tone and bearing from being in the form of a prayer or meditation before God: "Oh my God, the more I study, the longer I look at it, the more clearly do I see that Protestantism has produced a fundamental confusion in Christianity".[21]

Kierkegaard's Lutheranism.—Haecker, basing his opinion on the texts we have just quoted and on many other passages in the *Journal* and other works of Kierkegaard, believes that Kierkegaard, if he had lived, would have gone over to Catholicism.[22] This is admittedly only a hypothesis, and a dangerous one, but it indicates the direction Kierkegaard was taking in the last years of his life. There is no doubt that he was moving away, not only from the established Church in Denmark, but from Protestantism in general, as he became more and more aware of its impotence to express the full perfection of the Christian idea. Moreover, we have a declaration by him, dating from the end of his career, which enables us to define exactly the position he took up in the debate, which became ever more dominant in his thoughts, concerning the relative value of Protestantism and Catholicism from the Christian point of view. "Protestantism," he writes, "is from the Christian point of view quite simply false, a piece of dishonesty which falsifies the whole Christian conception of the world and of life from the moment it attempts to be not merely a corrective necessary for a given time and place, but a principle for Christianity. However, from saying this to entering the Catholic Church is a step I cannot take, but which I shall perhaps be expected to take; for men to-day have completely forgotten what Christianity is".[23] Certainly nothing could be clearer. It cannot be concluded from this declaration, however, that Kierkegaard, if he had lived, would not have abandoned Protestantism for Catholicism. Newman, a short time before his conversion to Catholicism, made a number of declarations of the same kind.[24] One thing alone is sure: his *direction* was towards Catholicism. All the rest is conjecture, and merely substitutes an abstract logic for the concrete, existential reality of Sören Kierkegaard.

Be that as it may, the influence of Lutheranism upon his thought remains profound. What seems to bring it out most clearly is above all the cultivation of anxiety and dread, which is at the heart of Kierkegaard's psychology and doctrine. If faith is anxiety, it is no doubt, Kierkegaard notes, because it inevitably brings one into conflict with the world ("I am not come to bring peace, but a sword"), but also and above all because it is a perpetual victory over doubt and despair. "A year of temptation is nothing compared with an hour of doubt", such as it is experienced by the hero of faith and the witness to the truth.[25] This Kierkegaard himself declares that he has learnt from Luther, for whom "grace is vain if it is not received by an anguished, tortured conscience".[26]

At the same time we may give its true significance to the assertion, so often made by Kierkegaard, that Christianity can consist only in a "personal relation to God". Assuredly, as we have said, nothing is truer than this claim, which is essential to Christianity at its most authentic. But in the form which Kierkegaard gives it nothing could be more Lutheran, if dread is the instrument of this personal relationship, the only means of feeling and experiencing personal communication with God. Horror, fear and trembling, despair, anguish and doubt, are permanent needs of the religious soul if it is deprived of the Church and the sacraments. Kierkegaard is incontestably marked out in this way.

From this derives the conviction, which never left him, that Luther's force and value were to have emphasized the capital importance of the category of "for oneself", of inwardness and subjectivity, of the individual and the unique. Luther's message on this point is expressed by the fact that he experienced and lived in his faith as something disturbing and at the same time as something redemptive. He was thus the corrective for fifteenth century Catholicism, which lacked, says Kierkegaard, "absorptive power, inwardness", and whose conception of the sacraments as something objective was "judaism".[27]

However, Kierkegaard also saw the dangers of Lutheran subjectivity, as we have observed above concerning his position with regard to the Church. A long note in the *Journal* in 1852 emphasizes one of them. Kierkegaard remarks that the Lutheran point of view, according to which faith is essentially the remedy for the anguished conscience, would cease to have any meaning, and would become mere twaddle, if, as one might suppose, there were no anguished conscience, or there ceased to be any. The objection will seem a serious one, not only with regard to materialist humanism or a humanism (as in certain forms of contemporary existentialism) such that despair is at bottom only a paradoxical form of absolute confidence in the purely human, but also with regard to a "degenerate Protestantism" as envisaged by Kierkegaard: in the absence of an absolute norm for faith, the tranquillity faith brings, according to Luther, and piety iself, will in the end coincide with prosperity and worldliness, for there will be nothing left but to enjoy peaceably this life and the advantages it brings, once tranquillity appears as the triumph of faith. Pure inwardness thus leads in practice to the denial of the most essential thing in Christianity: renunciation of the world and its glitter, the spirit of poverty and sacrifice.[28]

On another point Kierkegaard had entered a fundamental reservation as early as 1835, which is taken up again in a different form in his last works. "Does the Bible," he asks, "constitute the Church? No, the Church constitutes the Bible; and this is shown by the fact that it was written by Christians. The Protestant treats the Bible as though it floats above the Church like Mohammed's coffin between four magnets".[29] It is the very principle of the Reformation which is here at stake, in so far as it substitutes the Bible for the Church and hence replaces the authority of the Church by personal inspiration; whereas the Bible is internal to the Church, the interpreter of the Word which does not pass away.[30] But Kierkegaard did not succeed in correcting the misapprehensions of his thought concerning Catholicism, nor in seeing that the sacraments, which are certainly "something objective", are also conditions of inwardness and means to personal appropriation.

In the last resort, it is this point which reveals, in Kierkegaard, both the persistent imprint of Lutheranism and his powerlessness, right to the end, to find a firm and sure foundation for his faith. Despite his efforts, painful and moving as they are, he remained imprisoned within a conception which hid from him the meaning of the Church and its sacraments, and prevented him from understanding that they are the remedy for the anguish and doubt which assail the Christian soul, they are the sources of peace. For the Catholic knows where he can find Christ. The Church is always close to him; she envelops him in her presence and infuses him with her mysteriousness; for him she is the fountain-head of joy, the source of strength and serenity. He knows that Christ lives in her, that he will find Him and partake of His life precisely in so far as he remains completely faithful to her. There is no anguish which is not assuaged in the heart of him who keeps his eyes fixed upon the City on the hill, for from thence come down continually upon the world Certainty, Light, and Peace.

NOTES TO CONCLUSION, CHAPTER ONE

[1] Cf. *Journal*, 1849 (Haecker, p. 90): "A partisan is not an intensive *a*, but a privative *a*."

[2] Kierkegaard made a personal study of Luther's works only from 1846 onwards. Up till 1848, the *Journal* has scarcely anything but approval and admiration for Luther. ("Luther reconquered the concept of faith for his age." "What a consolation to read Luther!" "Luther's the master of us all.") From 1848 onwards, the tone changes and criticisms multiply. They become more and more energetic.

[3] *Journal*, 1847, VIII A 332.

[4] *Training in Christianity*, p. 71.

[5] *Commentary on the Epistle to the Romans*, III.

[6] P. 40ff.

[7] *Journal*, 1849, X^2 244 (Dru 1008).

[8] A note in the *Journal*, 9 February 1849 (Dru 873) puts the same point of view in a rather different form: "The end of Luther's sermon on I Cor. xiii, where he concludes that faith is more than love, is sophistry. Luther always wants to explain love as love of one's neighbour, as though it were not also a duty to love God. Luther really put faith in the place of the love of God, and then called love, love of one's neighbour". It may be observed that this standpoint of Kierkegaard's seems difficult to reconcile with the view, quoted above, that the opposite of sin is not virtue, but faith. Kierkegaard eventually writes (*Journal*, 1849, Haecker, p. 30) that "in Lutheranism, faith is a kind of fig-leaf to cover up what is least Christian."

[9] *Journal*, 1854, E. P. IX, p. 358 (Dru 1399).

[10] *Journal*, 1854, XI^1 A 61 (Dru 1304). Cf. *Journal*, 1849, X^1 A 154 (Dru 889), where Kierkegaard stresses a comparatively vulgar aspect of Lutheran polemic: "Luther's: 'Hear me, thou Pope' not to mention anything else, sounds to me almost disgustingly worldly, so that the sacred earnestness of a reformer concerned only with his own responsibility, who knows that true reformation consists in becoming more inward. Such an expression is just like a journalist's slogan."—1850, (Haecker, p. 153–4): "The great mistake is to take Luther for a reformer, for a reformer who wants to kick over the traces is a scandalous thing! If he had made it clear that the liberty for which he was fighting (quite rightly) would result in making the spiritual life infinitely stricter than it had been before, he would have had nobody on his side, for nobody will become a follower of someone who wants to make life harder."

[11] Cf. *Journal*, 1854, XI^1 A 61 (Dru 1304). Cf. 1852 (Haecker, p. 290): "Luther exposed the highest spiritual principle to pure inwardness. That can become so dangerous that we run the risk of lapsing into the lowest paganism."

[12] *Journal*, 1854, E.P. IX, p. 372 (Dru 1406).

[13] *Journal*, 1852 (Wahl, p. 660). (Cf. 1851, X^4 A 137 and 212, Dru 1192 and 1200). J. Wahl (p. 668, note I) thinks that Kierkegaard here returns to "some-

thing of the Kantian theory". It would appear rather, that he is here returning to one of the fundamental theses of true Christianity. Kant's theory is developed along quite other lines.

¹⁴ Cf. on a similar theme, *Journal*, 1850, X³ A 463, (Dru 1134), where Kierkegaard humorously declares that Protestants have done away with the Catholic canonization of ascetics and martyrs and substituted for it canonization of the *bourgeoisie*: and of course, he adds, the *bourgeois* are canonized by the last clerical order to appear in Protestantism: the office-seekers and place-hunters.

¹⁵ *Journal*, 1849, X¹ A 154 (Dru 889).

¹⁶ *Journal*, 1854, E.P. IX, p. 372 (Dru 1406).

¹⁷ Cf. *Journal*, 1837, II A 76 (Dru 122): "The recognition of the negative side of the reformation and the *possibility* of the estranged party's return to Mother Church (without their on that account having to return like prodigal sons) is surely expressed slyly by the fact that they had not the courage to do what the Catholics did to them—declare them heretics."

¹⁸ Cf. *Journal*, 1854, XI² A 305 (Dru 1327): "Surely Protestantism, Lutheranism is really a corrective; and the result of having made Protestantism into the regulative has been to produce great confusion." The question is "whether Protestantism would not—presuming that it degenerated—lead to a form of corruption to which Catholicism—presuming it degenerated—did not lead, and whether that does not show that Protestantism is not fit to stand alone."

¹⁹ *Journal*, 1854, XI¹ A 28 (Dru 1298). Cf. ibid., 1854, XI¹ A 198 (Dru 1326): "In order to make the absurdity, the dishonesty and the corruption of Protestantism manifest when—instead of being a necessary corrective at a given moment—it sets up as a religion, as Christianity: in order to get that made manifest it required a country which was not even assisted—as in Germany and in other countries—by having Catholicism close at hand . . . a country which even has a language all of its own."

²⁰ *Journal*, 1854, E.P. IX, p. 284 (Dru 1379).

²¹ *Journal*, 1854, E.P. IX, p. 305 (Dru 1385). Cf. ibid. XI¹ A 108 (Dru 1310): "Luther; your responsibility is great indeed, for the closer I look the more clearly do I see you overthrew the Pope—and set the public on the throne"—1854, XI¹ A 193 (Dru 1325): "The longer I study Luther the more clear does it become that Luther also made this confusion; he confuses what it means to be the patient with what it means to be the doctor. He is an extremely important patient for Christianity, but he is not the doctor; he has the patient's passion for expressing and describing his suffering . . . but he has not got the doctor's breadth of view."

²² H. Hoffding, *S. Kierkegaard als Philosoph*, 1902, p. 167, had already advanced this view.

²³ Quoted by Ruttenbeck, S. Kierkegaard, *Der Christliche Denker und sein Werk*, Berlin, 1929, p. 238 (Wahl, p. 381).

²⁴ Cf. Newman, *Apologia*, London, 1864, p. 308-309, 362: "8 April, 1841. I am afraid that in one respect you may be disappointed. It is my trust, though I must not be too sanguine, that we shall not have individual members of our communion going over to yours . . . I can earnestly desire a union between my church and yours. I cannot listen to the thought of your being joined by individuals among us."—"26 April, 1841, I think I never shall believe that so

much piety and earnestness would be found among Protestants, if there were
not some very grave errors on the side of Rome. . . . That I am an advocate
for Protestantism, you cannot suppose—but I am forced into a *Via Media*, short
of Rome, as it is at present."—"5 May 1841, I say this lest any lurking suspi-
cions should be left in the mind of your friends that persons who think with me
are likely, by the growth of their present views, to find it imperative on them to
pass over to your communion. Allow me to state strongly, that if you have any
such thoughts, and proceed to act upon them, your friends will be committing
a fatal mistake."—7 November 1844. I am still where I was; I am not moving.
Two things however, seem plain, that every one is prepared for such an event,
next, that every one expects it of me (his conversion to Catholicism). However, I do not think it either suitable or likely." The following year (1845),
Newman entered the Catholic Church.

25 *For Self-Examination*, p. 41–45.
26 E. P. 1851–3, p. 225.
27 *Journal*, 1852 (Haecker, p. 284).
28 *Journal*, 1854, XI² A 305 (Dru 1327).—In *Training in Christianity*, p. 92,
Kierkegaard had already stressed this point, showing that the system of an
Established Church leads to the transformation of the church militant into the
church triumphant, and to the deification of the established order: "The deification of the established order is the secularization of everything. The established order may be quite right in affirming that, so far as worldly things are
concerned, one must attach oneself to the established order, be content with
relativity, etc. But in the end one secularizes also the God—relationship, insists that this shall be congruous with a certain relativity, not essentially different
from one's station in life, etc.—instead of which it must be for every individual
man the absolute, and it is precisely this God-relationship of the individual
which must put every established order in suspense."

29 *Journal*, 1835, I A 108 (Wahl, p. 584).
30 Cf. *Journal*, 1838, II A 252 (F. & G., p. 84): "There are two factors in the
Christian life which must be harmonized. It is first of all a conviction, a certainty, both unshakeable, of our relationship to God, of His grace and love
without their being conceived however as abstractions, which might, through
a whole scale of modifications, eventually lead man to sin in order thereby
to become certain of salvation. Secondly, it is an empirical development."

II

PROFIT AND LOSS

Kierkegaard's Rationalism.—We can now attempt to judge Kierkegaard's work as a whole. It will be obvious, no doubt, that
Kierkegaard's psychology must always be taken into account. He
was outstandingly, to use his own expressions, a "problem man",
a "Janus bifrons". If the whole of his life was lived according to
two declensions, which change not only the endings of words,
but the whole words themselves, is it permissible to explain the
contradictory appearance presented, when they are confronted
with each other, by the noble ambition he revealed and the means
he used to fulfil it? For it is not without reason that it has been
asked whether, in spite of his own counsel, Kierkegaard does not
try to rationalize his conceptions.[1] It has been found possible,
indeed, to reproach him with erecting a Christian system by
asserting that Christianity can only be lived, with teaching dogmatically that existential truth can be communicated only in-
directly and that Christianity has no dogma.[2] Contradiction
rationalized, paradox justified, the irrational mediatized, the
absurd made intelligible, existential truth entrusted to the *professor
publicus* (or the writer, which amounts to the same thing), that is,
put under the protection of the universal and made subject to the
ethical: this would be the worst of defeats for Kierkegaard's
position.

What is even more serious is that it may be asked whether the
defeat could have been avoided. Kierkegaard was certainly not
unaware of this. He rebels against Hegel, whose ambition is to
rationalize everything; he wants, on the contrary, to start with
faith and the absurd, to take as his model thinker, not Hegel, the
typical *professor publicus*, enslaved to the universal, but the private
or subjective thinker, Job, or better still Abraham, the father of
the faith. For him the source of philosophy is no longer surprise,

as the Greeks thought, but despair and dread. All philosophy is thus involved in the "paradox". But is this Christian paradox, as Kierkegaard proposes it, anything more than that of our own transitory, individual thought struggling with the eternal? And how can this problem be solved without going outside subjectivity?

On the other hand, Kierkegaard is constantly concerned to mediatize the paradox and empty it of significance. He himself was aware of the tendency into which he slipped, as it were, in spite of himself. "I have tried to prove the necessity of the paradox, an attempt which shows a certain weakness, but which is something different from the speculative suspension of the paradox". If the paradox is necessary, how can it still be a paradox? It remains a subjective paradox as long as it is not known to be necessary: once it is recognized as such it falls into line again, so to speak. Kierkegaard is thus all too easily reassured on the point. Chestov observes very justly that Kierkegaard, who attacks Hegel so energetically, is always concerned to discover everywhere dialectical movement, natural development, transition. In the last analysis, he is repelled by the leap: he has a secret affection for mediatized actions. Thus he writes: "Faith is the paradox of the superiority of the individual over the universal". But he immediately makes a reservation: "But the individual, as a particular man, is superior to the universal only if he has previously been subject to the universal, and has become a man, a particular individual, by means of the universal". This reservation may well contain great wisdom; but unfortunately it is uncharacteristic of Kierkegaard, since here the leap is abolished, and faith apparently rests upon reason, and subjectivity upon the ethical.

This defeat is not surprising. It is inherent in the attempt itself, in this sense, as Kierkegaard does not fail to remark, that the paradox is never as paradoxical as it might be: it is never absolute paradox. Léon Chestov is on sure ground in reproaching Kierkegaard with having resigned himself to wanting to explain the inexplicable, to rationalize original sin, for example. How can one avoid giving an intelligible sense at least to the *terms* in which the inexplicable and the absurd are formulated? One must at least

resign oneself to conceiving the absurdity of the absurd and the
inexplicability of the paradox, otherwise how could one distinguish the paradox and the absurd as such? And this is in itself an
explanation. Chestov proposes a total self-immolation of the
reason in the face of absolute paradox.[3] But is not this the equivalent of nothingness? As Kierkegaard observes, the paradox
would disappear in its own fulfilment.[4] "That the Son of God
should have become a man is the supreme metaphysical and religious paradox. It is not the profoundest ethical paradox however, for this would arise only if the Son of God had not taken up
a negative, polemical attitude towards the State and the Church,
but had been a member of the spiritual power".[5] But Kierkegaard
at once adds, quite rightly, that one might take the paradox even
further, by supposing that God might have remained completely
unknown. In this, truly absolute, paradox, however, God would
have acted as an ironist, not as the God and Father of men. Moreover in other respects the paradox would have completely dis-
appeared. Thus the absolute paradox neither has been conceived,
nor is conceivable: it no longer exists; but a paradox which can
be enunciated and explained is no longer a paradox, in Kierkegaard's sense of the word. It is understandable that Kierkegaard
should write, concerning difficulties of this kind: "May God
help the unhappy intellect which is a prey to doubts of this
sort".[6]

Truth to tell, these doubts recur in many guises. One of the
most typical is the difficulty of a union between the subjective
and the historical. There is a historical Christ, and Kierkegaard
submissively accepts the evidence provided by the sacred texts.
But Christ cannot remain "objective". One must identify oneself
with Him through faith and love, through imitation and bearing
witness: it is in this that true contemporaneity consists. The
Christian life is essentially defined as the embodiment of Christ
within oneself. But it will be asked: how can one make present
Him who by definition is absent and in the past, how can one
annul the nineteen hundred years which separate Christ from us
to-day? Kierkegaard replies that this is the very form of the paradox, and that there would be no paradox if it could be justified

and rationalized. Christ, he says, "is and insists upon being the definite historical person He was 1800 years ago, and . . . this definite person, living under the conditions He then lived under . . . He is not, and for nobody is He willing to be, one about whom we have learned to know something merely from history . . . because there is absolutely nothing that can be 'known' about Him. . . . He is the paradox, the object of faith. But all historical communication is communication of knowledge, hence from history one can learn nothing about Christ".[7]

Kierkegaard, it is true, is careful to state that he is speaking here only of profane, not of sacred, history, for the latter "stands apart, outside history".[8] Profane history, no doubt, can reach as far as the literal sense of the facts, but sacred history alone can grasp their mysterious significance. Criticism may usefully bring more exact knowledge concerning the externals of revelation, the authors and the dates of the books of the Bible, but sacred history alone can bring to life and unify the abstract and inanimate data of history, and discern in the succession of events and human actions the unfolding of a divine plan, accessible only to faith. These views are perfectly correct, and we shall not contradict them. But it must also be observed that Kierkegaard's position gives them the appearance of a vicious circle. The problem is to know how precisely faith can set aside history, space and time, in order to become contemporary with Christ. To say that sacred history is the answer is clearly to give the problem for its own solution, if it is true that *sacred* history is in the first instance *history*, and as such within the scope of historical science and open to judgement by that science. The *Credo*, which is certainly, as Kierkegaard stresses,[9] an affirmation of subjectivity or personal appropriation (*I believe*), is also a solemn and truly fundamental affirmation of the historical reality of the Incarnation: Christ died *sub Pontio Pilato*, and history fixes the terminal dates of Pilate's proconsulate, just as it fixes the date of the census of Augustus Caesar, under the governorship of P. Sulpicius Quirinius. The whole faith of the Church is bound up with these historical facts, which can be situated and dated. "If Christ be not risen," writes St. Paul, "then is our preaching vain".[10]

This Kierkegaard admits and proclaims. But the problem here is one of logic and coherence. If sacred history, as he says, is outside history, how can it be grasped? How can contemporaneity be realized? What is to guarantee the effective reality of this contemporaneity? Kierkegaard replies: "Faith. Here, quite certainly, we have inwardness at its maximum proving to be objectivity once again".[11] But is it not apparent that faith cannot guarantee itself, and that subjectivity becomes objectivity only by a decision, and a passion, which will always run the risk of seeming arbitrary and gratuitous? Kierkegaard admits it when he makes faith something uneasy, an ever-threatened equilibrium above seventy fathoms of water. Finally, in this conflict of history and faith, it is faith which not only gives meaning to history but also guarantees and even creates history.

Such, in one of its aspects, is the irreducible conflict in which Kierkegaard is engaged, and which explains the dramatic appearance of his thought, divided between a fideism which excludes all reason and a rationalism which excludes all faith. He chose faith against reason. From that point onwards, however, he is no longer capable of thinking his faith, that is to say, of conceiving it intellectually as belief and paradox. Only silence remains. But it must be an inner silence too. Subjectivity thus becomes synonymous with darkness intelligible.

Kierkegaard's Christianity.—Is Kierkegaard a Christian? Our answer to this problem has already been given. What concerns us here is that the question could ever have been asked. For it seems an odd one, when one recalls the painful intensity with which Kierkegaard *lived* the tearing asunder, the separation, from *homo animalis* which Christianity demands. He strikes a note which is quite unmistakeable, and to us it seems certain that on the existential level his testimony is one of the most moving that we have. A Hegelian in spite of himself, the victim of a reason which was madly ambitious, an impenitent rationalist even in his defence of the "movement of the absurd", he paid a heavy price for his speculative follies. With such conflicting themes he not only wrote heart-rending music, but rent his own heart.[12] The best

16

testimony we can offer him is always to set aside the æsthetic standpoint when we approach him. An incomparable artist, a wonderful writer, even for the reader who knows him only in translation, in his presence, as in Pascal's, we can nevertheless think only of the message he brings.

Outside the plane of living experience, however, it may legitimately be asked if Kierkegaard is really a Christian, that is to say, if his position is really a Christian one. He doubted it himself, partly, certainly, from humility, but partly also because he was rightly aware of the contradiction in which he had involved himself by reducing everything to subjectivity, and at the same time making himself the poet of the religious, that is to say, expressing the religious in its outward aspect, as an object. It might also be observed that if, in his relations with the religious (as in his relations with Regina Olsen) he was a constantly unhappy lover, and if he raised unhappy love for God to the level of a metaphysical principle—for the essential element in the religious is despair, and its sign is dread—it was perhaps because he found a certain pleasure in tormenting himself and in tormenting others. In this way, does not his Christianity lead back to the æsthetic attitude, attempting to justify itself in the rôle of a herald? "The wrong path," he himself notes, "lies all too near, the wish to reform and awaken the whole world . . . instead of one's self".[13]

It would no doubt be more exact to say that Kierkegaard's attitude towards Christianity shows voluntary and painful tension, and by that alone is a genuinely Christian position. But on the religious plane, to which Kierkegaard, the religious poet, belongs in spite of all, it is difficult to decide whether the thorn in the flesh is that of an anguish truly nourished by Christianity itself and falling wholly within the Christian sphere, or whether on the other hand it is not the anguish of a conflict in which Christianity itself is in question. Certain of Kierkegaard's observations have led some critics to choose the latter hypothesis, which would also make it possible to give a truly pathetic significance to the defence of the "absurd". What is in any case disturbing is that with Kierkegaard the "supernatural", "grace", and "faith", sometimes seem to be the form assumed by the rational, sensual, and emo-

tional demands of a nature in rebellion against the limitations
placed upon it. In the last resort, Chestov is quite right in saying
that Kierkegaard is still under the spell of the incantation in which
the serpent sang the praises of the forbidden fruit.

In short, Kierkegaard is a man defending an untenable and
desperate position. Contradiction besets him on all sides, because
he lived as it were divided up between the religious man and the
poet, between the rationalist and the Christian, between the
believer and the unbeliever, between the dialectician and the
ironical critic of Christendom; he was these all at once, lacking any
higher means whereby they might be reconciled and pacified.
His thorn in the flesh was the feverish pursuit of a unity which the
circumstances of his life, his temperament and his ideas made impossible. Out of this impossibility he made an absolute principle.
He was assuredly a martyr, not to Christianity, as he said, but to
himself. And to have been aware of this was perhaps the deepest
source of Kierkegaard's despair.

His greatness is above all in the human, concrete testimony
which enlivens his thought.[14] Kierkegaard analyses with magnificent penetration "the terrifying adventure of the man God iso-
lates and crucifies for love". Here one can speak without hesitation of offence and rending apart. To consent to be "divested
of oneself", to hope in the night of dread, to leap, in spite of
appearances, beyond the tangled growths of anxiety, is for the
individual the most definite of paradoxes; this "movement of the
absurd" is the equivalent, as we have remarked, in the practical
sphere, of St. Paul's *contra spem in spe* and of the dark night of the
mystics.

We must not follow Kierkegaard, however, in legitimizing the
offence and the antinomy of the unhappy conscience. The conflict which convulsed him so profoundly bears the marks of an
event which was both personal and accidental. Though it is true
that the Christian life necessarily implies conflict and struggle,
that does not mean that every unhappy conscience is a Christian
one. Romanticism has so to speak methodically cultivated the
"unhappy conscience" as a style, without really transcending the
level of flesh and blood. Kierkegaard, for whom romanticism

was a constant temptation, has forcefully noted how far removed it is from Christianity.[15]

The whole problem for Kierkegaard was to find a way out of
subjectivity, which seemed to lead to the immanence of the self
within itself, and to a reason set afire with impossible demands.
We readily admit that "no philosopher has conveyed a clearer
sense of that 'otherness' which thought encounters, of the transcendental absolute".[16] But here a further doubt may be raised:
does not this transcendency have a psychological rather than a
metaphysical character? What is certain is that Kierkegaard's
example admirably illustrates the dramatic conflict engendered by
the abstract creation of a radical opposition between the spheres of
reason (immanence) and of faith (transcendency); far from leading
us to erect this conflict into the law of the Christian life, it should
rather induce us to avoid the paths which involve one in such
contraditions. Kierkegaard, moreover, himself hesitated before
this harsh rupture within the very heart of humanity: thus he
writes, after having sketched out a sort of mediation between the
ethical and the religious, that "God is the friend of order". But if
this is so, how should God impose upon man an endless conflict,
a form of divided and unhappy conscience, between the demands
of faith and the demands of reason, which latter is itself undoubtedly a part of "order"?

Here we have Luther's case again. Luther became conscious of
his Christianity only in anxiety concerning salvation, and succeeded in quelling this anxiety only by the "leap" of faith and the
"movement of the absurd". And it necessarily reappeared within
the tranquillity brought by faith, in order to make the latter
visible and sensible by the effect of contrast. Bremond has insisted
upon this point in connection with Saint-Cyran and also Pascal.
Kierkegaard himself remarks upon it in Luther's case: "That is
remarkable, it is the one thing necessary, and it explains everything Luther says: namely, that the whole doctrine must be related to the struggle of the anguished conscience".[17] Luther experienced his faith as an anxious thing and he made it a law of
faith. Thus Kierkegaard made his—truly tragic—speculative
embarrassments a condition of belief and of the religious, and he

transformed the failure of his efforts into an apologia of despair, of subjectivity, and of being "unto oneself". But at the same time he runs into the danger, which he very penetratingly attributes to Luther, of making belief disappear in subjectivity and inwardness, and of deifying immanence and the self.

It is not this insoluble conflict, then, which makes Kierkegaard of value for us. The monologue "before reality, which excites, attracts, and *does not answer*" [18] is not a rational ideal, and even less a Christian one, far from it, and Kierkegaard himself tells us so. "If one's right to knowledge is to have its full scope", he writes, "one must venture into the thick of life, on to the high seas, and raise one's voice, for God will perhaps hear the shout, and not stay upon the beach and watch the others fight and struggle, for that is the only way that knowledge acquires authentic value before the true Forum. This is something quite different from standing on one leg and proving God's existence, and then going on one's knees to thank Him".[19]   Yes, if the cry Kierkegaard utters out of the depths of that night moves us so profoundly, it is because, beyond all the ambiguities of a reason forced to abdicate through having asked too much, we feel that his passionate dialectic above all expresses the ardour of a soul which thirsted after God and His righteousness, and which deserved to hear the answer promised to all those who seek Him in tribulation.

Kierkegaard's Greatness.—Kierkegaard was not, any more than Pascal, a dogmatizing theologian. Mohammed objected most strongly to being taken for a poet, and the Koran for a poem. Kierkegaard protests with all his strength against the notion of regarding him as a prophet—because he wants to be only a poet.[20] "I ask nothing better," he writes, "than to be pointed out as the only one who *cannot* doctrinize".[21] To define his position he finds no more adequate term than that of "policeman of eternity" or "spy", a spy in higher service, in the service of the idea, whose function is to obtain information concerning errors, illusions and doubtful matters. The police employ people who often have a shady past, and thus have a hold over them to exact complete obedience. So also does Providence, "but an infinite difference

distinguishes her from the police: in her compassionate charity
she makes use of such a man out of love, saves him and disciplines
him by making use of his wisdom, which thus is sanctified and
consecrated". Kierkegaard was a troubled soul who sought to
grasp, and to make others grasp, the true meaning of Christian
reality. Hence we have more liberty in understanding his message,
which, in spite of himself, has the aspect more of a confidence
than of a doctrine.

Kierkegaard teaches us the necessity of choice, and no lesson is
more opportune than that. Choice is the most uncommon thing
of all in our time, not only in the realm of action, but also in that
of the spirit. This age cultivates confusion of ideas, and relies
now upon statistics, now upon recourse to origins, to resolve
conflicts.[22] It is characterized by luke-warmness and flabbiness,
which are in direct proportion to its agitation: what it wills and
thinks is always only "up to a certain point"; "yes" always
squints across at "no", and "no" at "yes". All the mysteries,
human and divine, are reduced to problems whose solution is so
cheap that its mediocrity can safely be revealed. It is always a
question of spiriting away difficulties, filling in ditches, annulling
differences, finding compromises—of making cleverness the rule
of thought and action.[23] The spirit of synthesis is reduced to the
all-too-easy tactic of mingling contraries, which is exactly the
opposite of Pascal's and Kierkegaard's precept to "maintain
contraries". The habit of thinking extensively—democratically—
the cult of the mass, ruins the universal for the benefit of the
general and makes the personal a monstrous paradox. The entire
age tends to become a committee. The taste for gregariousness
poisons even intellectual life: ideas have the dreary, mournful
banality of dirty crumpled banknotes. The impersonal is king;
the general claim to absolute independence coincides oddly with a
state of affairs where individuals, in both thought and life, sink
defeated into the anonymity of an all-including "they". Reason
is adorned with a capital letter, but has lost its face, which is the
face of God. The fiduciary inflation of "intelligence" has made us
forget the Supreme Intelligence. Truth and morality have become mere poetry and oratory. The word and the gesture take

the place of life. The *professor publicus* has triumphed: truth is passed from mind to mind, like cash from hand to hand.

Against all this, to save us from the downward rush into the impersonal and the mechanical, Kierkegaard can be an incomparable master. No doubt he is terribly lacking in the sense of community spirit, of the value of the social—which are the opposite of the gregarious and of the mass, and are the most necessary conditions for the health of the personality—and also, to tell the whole story, in the sense of the Church and of the communion of saints, of the intimate connection of the mystery (and the offence) of Christ the God-Man with the mystery (and the offence) of the Church, the Body of Christ. A strange lacuna indeed, in a thinker who insisted so much upon the vital quality of oppositions and the tensions to which they give rise.[24] The fact remains, none the less, that Kierkegaard teaches us true greatness, which is spiritual, and, more precisely, Christian. His message, in its most general sense, consisted in saying that Christianity is a serious affair, that the believer has his back to the wall, that he must feel "upon his skull the whole weight of infinity", that doctrine and life must overlay each other completely, and that the Christian's task is, not to settle into a comfortable and quiet conformity, but to establish himself in a personal relationship with God, a personal relationship which must express itself in the character of a witness and an imitator of Christ, with all that this involves in the shape of hostility and persecution from the world.

To become a Christian: that is the summary of Kierkegaard's message. For the Christian everything comes back to this incessant and painful, but glorious, task, since he identifies it with Christ, in order to become like him. For if one must be an "Individual" or a person, if one must give one's life the character of unity, which is also that of truth, of goodness and of being, the surest and in truth the only way is to sacrifice everything to the one thing necessary, that is, to become a Christian. If one must work to develop within the personality the heroic virtues, to destroy egoism and replace it with universal brotherly love, again the only way is to become a Christian, because "the love of God and the love of one's neighbour are like two doors which can be

opened and shut only at the same time".[25]   Finally if one is to
abjure the bitter and bloody enmities of the tribe, to raise oneself
up to the sense of universal brotherhood in a common destiny
which does not end on this earth but flows on into eternity, there
is only one path open, which is to become a Christian.[26]

Such is the secret, known to all since Christ, which alone is
capable of setting man upon the road to true greatness, by giving
his efforts, among the hostile forces he must each day face and
conquer, the character of a history unified by the spiritual ends
in which the human destiny finds its perfection.   For "man's
eternal dignity consists in the fact that he can have a history, the
divine element in him consists in the fact that he himself, if he will,
can impart to this history continuity, for this it acquires only when
it is not the sum of all that has happened to me or befallen me but
is my own work, in such a way that even what has befallen me is
by me transformed and translated from necessity to freedom".[27]

Kierkegaard has written: "What I *will*, what I require also of
everyone whom I admire, of every one I am in any real sense to
recognize, that by day he should think only of the categories
of his life and dream of them by night".[28]   Kierkegaard, was such
a man, thinking day and night of the domant idea of his life,
which was that of "becoming a Christian".   He has said so himself
in moving terms, speaking in the past tense, as he supposed his
biographers and interpreters would speak of him (for if one lives
looking forward, one understands looking backward), and this
judgement upon himself and his own work has been fully ratified
by posterity.   "He himself was 'that individual'," he writes, "if
no one else was, and he became that more and more.   It was the
cause of Christianity he served, his life from childhood on being
marvellously fitted for such a service.   Thus he carried to completion the work of reflection, the task of translating completely
into terms of reflection what Christianity is, what it means to become a Christian.   His purity of heart was to will only one thing.
What his contemporaries complained of during his lifetime, that
he would not abate the price, would not give in, this very thing is
the eulogy pronounced upon him by after ages, that he did not
abate the price, did not give in.   But the grand enterprise he under-

took did not infatuate him. Whereas as an author he had dialectically made a survey of the whole, he understood Christianly that
the whole signified his own education in Christianity. The
dialectical structure he brought to completion, of which the
several parts are whole works, he could not ascribe to any man,
least of all would he ascribe it to himself; if he were to ascribe it
to any one, it would be to Governance, to whom it was in fact
ascribed, day after day and year after year, by the author, who
historically died of a mortal disease, but poetically died of longing
for eternity, where uninterruptedly he would have nothing else
to do but to thank God".[29]

[1] J. Wahl, *Études kierkegaardiennes*, p. 434.

[2] We have seen however that this last imputation is not justifiable.

[3] Cf. L. Chestov, *Athènes et Jérusalem*, Paris 1938, p. 209 ff.

[4] *Journal*, 1843, IV A 62 (F. & G., p. 162).

[5] *Journal*, 1843, IV A 103 (F. & G., p. 171).

[6] *Journal*, 1843, IV A 62 (F. & G., p. 162).

[7] *Training in Christianity*, p. 26-8.

[8] *Training in Christianity*, pp. 28, 33.

[9] *Journal*, 1836, I A 56 (Dru 15).

[10] I Cor. xv, 14.

[11] *Journal*, 1849, X² A 299 (Dru 1021).

[12] Cf. *Journal*, 1848, IX A 86 (Dru 778): "It seems to me that I have written things which would move stones to tears—but contemporaries are only moved —to scorn and envy."

[13] *Journal*, 1849, X¹ A 513 (Dru 937).

[14] On this point cf. the observations of G. Thibon, in *Études Carmélitaines*, April 1938, p. 149.

[15] This does not force us to deny the affinities or analogies between them, of which the chief is the divided conscience or duality of romanticism. Cf. *Journal*, 1836, I A 140 (Wahl, p. 579): "Properly speaking, the romantic element resides in the fact of two halves of an idea being separated by something which remains between them. When Adam was created, the idea of Adam needed to be completed by Eve. . . . Eve arrives, and there is no more romanticism, there is tranquillity. Man is created, and sins. This fact demands a complement, which is Christ. Romanticism has developed in nations which have become aware of this division of existence into two. Christ comes, and there is tranquillity. Christ's second coming might be treated in the same way." The *Journal* for the years 1836-7 contains numerous fragments on this theme.

[16] J. Wahl, *Études kierkegaardiennes*, p. 451.

[17] *Journal*, 1846, VII A 192.

[18] J. Wahl, loc. cit., p. 452.

[19] *A Literary Discussion*, VIII, 95 (Geismar, p. 84).

[20] *Journal*, 1849, X¹ A 510 (Dru 936).

[21] *Unscientific Postscript*, p. 249 f. Cf. *The Point of View*, p. 75: "And now as for me, the author, what, according to my opinion, is my relation to the age? Am I perhaps the 'Apostle'? Abominable! I have never given an occasion for such a judgement. I am a poor insignificant person. Am I then the teacher, the educator? No, not that at all; I am he himself who has been educated, or whose authorship expresses what it is to be educated to the point of becoming a Christian. In the fact that education is pressed upon me, and in the measure that it is pressed, I press upon this age; but I am not a teacher, only a fellow student."

[22] *Journal*, 1846, VII A 15 (Dru 562): "In the end physics will displace ethics